# Comparative Public Administration

This accessible introduction to the system of public administration uses a clear, country by country analysis of the contemporary system of public administration and management in a number of significant countries. It examines the extent to which new public management, politicians and public opinion can influence bureaucracies in various countries and in addition, it explores the role of public administration systems within the wider political systems and democratic frameworks of their states.

The new edition revises and updates several of the original country studies including: the United States, France, the UK, the Republic of Ireland and Italy, and adds four more chapters on Greece, Russia, India and China. Each chapter is written to a common framework, which covers the following issues:

- political culture
- the constitutional framework
- the civil service
- public sector agencies
- federal and local government
- financing the system
- co-ordination of the system
- managing the system
- accountability, secrecy and openness
- democracy
- further developments and the financial crash.

This textbook is essential reading for students of comparative public administration.

**J. A. Chandler** is an emeritus professor of Local Governance at Sheffield Hallam University and author of several books on local government, including *Explaining Local Government* (Manchester University Press, 2009). He has also edited *Local Government in Liberal Democracies* (Routledge, 1993) and *The Citizen's Charter* (Dartmouth, 1996). He is completing *Explaining Public Policy* to be published by Routledge in 2014/15.

'The book provides an agile and effective introduction to the administrative system of a number of important countries. This is a useful contribution that will introduce students to the growing field of comparative public administration.'

Edoardo Ongaro, *Professor of International Public Services Management, Northumbria University, Newcastle, UK*

'This is an insightful account of an important though often neglected area of the political process. Written by country experts, and drawing on examples from China, Europe, India, Russia and the United States, it provides the reader with a clear and topical analysis of the workings and impact of public administration.'

Dr Hugh Atkinson, *Department of Social Sciences, London South Bank University, UK*

Praise for the first edition:

'*Comparative Public Administration* offers students an easily accessible yet profound analysis of the structure of the state in Western Europe, the US and Japan. This rich volume suggests new and promising methods of research into how the state operates in advanced countries.'

Jan-Erik Lane, *University of Geneva, Switzerland*

# Comparative Public Administration

## Second edition

**Edited by**
**J. A. Chandler**

Routledge
Taylor & Francis Group

LONDON AND NEW YORK

First edition published 2000

Second edition published 2014
by Routledge
2 Park Square, Milton Park, Abingdon, Oxon OX14 4RN

and by Routledge
711 Third Avenue, New York, NY 10017

*Routledge is an imprint of the Taylor & Francis Group, an informa business*

*British Library Cataloguing in Publication Data*
A catalogue record for this book is available from the British Library

*Library of Congress Cataloging in Publication Data*
Comparative public administration/edited by Jim Chandler.
– Second edition.
pages cm
Includes bibliographical references and index.
1. Public administration. I. Chandler, J. A.
JF1351.C5855 2015
351—dc23
2013047764

ISBN: 978–0-415–56927–9 (hbk)
ISBN: 978–0-415–56928–6 (pbk)
ISBN: 978–1-315–77197–7 (ebk)

Typeset in Baskerville
by Florence Production Ltd, Stoodleigh, Devon

MIX
Paper from
responsible sources
FSC
www.fsc.org   FSC® C013604

Printed and bound by CPI Group (UK) Ltd, Croydon, CR0 4YY

# Contents

# Notes on contributors

**J. A. Chandler** is an emeritus professor of Local Governance at Sheffield Hallam University. He has written extensively on British and comparative local government and is currently completing a book for Routledge on public policy.

**Neil Collins** is Professor and Dean of Commerce at University College Cork. He is a recognised expert in the study of corruption in Irish politics. He is author of a standard text on the local government management system in Ireland.

**Howard Elcock** is Professor (emeritus) of Government at Northumbria University. He was educated at The Queen's College Oxford and previously taught at the University of Hull. He also taught for two sessions at the State University of New York College at Fredonia and in several European and Asiatic countries. He has over 100 publications, including books on political leadership, local government and public administration. He now divides his time between England and Greece.

**Thomas Johnson** specialises and writes on Chinese environmental policy and civil society and is currently an assistant professor at the City University of Hong Kong.

**John Kingdom** is a former reader in politics at Sheffield Hallam University. He is author of *Government and Politics in Britain* (Polity Press) and has just completed the fourth edition of this leading text book.

**Marina Nistotskaya** is a research fellow at the Quality of Government Institute in the Department of Political Science at the University of Gothenburg, Sweden. Her research interests include comparative public bureaucracy, economic development and post-Soviet government and politics. She has published on causes and consequences of non-politicised bureaucracy in a comparative perspective.

**David Pell** is an associate lecturer in Sheffield Hallam University Business School and part-time tutor in politics for the Open University. He specialises in environmental studies.

**Aodh Quinlivan** is a lecturer at the University College Cork and former local government officer who publishes on Irish public administration and management. His latest book is *Inside City Hall Politics – A Year in the Life of Cork City Council* (Cork: Echo Publications, 2011).

**Emmanuelle Schön-Quinlivan** is a lecturer in Politics with the Department of Government at University College Cork, Ireland. She specialises in European Union politics, public management and institutional change. She has published extensively on the impact of the Kinnock reforms on the European Commission.

**R. E. Spence** has retired as a principal lecturer at Sheffield Hallam University Business School and has published several papers on contemporary Italian politics.

**Guohui Wang** is a lecturer in the Department of Public Administration in the School of Economics and Business at Yantai University.

# Preface and acknowledgements

This is the second edition of a study of public administration in major countries that was first published in 2000. The new edition includes updated material on the United Kingdom, Ireland, France, Italy and the United States of America and also adds new chapters on Greece, Russia, the People's Republic of China and the Federal Republic of India. The book is intended to provide easily accessible introductions to the policy-making and implementation structures and process of the selected nations, and is structured to allow readers to easily compare specific aspects of different administrative systems. Each chapter is written by a country specialist and established authority in the study of public administration and management, with several contributors updating their contribution to the first edition. The chapters are designed to be more than simply a description of the machinery of government, but also a consideration of how far in each country, the system of public administration facilitates open democratic government. In view of the economic crises that became visible in 2008, a further issue is how far public administration has been susceptible to retrenchment and privatisation. The conclusion will debate some further considerations on developments within the administrative systems studied in this volume during a period of austerity.

The study will be of value to students from 'A' level to postgraduate level who require a background in and understanding of the management and administrative structure of significant developed states. It will provide a description of the administrative systems of each state and, for more advanced scholars, a platform for more theoretical comparison between the institutional arrangements, functions and development of these systems.

I would finally like to thank all the contributors to this volume who have taken much time and effort to develop each chapter. Despite demands upon their time to undertake research for publication in major academic journals as required by their universities they have demonstrated through this work a commitment to communicate to a wider interested audience.

# Abbreviations

| | |
|---|---|
| ARC | Administrative Reform Commission |
| BJP | Bharatiya Janata Party |
| C&AG | Comptroller and Auditor General |
| CBRC | China Banking Regulatory Commission |
| CCP | Chinese Communist Party |
| CPI | Corruption Perception Index |
| CRS | Cadre Responsibility System |
| EC | European Community |
| ECB | European Central Bank |
| EFSF | European Financial Stability Facility |
| EMU | European Monetary Union |
| ENA | École Nationale d'Administration |
| EPA | Environment Protection Agency |
| ESB | Electricity Supply Board |
| EU | European Union |
| FOI | Freedom of Information (Ireland) |
| Foi | Freedom of Information (Russia) |
| GDP | Gross Domestic Product |
| HSE | Health Services Executive |
| IAA | Independent Administrative Agencies |
| IMF | International Monetary Fund |
| INC | Indian National Congress Party |
| IT | Information Technology |
| LDC | Local Development Companies |
| LPC | Local Peoples Congress |
| M5S | Il Movimiento Cinque Stelle |
| NAO | National Audit Office (USA) |
| NDRC | National Development and Reform Commission |
| NGO | Non-government Organisation |
| NPC | National People's Congress (China) |
| NPM | New Public Management |
| OECD | Organisation for Economic Co-operation and Development |
| PLA | People's Liberation Army (China) |

| | |
|---|---|
| PPP | Public Private Partnership |
| PRC | People's Republic of China |
| QUANGO | Quasi Autonomous Non-governmental Organisation |
| SARS | Severe Acute Respiratory Syndrome |
| SASAC | State Owned Assets Supervision and Administration Commission of the Central Council (China) |
| SC/ST | Scheduled Castes and Tribes |
| SERC | State Electricity Regulatory Commission |
| SMI | Strategic Management Initiative |
| SSB | State Sponsored Bodies |
| UK | United Kingdom |
| UNESCO | United Nations' Educational, Scientific and Cultural Organisation |
| UPSC | Union Public Services Commission |
| USA | United States of America |
| VAT | Value Added Tax |
| VC | Organic Law of Villager's Committees |

# 1 Introduction

*J. A. Chandler*

Public administration is a practice that is constantly in the news. It relates, for example, to debates on the advantages and disadvantages of privatisation, the extent of corruption or dedicated altruism among public servants, the degree to which local government values a sense of community, or whether we are increasingly being dominated by faceless administrators in Brussels or Washington. Public administration is a practice, whether we realise it or not, that continually affects our lives. It is, nevertheless, one of those many concepts that, while theorists know what they mean by the idea, is difficult to concisely frame as a subject area. As Greenwood and Wilson observe any simple definition is doomed to failure (1989: 1). As an academic subject public administration encompasses the study of the development and maintenance of policy by members of governments, public agencies and public sector employees and the practice of putting the authoritative decisions they have made into practice. A public body is one that is established and sustained by the constitution or authoritative governments of a nation or nations. As such, public administration can be seen as a branch of political analysis, although, like any subject area, it will also touch on other disciplines such as, in this case, ethics, economics or management theory. The boundaries of what is public and private are, however, not always clear-cut but can fade imperceptibly into one another as both sectors are necessarily closely entangled in the complex network of relationships that form a social system.

The development of New Right theory has created a fashion for denigrating the term 'public administration' as old fashioned, instead concentrating issues of developing and regulating public provision of services and values under the phrase 'public management'. Within the use of this term is a concentration on effectiveness and efficiency, paralleling the dominant capitalist ideology of seeing progress as the development of profit through private competition. Public administration is, however, not solely about profit, growth and efficiency, but is also concerned with wider concerns such as ethics, human rights, democracy and well-being. Moreover, most private business management is relatively small-scale and concentrated on a limited range of products. The practice of public administration is, generally, not a matter of small scale provision, and covers a wide range of basic human needs. It involves, as this book shows, a multitude of interconnected organisations that need substantial financial and human resources to undertake their functions to ensure a framework for sustaining reasonable living standards for large populations.

## The comparative approach

It is important, even at the most introductory phase of any national survey, to adopt a comparative framework and not simply study the social arrangements for a specific nation. We cannot fully understand the social and governmental structures of any particular country unless we have a knowledge and understanding of other regimes. We may know the basic structure of the institutions of a country and how the various elements of this structure interrelate to establish and implement public policy, but we cannot appreciate whether the institutions are particularly efficient, democratic or ethically sound without comparison with other countries. For example, efficiency and democracy are not, in practice, qualities that can have absolute values attached. Just as it is physically impossible to develop a thoroughly efficient engine, it is impossible to conceive of a government that could achieve absolute efficiency for the management of its health or social services. It would be even more problematic to discern what could be required to produce a perfect democracy. It is, therefore, only possible to make any judgement on the effectiveness or ethical acceptability of the systems that govern our lives if we can compare them. The British, American, Russian or Chinese political systems are, for example, only more or less democratic than each other, and are not measured against a hypothetical and unpractised ideal situation.

## The structure of the chapters

Although designed to be a preface to comparative study this work cannot claim to be a fully comparative analysis in the sense that the authors do not make any general theoretical claims concerning the differences and similarities in systems of public administration. As an introduction to comparative study the book is, however, structured to make it possible to show how each particular country or administrative system that is included differs, or is similar to, others systems in specific structural areas. Hence, each author presents a chapter that is structured to a common format so that it is easier to gain an impression of how, for example, the civil service or local government system of one particular country may differ from another. The sections into which each chapter is divided are as follows.

### *Political culture*

It is not possible to make much sense of any social system without setting it in the context of the economic and social structure of society, the prevailing ideological values of its citizens and some concept of the historical developments that underlie the evolution of these predominant values. In this section the authors, therefore, provide a brief description of the process of establishing the nation, the extent of consensus or conflict in the system over territorial arrangements, and the principal ideological tendencies within the state. Most authors have expressed the nature of ideological division through brief descriptions of the values of the major political parties in their area of specialisation.

## The constitutional framework

This section will provide a brief account of the central policy-making structures of government and, in particular, a survey of the division of power and resources between central bureaucracies, ad hoc agencies, federal and local governments, and the extent to which the private sector is involved in the implementation of public policy.

### The civil service

At the heart of policy-making and often the process of implementation within government are the permanent bureaucrats attached to central government departments. This section will describe the structures of the civil service of each country, its relative power within the governmental system, the pattern of recruitment, promotion and training within the service and the prevailing values of senior civil servants. An important issue discussed in each chapter is the extent to which civil servants are close to the policy-making process and have partisan links with the governing political parties. The section will also consider the prestige of the service within a state, management styles and the impact of demands for efficiency.

### Central government agencies

While the civil service may be identified in the public mind as the quintessence of public bureaucracy, in many regimes, much of the task of implementing policy and even determining policy is in the hands of public bodies that are not directly responsible to a specific government minister or department. The many organisations established by government but not directly subordinate to a government department are referred in the study as central govern-ment agencies. As the book will show the extent to which different political systems have established agencies differs considerably and a wide variety of organisations may be placed in this category. For each country studied this book will provide a survey of the extent and type of agencies concerned with centralised administrative tasks and the structure and powers of some of the major agencies. The section will also consider the use made of agencies as a means of furthering private sector business practices within the public sector.

*Federal and local government*

Several of the countries analysed in the book are federal systems or, as in Britain, are moving in this direction. In these regimes major sub-divisions of the state are guaranteed sovereign power over certain specified policy-making and administrative tasks and, therefore, the federal units to some extent share power with the central government. Normally the powers of the federal units are guaranteed under a written constitution that stipulates what the federal and central government may or may not do. An effective federal system also requires that the constitution cannot be changed without the consent of at least a majority of the federal units of government.

In both federal and non-federal states some measure of power and responsibility is also devolved to local governments, which, unlike ad hoc agencies, are controlled by politicians responsible to their local citizens and usually subject to popular election. The book will provide a description of the structural arrangements for these units of territorial devolution and decentralisation. The section will consider the policy-making powers of sub-national governments, their resource base, their elected political structures and their bureaucratic services. An important aspect of the role of federal and local government is its relationship with national government, and this may ensure that in some systems, such as that of the United States, devolved governments have considerable authority, whereas in others, such as the British system, its powers are far more restricted.

## Financing the system

Any discussion of the administrative arrangements of a state must also consider how the various structures are financed. Most agencies and local governments can achieve little independently of central government unless they have independent powers to raise revenue through taxation or sales of services. An organisation that is wholly beholden to central government for its resources can easily be bent to the will of the paymaster. As a public organisation central government, let alone its agencies and local government, cannot be given complete power over its finances without instituting some independent means of checking that it is using its resources for the public good.

## Co-ordinating the system

Administrative systems are, as can be seen from the preceding paragraphs, complex organisations made up of a variety of central offices, agencies and federal or local governments. It is, especially for the more complex administrative systems, important to provide some understanding of how the elements of the system work together.

## Managing the system

Earlier in this introduction it was indicated that an important theme of this book is the extent to which administrative systems in liberal democracies are changing under the impact of new public management. This section will open a discussion on changes in the systems of each country and the extent to which they are being moved towards a managerial emphasis on efficiency, effectiveness and economy.

## Accountability, secrecy and openness

Bureaucracies, whether at the national or local level, should be subject to scrutiny and made accountable to legislatures and ultimately to their citizens. The extent to which the administrative structures within the state are accountable will, in part, be determined by the extent to which their activities are open to public scrutiny and each chapter will consider how far the administrative systems of each country facilitate open government. Open government alone does not, however, ensure democratic accountability. This must also be secured by establishing means that enable citizens or organisations to secure redress against government and bureaucracy through the courts or tribunals and offices such as the ombudsman.

## Democracy and the administrative system

The penultimate section of each chapter summarises the preceding arguments on accountability and open government to discuss the extent to which the administrative system of a particular state provides an effective, open and accountable system that enhances democracy within the nation. The section may also consider the problems of ensuring accountability within a more commercialised and competitive management structure.

## Further developments and issues with the system

The final section of each chapter discusses the extent of pressures for change to the administrative system in the country under discussion and, therefore, the future changes that may take place in their bureaucratic systems in the near future. In particular, authors have in their concluding remarks if not in the section on public finance, considered how far the system of public administration in their particular nation state has been retrenched and subject to privatisation as a consequence of the world recession that followed the crash in the banking sector in 2008. This issue is also taken up as a major theme in the concluding chapter of this edition.

## The choice of countries

The book discusses public administration in a range of relatively stable nations with extensively developed or developing economies. The countries studied are, therefore, comparable from the point of view that they are all capable of extensive spending per capita on public services and have populations that generally accept the prevailing structure and legitimacy of the systems of government. The choice of systems that are studied within this framework in part reflects examples of very different constitutional and administrative systems. States with a relatively long liberal-democratic tradition are featured and include the United States, with its presidential and federal system, as opposed to the parliamentary systems of West European countries. The study also includes states of differing population size so that contrasts may be made between, for example, Ireland and Greece, as smaller liberal democracies and the much larger states such as France or the United States. The second edition of this book has also included chapters on three major economic powers – Russia, China and India. Russia and China represent regimes that have rapidly evolved from communist to capitalist economies but have still, to varying degrees, yet to embrace a pluralist and liberal-democratic tradition. India has sustained the liberal democracy bequeathed to it on independence, more perhaps through the necessity of balancing power in such a populous and diverse country, but has yet to establish a society that is fully developed for both the poorest and the elite policy-makers within it.

## References

Greenwood, J. and Wilson, D. (1989) *Public Administration in Britain Today* (2nd edn) London: Unwin Hyman.

# 2 The United Kingdom

*John Kingdom*

The structures and process of British public administration have evolved over centuries to create a variety of state bodies with varying histories, functions and patterns of accountability and control. These include the civil service (the central government bureaucracy), a large army of local public servants serving an elective system of local government, a mammoth institution administering the state-provided National Health Service (NHS) and, under the acronym 'quango', a large miscellany of institutions playing executive, consultative, advisory and regulatory roles. In addition there is a complex of tribunals and inquiries, an ombudsman system and the judiciary with responsibility for the administration of justice.

The architecture of the modern state was drawn largely in the nineteenth century when the rising industrial bourgeoisie sought a means of supporting the emerging capitalist economy. A number of major reports and acts of parliament provided a blueprint for an efficient and meritocratic civil service and a system of prudently managed local authorities. By the opening of the twentieth century an ethos of political impartiality, permanence and public service prevailed. Public administration was seen as different from that in the private sector. Reconstruction following the Second World War saw the enlargement of the functions of these institutions, together with the creation of the NHS and the nationalisation of a number of major industries in the form of public corporations.

From 1979, with the advent of the Thatcher government there was a drive to supplement the traditional public service values with an emphasis on the 'three Es' (economy, efficiency and effectiveness). This entailed the rise of a movement termed 'new public management', where the assumption was that the managerial methods and ethos of the private sector could be profitably introduced into the public sectors (see Elcock, 1991 and Jarvis, 2002). The approach was largely continued after 1997 by the New Labour government of Tony Blair. Public administration was also to be affected by developments in political institutions, including devolution and structural changes in the judiciary. In 2010 the general election saw the creation of a coalition government committed to resolving a huge national debt crisis with cuts in the public sector. Talk of the 'big society' suggested a nostalgic vision of more voluntary (and less state) involvement in the lives of people.

# Political culture

## *Background: the people*

Although genetic analysis indicates that around 80 per cent of British DNA comes from an indigenous population settling in Britain around 12,000 years ago, the modern population embraces many ethnic minorities. Centuries of history have seen colonisation by Celts, Romans, Anglo-Saxons, Danes and Normans. Successive settlements have added to the gene pool and to social patterns, political life and the language itself. Although the Norman Conquest, in the emblematic year of 1066, was the last time the island nation was successfully invaded, a largely peaceful influx of other races and nationalities, often seeking refuge, has never ceased. The medieval period saw numbers of Jewish settlers and at the end of the seventeenth century the country became host to Huguenots escaping persecution in France. The Irish potato famine of the eighteenth century produced a further injection into the body politic.

The post-war, post-colonial era saw further waves of immigration following the 1948 British Nationality Act bestowing citizenship upon all Commonwealth citizens. First came large-scale migration from the Caribbean, to be followed from the 1960s by arrivals from India and Pakistan. The break up of the Soviet empire, the widening of the European Union and the legal establishment of European citizenship has produced immigration from Eastern Europe. In addition there has been a great increase in the numbers seeking asylum from countries all over the world.

This amalgamation of races and nationalities has produced a modern population that calls itself the British. Yet, despite the celebration of 'This happy breed of men' by Shakespeare's John of Gaunt in *Richard II*, such a breed could hardly justify any claim to be a race. The diversity extends beyond the common people to royalty itself, with a succession of wives, consorts and rulers imported from the royal blood lines of Europe. Not until the First World War did the Saxe-Coburg-Gothas, with Germanic lineage, rebrand themselves as the very British-sounding Windsors.

Today the British population numbers some 62 million with an overall density one of the highest in the world. Recent immigration and fertility patterns mean that the minority ethnic groups have a younger age structure than the white population. However, an anticipated ageing of these groups is expected to change this.

## *Geography*

John of Gaunt was right about the geography, however. As a 'precious stone set in the silver sea' the island was indeed a 'fortress built by Nature for herself, Against infection and the hand of war'. Protected by its oceanic moat Britain was able to develop formidable sea power and through colonisation was to preside over the largest empire the world had ever seen. The industrial revolution of the eighteenth and nineteenth centuries saw military power transformed into the more stable economic power, as raw materials from the empire were imported into Britain to be transformed into profitable manufactured goods. The enterprise was assisted by a slave trade, which was not abolished in the British empire until the Act of 1807. Britain was the dominant world force. The economic doctrines of *laissez faire* and comparative advantage gave the position theoretical and moral justification. The new economic class played a significant part in shaping the modern state.

### Continuity

Despite periods of social and industrial unrest Britain has not experienced the trauma of social revolution that has featured in the history of many nations. A civil war of the seventeenth century was a dispute within the aristocratic class rather than a social revolution and the brief republican period was soon brought to an end with a restoration of the monarchy in 1660. The result of this has been an evolutionary development that has never required a formal writing of the constitution to mark a new beginning. Consequently, a significant number of institutions and practices have persisted, including the monarchy itself. Not until the advent of the 1997 Labour government was a serious attempt made to remove the hereditary peers from the upper house of parliament and even in that 'reform', 92 of their number were allowed to remain. Similarly, a process of devolution was a largely incremental move falling well short of the independence demands of nationalists. For critics the evolutionary nature of the system has stood as a bar against modernisation of the constitution. Even so developments since 1979 have made it possible to speak guardedly of a new British constitution (see Bogdanor, 2009).

### Attitudes towards authority

British political culture has often been characterised as deferential, one in which citizens generally respect and accept the forces of the state (see Almond and Verba, 1963). The absence of a popular revolution, the failure of any communist or socialist party to take root and the persistence of the ancient symbols of power mentioned above stand as testament to this. With industrialisation, capitalism took root with relative ease and the great depression of the inter-war years was borne with stoicism; a general strike of 1926 collapsed for lack of popular support. In this climate the Conservative Party was regularly able to count on a substantial element of working-class support.

However, from the 1960s the deference theory began to look less appropriate, as people from lower-class backgrounds began to break through social barriers in fashion design, theatre, popular music and business. Today tabloid newspapers can adopt an irreverent tone when reporting the activities of establishment figures, including royalty, and serious media commentators will grill politicians in a manner unknown in the early post-war decades. A confrontation with the miners precipitated the fall of the Conservative government in 1974 and mass demonstrations against the Community Charge, introduced by the Thatcher government to replace local rates, led to the abandonment of the tax and contributed to the fall of the prime minister.

In 1980 Almond and Verba revisited the political culture and found the greater cynicism to be confined to only a minority (Kavanagh, 1980). In the 1980s people returned neo-liberal governments. Thatcher was able to defeat the miners in an epic struggle and enact a raft of anti-trade-union legislation. When the Labour Party took power in 1997 it did so under the leadership of a public-school- and Oxbridge-educated lawyer. Tony Blair was at pains to expunge all traces of socialism from his polished political rhetoric and promised 'fairness not favours' to the trade unions, the founders of the party. The public schools, the aristocracy and the monarchy remain and in December 2005 the Conservatives elected David Cameron as leader, confident that this Eton-educated distant relative of the Queen would be able to secure the popular vote. The thousands lining the streets for the Queen Mother's funeral in 2002 could give little hope to any with republican sympathies. Although Prince Charles's failed marriage to Princess Diana brought the popularity of the monarchy to a low ebb, the engagement and marriage of his son William to commoner Kate Middleton was greeted with rapture by the tabloids.

Yet the picture remains unclear so far as politicians are concerned. Public opinion polls and attitudinal surveys reveal declining levels of trust in politicians and the political system. Such feelings were fuelled by the financial crisis in which politicians appeared too weak to regulate bankers' bonuses, a great MPs' expenses scandal (that saw some inidividuals convicted in court) and broken manifesto pledges.

## Social stratification

Coupled with the idea of deference is that of social class. While this is present to some degree in most societies, it has been a particularly salient factor in Britain where attitudes towards redistributive policies are more closely related to relative wealth than in comparable nations (Evans, 1993: 133–4). As much as enterprise and invention, the industrial revolution was fuelled by mass labour in a social development that produced the divide between bourgeoisie and workers, and in which Karl Marx saw the volatile mix for cataclysmic class war. While this never happened, the two major political parties have historically reflected a class divide, with the Labour Party formed from the trade union movement and the Conservatives representing the interests of both aristocracy and the emergent capitalist class.

In the modern era of mass democracy both parties have sought to widen their appeal to garner support from the centre. Prime ministers, including the Conservative John Major, himself from an economically impoverished background, and Labour's Tony Blair, from a privileged one, declared Britain to have become a 'classless society'. Yet reference to class continues to colour political rhetoric and debate, and the gap between rich and poor has widened. It became possible to speak of both an 'underclass' and a 'super class' (Adonis and Pollard, 1997). Regular surveys show the divide to be reflected in life chances, educational attainment and health status. While the social structure of modern Britain cannot be characterised in terms of a simple dichotomy between working class and bourgeoisie, social stratification remains. Beneath an aristocracy of those with ancient titles and large estates exists a middle class, which can itself be sub-divided into upper and lower strata. Beneath this is a category sometimes termed the 'underclass'.

In 2008 government minister Harriet Harman set up a National Equality Panel to investigate inequalities. Reporting in January 2010 this found that social class still determined life chances in Britain and that 'deep-seated and systematic differences' remained between social classes. Despite a reign of 13 years, a Labour government had failed to bridge the gap (Cassidy, 2010).

A report by the Joseph Rowntree Foundation found that, in 2008–09, 13 million people could be classed as in poverty. Moreover, 44 per cent of these were in 'deep poverty', with a household income one-third below the poverty line, the highest proportion ever recorded (Parekh, MacInnes and Kenway, 2010). There is a political consequence in the imbalance in that the underclass, characterised by poverty, homelessness, unemployment, drug dependency and political apathy, has a voting turnout lower than that of the wealthy.

### Gender

The political structure that emerged from the reforming era of the nineteenth century was one dominated by males. Women only gained the right to vote after a prolonged and bitter struggle that involved imprisonment, hunger strikes and forced feeding. Despite considerable advancement, overall women tended to be among the most deprived sections of the population (Devine, 1997: 44). An increasing casualisation of the workforce was to intensify the inequality with women in low-paid, part-time jobs while their husbands often suffered redundancy (Hutton, 1996: 106). Various government initiatives have been instigated involving the setting of targets for recruitment and promotion and the creation of women's units. However, it can be argued that the political system itself serves to institutionalise and reproduce inequalities between the sexes (Lovenduski, 1996). The effect can be amplified by the subservient positions in which various religions place women.

In political life women continue to be outnumbered by men in all aspects; in parliament, the civil service, local government, trade unions and the police service. The same position exists in areas such as banking, business, management and the law. Mrs Thatcher did little to promote her female colleagues and the cabinet of John Major was markedly gentlemen only. Blair moved things forward with a cabinet containing a record number of five women, although none was in a senior position. However, in 2006 he made Margaret Beckett Foreign Secretary. Gordon Brown's first cabinet in June 2007 included five women. In May 2010 David Cameron appointed four to his cabinet of 23, with one of them, Theresa May, in the senior position of Home Secretary. Clearly there have been advances but Britain remains behind other comparable democracies in this respect. According to the Centre for Women and Democracy, women make up 53 per cent of Spain's cabinet, 50 per cent of Sweden's, 38 per cent of Germany's, 33 per cent of France's and 31 per cent of America's (Dodd and Gentleman, 2010).

### Race

The 1991 census showed some 3 million people in Britain belonged to an ethnic minority. By 2001 this had risen to 4.6 million (or 7.9 per cent). Society is often described as multicultural, yet racism remains. The imperial dominance enjoyed by Britain was to bequeath a notion of racial superiority that survives in the national psyche as both patriotism and xenophobia. The waves of post-war immigration met with considerable hostility from within the resident population. In the post-9/11 atmosphere those of Asian extraction were to experience renewed levels of racism. Various studies and reports reveal that people from nearly every ethnic minority group are paid less for comparable work than white men and women.

The issue assumed particular salience after the murder of the black teenager, Stephen Lawrence, in April 1993 at a bus stop in south east London. Failures in policing led to an inquiry, and the resultant Macpherson Report (1999) identified institutional racism within the police service, involving unwitting prejudice, ignorance, thoughtlessness and racial stereotyping (para 6.34). Racism, institutional or otherwise, is not the prerogative of the police service. The report suggested that other agencies including, for example, those dealing with housing and education also suffered from the 'disease' (para 6.54). Although the report occasioned critical backlash and accusations from opposition spokesman William Hague that it would lower police morale, it led to the enactment of the 2000 Race Relations Amendment Act, extending the application of the Race Relations Act 1976 to the police and other public authorities. Efforts are regularly made to redress racial imbalance but, in 2004, Trevor Phillips, chair of the Equality and Human Rights Commission, could still refer to 'the scandal that more than half of Whitehall's departments have no ethnic minority staff at senior level' (Phillips, 2004).

The position is reflected in government. David Cameron worked strenuously to increase the diversity within the Conservative Party and, in 2010, included life peer Baroness Warsi in his cabinet as minister without portfolio. The only ethnic minority member, she was also the first Muslim woman to serve in a British cabinet. She also became co-chairman of the party.

## *Insularity*

Geographical insularity can promote cultural insularity and this has been particularly pronounced in attitudes towards Europe. Despite playing a key role in the allied victory over fascism in the Second World War Britain disdained entry into the European Coal and Steel Community in 1951 and the European Common Market in 1957. Even after entry into the European Community in 1973 scepticism remained in both the population and the political class. History decreed that Britain could and should stand alone. In addition there was a conviction that a 'special relationship' with the USA would secure a seat at the top table in international diplomacy. The anti-European strains existed in both major parties. Within Labour, the left suspected the free-market ambitions of the project, while right-wing Eurosceptics in the Conservative Party saw a creeping socialism. This fear was stridently expressed by Margaret Thatcher when Prime Minister. Indeed, Euroscepticism threatened to tear her party apart during its period in opposition after 1997. There was also a feared loss of 'Britishness'. Conservative leader William Hague fought, and lost, a general election on a slogan to 'save the pound'. In the event, the Labour government, under the financial stewardship of Chancellor Gordon Brown, showed itself no less willing to preserve the currency as Britain remained steadfastly outside the Eurozone. Only the Liberal Democrats express enthusiasm for the European project. It can be argued that it has been a structural crisis within the party system that fuelled Euroscepticism within domestic politics (Gifford, 2008: 7). This is not to say that Britain does not engage with the European Union; local authorities and the devolved nations regularly lobby at Brussels and can gain much from EU structural and regional funding. The insularity extends to the general population, with views confirmed by much of the press. Governments stoutly resist calls for referendums on European matters.

## *Religion*

Despite its claims to be a secular state, religion and religious symbols permeate Britain's political culture. There is an established church, of which the Queen is the head, and bishops of the Church of England have long continued to sit in the House of Lords. The lower house, the Commons, begins each day with prayers. Most political figures profess religious faith. While much of this may be seen as symbolism, in a more secular age the growing Muslim population, with a belief that religion and religious laws should influence politics, adds to political and racial tensions.

## The constitutional framework

Although a unitary state, the UK contains a local government system, and three devolved assemblies governing Wales, Scotland and Northern Ireland with varying degrees of autonomy. It is a constitutional monarchy with the

Queen as head of state. The country is exceptional in not having a written (or codified) constitution that the Queen's subjects can peruse as a single document. However, vestiges of royal power (the Royal Prerogative), which are exercised by the government, and the varied body of statutes, common law decisions, legal opinions and conventions provide for a regularised and orderly liberal democratic system. The 1998 Human Rights Act, incorporating the European Convention on Human Rights into British law, strengthened the constitutional rights of people by replacing a confusing body of common law and statute. In addition, various pieces of EU legislation may also be regarded as adding to the constitution.

In its present 'unwritten' form the constitution occasions considerable debate. It leaves the structures of government vulnerable to political manipulation. Many of the changes made to local government during the Thatcher era illustrated the uncertainty (Elcock, 1991: 210). Labour's devolution was accomplished with similar constitutional ease. For reformers a written constitution is the *sine qua non* of political modernisation. This is discussed later.

The central government comprises a bicameral legislature, an executive and a judiciary. However, contrary to the view taken in the eighteenth century by the French jurist Montesquieu, the constitutional separation of these three arms of government is by no means complete and was more accurately described by Walter Bagehot in the nineteenth century as a *fusion* of powers.

## The legislature

Parliament is located in London on the banks of the Thames in the Palace of Westminster (by which metonym it is often known). It is a bicameral legislature with a popularly elected lower chamber (the House of Commons) and an upper chamber (the House of Lords) formed largely by appointment but also containing 92 members of the ancient aristocracy. The latter once dominated the House and their position was eroded through a gradual process of democratisation. For most legislation the process begins in the Commons before passing to the Lords, which, with no power of absolute veto, can only delay legislation and suggest amendments. The process is not complete until a bill has passed before the Queen for Royal Assent. However, today this is a mere formality.

The Members of Parliament (MPs) sitting in the Commons are elected to represent single-member constituencies with populations of around 69,000 (to be increased in 2015). Male MPs outnumber their female colleagues by around 5 to 1. There are relatively few members from ethnic minorities. The electoral system is based on simple plurality (first-past-the-post): the candidate with most votes is elected with no requirement for an absolute majority. The system is much debated and there are regular calls for some form of proportional representation (PR). The fact that this is used in elections to the European Parliament and the devolved assemblies lends weight to the call. Advocates of the status quo reply that the system produces strong government. While this is so, it does so by grossly over-representing the winning party's support in the country. Labour's 1997 'landslide' of 418 seats to the Conservative's 165 was achieved with only some 43 per cent of the popular vote. The coalition government formed after the 2010 general election held a referendum on a limited electoral reform, which would have introduced an alternative vote system, but this was decisively rejected.

The electoral system tends to inhibit the emergence of a range of political parties so that it has been common to refer to the system as bipartisan. Yet this interpretation was increasingly undermined by a growing Liberal Democrat presence. The party entered the 2010 general election with 63 seats and, although falling to 57, was able gain a taste of power as the minor partner in a Conservative-led coalition.

The bipartisan nature of politics is institutionalised in the very structure of the Commons, with two sets of benches facing each other in confrontational manner, rather that the semi-circular configuration found in many chambers. Party loyalty is a pre-eminent requirement and certain MPs are appointed as 'whips' with the task of ensuring this, sometimes exerting immense pressure on their colleagues. Such discipline is crucial for a government because it is parliament that creates and supports the executive. However, this is not to say that rebels do not exist. From 2001 a number of Labour MPs opposed the government on a range of key issues, including fox hunting, anti-terror measures, university fees, NHS reforms and the invasion of Iraq (see Cowley, 2005).

### The executive

The executive arm of government comprises thousands of state servants delivering government policy in a variety of institutions. At its heart is the core executive, consisting of government ministers, top civil servants and a miscellany of political advisors from various disciplines.

The political impetus comes from some 100 ministers from the party (or coalition) that can command a majority in the Commons. These form the government and at its heart is the body of around 20 or so cabinet members, most of whom are drawn from the elected house although there are usually a few from the Lords. Since cabinet members are effectively leaders of both the executive and parliament, the system undermines any idea of a separation of powers and the legislature has followed the party line for much of the time. However, rebellions can occur, and dissent in the House of Commons has been shown to have increased significantly since 1970 (Norton and Cowley, 1999). Yet, while sometimes significant and always politically exciting to the media, these occasions remain relatively rare. The House of Lords, the 'Upper House' in this bicameral parliament, has seen a gradual erosion of its powers and authority, so that it has offered no serious impediment to the executive.

However, reforms introduced by the New Labour government (see below) have seen some spirited opposition and increased its potential as a revising chamber.

This concentration of power goes even further in the position of the prime minister. The formal invitation by the Queen to become her first minister bestows inestimable power. Foremost comes patronage, the ability to make or break the careers of colleagues. All cabinet members must be appointed by the prime minister and the regular threat of cabinet reshuffles will ensure that all will remain largely compliant. Beyond the cabinet are a host of other official positions subject to prime ministerial patronage. This power has been increasingly used to create policy units and think tanks, operating as satellites around the official residence of Number 10 Downing Street, and serving in the manner of a personal department.

Commentators speak of the 'presidentialisation' of the office. Yet this is a 'president' whom none of the people have elected apart from those in one particular constituency. However, it can be argued that voters are led by the mass media to treat the general election as a contest between the party leaders, and this can bestow legitimacy. During the 2010 general election campaign a series of TV confrontations between the party leaders did indeed resemble US presidential debates. As politics changes, prime minsters have increasingly devoted attention to media management (see Seymour-Ure, 2003).

Yet the prime minister has an Achilles heel. The position is gained only through the leadership of the party and if this is removed all else falls away. This was the case with one of the most dominant figures of the post-war era. When, in 1990, Margaret Thatcher was challenged by Michael Heseltine for the leadership of her party, the support of her colleagues wavered, leaving her with little alternative but resignation. Her successor, John Major, himself encountered party opposition and was never able to exploit the full potential of the office. Even Tony Blair who, as Labour Prime Minister from 1997, dominated the political scene for many years, was forced to relinquish the leadership in 2007 because of discontent within the party over his domestic policies, the invasion of Iraq and the presence of an ambitious and well-supported rival, Chancellor of the Exchequer, Gordon Brown.

However, for as long as the party is happy, the British prime minister enjoys a degree of power in government that dwarfs that of the US president and can be envied by would-be dictators around the world.

### *The judiciary*

Composed of judicial figures of varying rank, this third arm of government has not enjoyed the same power given to those judiciaries operating under a formal constitutional separation of powers. Indeed, the position of the judiciary was a denial of such a separation. Senior judges were part of the legislature, sitting in the House of Lords as Law Lords. In addition the House of Lords acted as the final Court of Appeal and the Lord Chancellor was head of the judiciary, the speaker in the House of Lords and, with a seat in the cabinet, a senior member of the executive.

However, since 1979 there have been changes. A catalyst came with the passing of the 1998 Human Rights Act, which incorporated the European Convention on Human Rights into British law. Prior to this, judges had no power to question the constitutionality of new legislation but this Act allowed them to consider whether it was in compliance with the Convention. Although the principle of parliamentary sovereignty was maintained, so that judges could not over-ride an Act, they were given the ability to ask parliament to think again through the issue of a declaration of incompatibility. This would invite correction by means of a ministerial issue of a 'remedial order'.

Further important reforms came in a Constitutional Reform Act of 2005. This formally recognised the independence of the judiciary, barring government from attempts to influence its decisions. In addition the judicial functions of the Lord Chancellor were transferred to a president of the Courts of England and Wales (a new title given to the Lord Chief Justice) and the judicial functions of the House of Lords were passed to a newly created Supreme Court to be located at Middlesex Guildhall, a separate building on the other side of Parliament Square. The Act also created an independent Judicial Appointments Commission, responsible for recommending judicial appointments to the Secretary of State for Justice. May 2007 saw the changes spreading to Whitehall with the creation of a new Ministry of Justice formed by merging certain functions of the Home Office with those of the Department for Constitutional Affairs (formerly the Lord Chancellor's Department). This assumed responsibility for courts, prisons, and probation in England and Wales.

## The civil service

The zone of power does not end with the cabinet or prime minister. Closely enmeshed into this core executive are the senior civil servants, shadowy wielders of influence, traditionally operating with impartiality and permanence behind a cloak of anonymity. Beyond the core, mostly in the form of executive agencies (see below), exists a mammoth organisation of around half a million employees working in London and around the country (see Burnham and Pyper, 2008).

The civil service is the government bureaucracy. It is structured in some 20 functionally defined departments, some of which retain ancient titles reflecting the origins of the service as sections of the royal household. Finance rests with Her Majesty's Treasury, the most dominant department with a pervasive influence throughout the service. Many of the newer departments reflect a developing range of social and economic responsibilities such as education, social security and business. Each is headed by a senior minister or secretary of state responsible to parliament for all that takes place under his or her stewardship.

The modern form of the service owes much of its character to a series of reforms following the Northcote–Trevelyan report of 1854. Before this the administration of government business was carried out by a variety of separate bodies that had evolved from the royal household. These were staffed on the basis of political patronage and nepotism with employees sometimes financed by bribes. Inspired by the model of the Indian Civil Service created to administer the colonial territory, the report called for entrance on the basis of merit. It also advocated permanence so that employees would not change with governments and could develop professional careers. This in turn called for political neutrality and anonymity to shield officials from public controversy. These principles of permanence, anonymity and neutrality were to define the modern service.

In addition, the various sections were amalgamated into a single Home civil service. Within the organisation employment was hierarchical. The Northcote–Trevelyan report depicted the work of officials in terms of intellectual level. This was to be reflected in a structure that distinguished between an administrative grade at the top concerned with policy formation at ministerial level, an executive grade responsible for implementation, and a clerical grade to undertake routine tasks. A new meritocratic appointments system recruited entrants to these grades with little expectation that those from the lower echelons would ascend to the heights of the administrative grade. Thus recruitment tended to reflect the class structure in society with entrants to the administrative grades coming from the Oxbridge universities, and usually educated in the prestigious public schools. These would work closely with ministers in the formation of government policy.

As Britain moved into a modern era critics were to argue that the power of the top civil servants was too great; termed 'mandarins' they were alleged to dominate ministers. The relationship was made the subject of a highly successful TV sitcom, 'Yes Minister', the running joke being that the sub-servient 'Yes' invariably meant 'No'. Today this mandarin class form the senior civil service and account for around 0.9 per cent of the total workforce.

Below come a number of management grades including Senior, Higher and Executive Officers. Next come lower grades making up just under half of all civil servants. Most civil servants do not populate the corridors of power, they work in executive agencies with the duty of implementing rather than making policy. In 2009 around 80 per cent of employees worked full-time, just over half being women. There is also a part-time workforce, of which women make up some 85 per cent.

## Central government agencies and non-departmental public bodies

The creation of the civil service agencies is a relatively new innovation, following a 1988 report from the Efficiency Unit under Sir Robin Ibbs. Entitled *Improving Management in Government: The Next Steps*, it argued that the routine executive functions of the service should be structurally separate from its policy advice role. The administration of policy was to be entrusted to agencies under parent departments but with a degree of autonomy from them. There were important managerial implications in this reform and these are discussed later.

The administrative arm of the state extends beyond the civil service. Popularly known as quangos, a further range of public bodies, with varying degrees of autonomy from government, exist within the public sector. Officially termed Non-departmental Public Bodies (NDPBs), these perform various functions that are deemed to be better removed from the direct line of ministerial control and accountability. Members are appointed by ministers on the basis of experience, expertise or a representative capacity. These bodies are served by permanent administrative staff, some of whom, such as those in the Health and Safety Executive, are civil servants.

There are various types of quasi-autonomous bodies. Executive bodies perform administrative, regulatory and/or commercial functions such as protecting the environment, regional development and managing national museums and galleries. Advisory bodies provide ministerial advice on a wide range of issues such as the schools curriculum, wage levels and standards in public life. Tribunals serve a judicial purpose in specialised fields of law, such as housing and employment. There are also Independent Monitoring Boards of Prisons, Immigration Removal Centres and Immigration Holding Rooms acting as independent watchdogs.

Although operating at an arm's length from government, quangos are by no means free from political controversy. Their number and cost are also questioned. In 2009, there were 766, accounting for a total expenditure of £46,487 million. There are also questions over the use of ministerial patronage, with allegations of a 'gravy train' of the 'great and the good' moving from one quango to another and enjoying prestige and power without ever coming before the electorate. They can also provide lucrative jobs for ex-politicians. For example, in 2010 the head of the Food Standards Agency, with a salary of £45,000 for a two-day week, was Lord Rooker. As government minister Jeff Rooker, it was he who had created the agency. A constitutional issue also arises with a loss of democratic accountability inherent in their autonomy. Opposition parties regularly promise a 'cull of the quangos', only to lose their enthusiasm once in office. The 2010 coalition declared its intention to wield the axe with zeal greater than anything seen before.

## Federal and local governance

As a unitary state all political sovereignty in Britain lies with the Westminster government. However, in a major reform, political devolution was introduced in 1998, with the establishment of separate elected assemblies for Scotland, Wales and Northern Ireland. There is also a well-established tradition of local government stretching back many centuries. Moreover, since 1973 the UK has been a member of what is now the European Union. Hence, the British can be said to live in a system of multi-level governance.

## Devolution

The politics of devolution cannot be fully understood without reference to history, and a number of predecessor institutions (Mitchell, 2009: 13). Such details are beyond the scope of this chapter (see Mitchell, 2009). It is the relatively small province in the north of Ireland that turns 'Great Britain' into the 'United Kingdom'. Yet, though small, it has proved a running sore on the body politic. Bitter and violent feuding between Catholic republicans (wanting a united Irish Republic) and Protestant loyalists (wanting continued union with Britain) have blighted the British polity for many years. This was resolved by the 'Good Friday Agreement' of April 1988, which accepted the principle of a power-sharing executive. In an election of June 1998, 108 Members of the Legislative Assembly (MLAs), six from each of the province's 18 Westminster constituencies, were elected using the single transferable vote system. Ministers are appointed using a system (d'Hondt) that awards places in proportion to party strength in the Assembly. This means that all those with a significant number of seats gain at least one representative. The executive is served by a civil service.

The new executive received immediate responsibility for certain Transferred Matters including education, health, social security, environment and agriculture. The Assembly has the power to enact primary legislation in these areas. Acts passed must be accepted by the Secretary of State for Northern Ireland and receive Royal Assent. The Assembly sits at Parliament Buildings at Stormont in Belfast. The career of the Assembly has been fraught with sectarian disputes and it has been suspended on several occasions. The sensitive areas of policing and criminal law were classed under Reserved Matters and only transferred to the Assembly in 2010 amid considerable political tension and threats of further suspension.

Wales and Scotland gained devolution in an altogether more peaceable manner. Both had nationalist movements and both were granted referendums in 1997 by the Labour government. In addition, both adopted the additional-member voting system and went on to establish coalition governments.

The 129-member Scottish Parliament received primary legislative powers in certain domestic areas such as education, health and prisons, and the right to raise or lower the basic rate of income tax by up to 3p. Yet demands for full independence led to the referendum in September 2014. The 60-member Welsh Assembly, or Senedd, had no tax varying or primary legislative rights. This left some dissatisfaction in Wales and the 2006 Government of Wales Act allowed the Assembly to pass legislation (Assembly measures) in areas such as health, education, social services and local government, subject to permission ('legislative competence') on a case-by-case basis from Westminster. The Act also made provision for a future referendum on increasing the Assembly's powers to the level of the Scottish Parliament's – including the ability to vary tax rates. This came in March 2011 and the result was an emphatic two-to-one majority saying 'Yes'.

In all the devolution settlements, matters judged to be of national importance, such as defence, taxation and foreign policy, are exempted, to remain the responsibility of Westminster.

## Local government

Britain has a long-established system of local government deriving from parishes, boroughs and counties. What may be termed the modern system grew up in the nineteenth century under the pressure of the industrial revolution, which saw major improvements in municipal government to facilitate the rise of the industrial towns. The Municipal Corporations Act of 1835 modernised the system with prudent accounting, democratic elections and a widening range of functions. Since this time there have been many reforms and reorganisations to the system in terms of both structure and internal organisation.

At the heart of the system is the principle of local democracy based on local elections. This uses the first-past-the-post-system, with councillors serving four-year terms. Although there are independent candidates, most local battles are between the main political parties, and councils are usually seen as being under the control of one or other or some form of coalition of them.

Geographical, demographic and industrial factors have produced a complex structure. There are large, sparsely populated rural areas, industrial towns with surrounding conurbations and a particularly dense concentration of population in the South East around London. The result is a number of different types of authority.

Today the major units of local government are 'unitary' authorities, with a single council responsible for the majority of functions in its area. This model applies in the whole of Scotland, Wales and Northern Ireland. In England it applies to 36 authorities in the northern conurbations and 47 other rural 'shire unitary' areas. In the conurbations policing, passenger transport, and fire and civil defence are run by joint authorities. Police authorities are now controlled by an elected police commissioner. The extensive Greater London conurbation is administered by 32 London Borough Councils with powers similar to those of the unitary authorities, but there is also a Greater London Authority under an elected mayor with responsibility for policing, passenger transport and economic development across the Greater London area. Some of the unitary areas and London Boroughs act jointly in areas such as waste disposal.

The rest of England has a two-tier structure, with functions shared between a top-tier county authority, responsible for wide-ranging functions such as education, strategic planning, passenger transport, transport planning, highways, fire, social services, libraries and waste disposal and a number of constituent district councils administering housing, planning applications, leisure and recreation, waste disposal and environmental health. At a communal level there are parish councils (community councils in Scotland and Wales) covering small areas, with various responsibilities such as litter, parks, public clocks, allotments and maintenance of the village hall. They also have a consultative role in planning applications.

### Non-elective local governance

Not all locally administered functions are the responsibility of the elected councils. Before the modern system of local government was formed there existed various boards administering services such as education, sanitation, burial and the poor law. Most of these were gradually taken over by the elected councils. However, the 1980s saw the rise of a new generation of non-elected bodies as the central government sought to reduce the role of the elected councils, many of which opposed its policies. In an evocation of an earlier age the new range of non-elected authorities was dubbed the 'new magistracy' (Stewart 1992, 1995). Towards the end of the 1990s non-elected functionaries outnumbered elected councillors by a ratio of 3:1 (Hall and Weir, 1996).

The internal management of local authorities has been subject to various reforms that have generally sought to centralise the power structure with cabinet systems, chief executives, council leaders and even elected mayors. Much of this reform has been Westminster-driven and is discussed in the section on central–local relations below (see Chandler 2009).

Another non-elected arm of the state is the National Health Service created in 1948: a vast undertaking, with more employees than any other organisation in Western Europe. In the immediate post-war years there were some expectations that the NHS would be administered by the elected local authorities but opposition from the medical profession resulted in a complex system of appointed boards at regional and local level. These have been subject to constant revision and are currently termed NHS Trusts.

### Financing the system

Public expenditure rose steadily in real terms from the beginning of the twentieth century. Two world wars precipitated sudden rises, which, although falling back during peacetime, remained higher than before. The emergence of the welfare state, with a popular acceptance of an era of 'big government', and the government's adoption of Keynesian economic management enhanced the upward trend. The financial crisis of the 1970s saw some concern over the level. Governments began to move away from the Keynesian doctrine and, under Thatcher, a neo-liberal agenda became the new orthodoxy, to be followed by New Labour under Tony Blair. The world banking crisis in the opening decade of the twenty-first century saw a revival of interest in the economic management role of the government. The 2010 coalition made the reduction of the national debt one of its top priorities, promising public spending cuts and introducing a rise in VAT to 20 per cent.

In the fiscal year 2008–09, Total Managed Expenditure, comprising spending by the entire public sector including central government, local authorities and other public organisations, stood at some £631 billion. This was 43.2 per cent of UK national income and amounted to about £13,000 per adult. The largest spending areas (in £bn) were pensions (110), health (110), welfare (88), education (80) and defence (42). Central government accounted for 74 per cent of public expenditure; the remaining 26 per cent was spent by local government. The government's spending is financed mainly from taxation and borrowing, with a smaller amount from trading activities. The proportion of taxation to GDP is 35.8 per cent.

The political head of British public finance is the Chancellor of the Exchequer, the ancient title a reminder that he was once the keeper of the royal purse. The chancellor is the most powerful minister in the cabinet, a rival to the prime minister, and relations between the two can often be tense and fractious. The present system owes much to Gladstone's nineteenth-century reforms. As chancellor he instigated an annual financial cycle comprising an estimate of each department's future expenditure, a budgetary process determining the way the money would be raised and an accounting process to ensure that it had been used properly. Constitutionally the Commons lies at the heart of the process. It must agree the proposed spending levels, authorise the taxation needed and be satisfied with the auditing process. (This is an area where the House of Lords had no power to amend or delay.) Yet in much of the process parliament's role is little more than ceremonial. However, it does bare its teeth somewhat in the auditing process through its Public Accounts Committee.

Throughout the processes, the detailed work is done by the chancellor's department, Her Majesty's Treasury. The first stage, which was originally known as the estimates process, entails a series of bilateral meetings between Treasury officials and the senior members of the departments. Various reforms have been introduced as the process became known as the Public Expenditure Survey and, under Chancellor Gordon Brown in the 1997 Blair government, the Comprehensive Spending Review. Some of the changes were seen by critics as cosmetic in order to generate confidence in the prudence of the government, but the essential purpose is to establish what each department may spend in the coming years. The purpose of these 'bilaterals' is negotiation. The departmental representatives will make a bid for Treasury consideration. Traditionally seen as parsimonious in its approach, the Treasury's goal is to restrict public expenditure. Civil servants and departmental ministers can often see ambitious plans crushed by its 'dead hand'. When the process is completed, three-year expenditure projections are presented to parliament in a White Paper. Parliament will debate these but, whatever criticisms are voiced, the estimates will be agreed and legislative approval will be given in the form of the Consolidated Fund Act, the Consolidated Fund being the government's bank account lodged with the Bank of England. During the course of the following year departments may request approval for supplementary estimates, depending upon circumstances.

The executive cannot raise taxes without parliamentary approval and the chancellor, with his traditional red box, presents the budget to parliament, which is made manifest in the Finance Bill. Beyond raising money for public expenditure, the budget is a key instrument for governments wishing to manage the economy through fiscal policy.

Drawn up in the bowels of the Treasury, the budget involves a consideration of the implications for the economy of various tax possibilities, and representatives of diverse economic interests will be consulted. Traditionally all this took place under a cloak of secrecy but increasingly leaks and pre-budget statements have made the process more transparent. Yet Budget Day remains a special day in the parliamentary calendar, the Commons will be packed and the media will turn out in force. The chancellor outlines the state of the economy and announces the government's revenue raising proposals. Once again, although debate over several days may be fierce, the House will not actually reject the proposals and the Lords will have no say in the matter.

It is in the auditing process that MPs can begin to flex their muscles. This they do through the oldest and most revered of their scrutiny committees – the Public Accounts Committee (PAC). Established in 1861 the PAC is an all-party committee but always chaired by a member of the opposition. The committee can hold hearings, call for papers and compel witnesses to attend. It also has the services of a key figure, the Comptroller and Auditor General (C&AG), who heads the National Audit Office (NAO). Originally concerned with the Whitehall departments, the remit of the C&AG now extends to other non-departmental public bodies. Following reports from the NAO the PAC can conduct deeper enquiries and has uncovered some serious malpractices. For example, it revealed that, in 2006, 36 out of 59 completed schemes for road building projects were costing 40 per cent more than originally estimated.

Beyond Whitehall most other public bodies, including the devolved assemblies, a variety of quangos and local government, are much concerned with the central financial processes that determine the grants they will receive. The announcement of the level of the Revenue Support Grant is a red letter day on the calendars of local councils and will have a bearing on the size of the council tax they will levy.

## Co-ordinating the system

Britain has a cabinet system of government that brings together some 22 ministers and their senior civil servants in the formation of policy. Most ministers head government departments, which means that overall policy can be co-ordinated at the highest level.

However, while opportunities for multiple communications exist between departments, interests and politicians, it remains a point of criticism that Britain lacks a system of fully 'joined-up' government. This is a product of the sheer volume of work expected of officials and politicians and the fact that ministers, departments and interest groups are also concerned with their self-interest, each fighting corners in a never-ending quest for a share of government resources. Highly focused on their individual portfolios, ministers can become blinkered and uninterested in the synoptic picture. Efforts have been made to combat this. Experiments were made with smaller cabinets of 'super ministers' with wide-ranging remits and in the 1970s a Central Policy Review Staff was created as a 'think tank', but it encountered opposition from the traditional departments. Another vehicle for co-ordination comes in the form of cabinet committees composed of ministers concerned with a particular area but also bringing together civil servants and other interested parties. These are often seen as the real centres of policy-making, relegating the full cabinet's role to that of rubber-stamping. In addition there are interdepartmental official committees operating within Whitehall bringing together senior civil servants from various departments.

Above all is the Cabinet Office headed by the Cabinet Secretary. A key section is the Cabinet Secretariat, which prepares agendas for the cabinet and its committees and conveys policy decisions to departments. Also within the Cabinet Office are units that can consider policy across departments (Burch and Holliday, 1996) and, during the Blair premiership transformed the Cabinet Office into a de facto prime minister's department. The Treasury itself plays a significant co-ordinating role in the spending reviews. In addition there are numerous informal contacts between senior officials in what is sometimes termed the 'village' of Whitehall.

There are also policy networks formed between a vast range of interest groups, politicians and officials. The civil service remains the prime target of those seeking policy influence. Leading figures representing large private corporations, financial institutions, confederations of business interests, leaders of charities and other voluntary societies and trade unions become very familiar with the architecture of the Whitehall corridors. Close relationships can form between them and the bureaucrats working in their particular fields. Some of these are institutionalised in the form of official consultative and advisory bodies. The mechanism is oiled by professional consultancy firms, sometimes employing the very people who once worked as politicians and officials.

The issue of co-ordination within the system of public administration also applies to the relationship between the elected local authorities and the central government. Central grants provide the lion's share of local government funding, a condition resulting in Westminster having a dominant voice in local affairs. Central control can concern the nature and extent of service provision and influence the level of council tax. Councils have been directed to contract out the provision of various services to private providers and enter into public–private partnerships. They have also been made to use private finance initiatives (PFIs) for capital projects.

There is a political dimension to the relationship. A local authority can fall under the control of a different party to that in government, resulting in ideological confrontation. Central–local relations reached high levels of acrimony during the 1980s when the Conservative government under Thatcher sought to make cuts, contract out services, promote the sale of council houses and impose a community charge, which became known as the 'poll tax'.

## Managing the system

Management within public sector organisations was to become a major issue from the 1980s. With a New Right suspicion of the state, the Thatcher government argued, in a proclaimed quest for efficiency, effectiveness and economy (to be known as the 3Es), that much could be learned from the practices of the private sector. A wave of reform, sometimes described as New Public Management, saw the introduction into public organisations of professional consultants, advisors from the private sector and gurus from a burgeoning academic discipline: management studies. Practices such as market testing, to see if private firms could do aspects of the work better or more cheaply, and the appointment of outsiders to top positions were introduced.

Following the 1988 Ibbs Report, *Improving Management in Government*, large segments of government departments were hived off as executive agencies. Although still part of the civil service the agencies would have much greater autonomy from their parent departments and be under chief executives with managerial roles more akin to that found in the private sector. They and their colleagues would be motivated with performance-related pay and bonuses. By the mid-1990s the agency model had become the principal instrument for the delivery of public services, with around three-quarters of all civil servants so employed. For critics this created a fundamental constitutional problem in that it undermined individual ministerial accountability to parliament. This is examined below. Subsequent analysis has suggested that claims of a managerial revolution have been somewhat overstated and some new problems created concerning fragmentation and communication (see James, 2003).

The managerial baton was picked up by New Labour with enthusiasm, with the term 'modernisation' employed to clothe the 3Es with futuristic promise. One insider's view, published in 2007, details a potpourri of institutional restructuring, management techniques, administrative procedures, mission statements, targets and strategic reviews pursued robustly throughout the public sector (see Barber, 2007). Critics argued that the process entailed a de-professionalisation of public sector workers and some of the language (delivery chains, deliverability, choice, challenge) sounded an Orwellian ring.

Local government also felt the winds of managerial reform. The system that had evolved up to the 1960s was one based on separate, functionally defined departments administering services such as education and social services, each overseen by a committee of elected councillors. These committees held a high degree of authority, effectively making policy in their areas, and their chairs could be prominent public figures. However, the problem with this model was seen as a lack of co-ordination between services, and two reports, Maud in 1967 and Bains in 1972, recommended forms of corporate management based on the private sector, with a management board (often termed a Policy and Resources Committee) composed of a small number of senior councillors. In addition, the head of the local bureaucracy would become the chief executive, with a dynamic leadership role. This figure would replace the old-style Town Clerk, usually a lawyer with little business or administrative skill.

Authorities responded with varying degrees of enthusiasm to these recommendations but during the 1980s, with the rise of the New Public Management, things were taken further as the contracting out and private–public partnership initiatives altered the managerial climate. The New Labour government sought to maintain the momentum and introduced a Local Government Act in 2000, which required local authorities to adopt one of three managerial models: a directly elected mayor who would appoint a cabinet of senior councillors, a council leader elected by the council who would also select a cabinet, or a directly elected mayor who would work with a manager appointed by the council. In all cases the powers of the ordinary councillors would be reduced and the parliamentary term 'backbencher' gained currency. The change to an elected mayoral system had to be confirmed by local referendums and the idea did not prove immensely popular. By 2009, 37 of the 152 major authorities had put the question to their electorates, with only 12 saying 'Yes'. One of these concerned the Greater London area, but the mayor of London, presiding over 32 London Boroughs was created under separate legislation and enjoyed significantly fewer powers than the other mayors. While analysts could approve the quest for efficiency and strong community leadership, the domination of central government, particularly in finance, left scepticism over the future of local democracy (see Stewart, 2003). In May 2012 central government compelled 11 of the largest cities to hold referendums but only the people of Bristol voted for the elected mayoral system.

The managerial movement also spread to the National Health Service. Here the Griffiths Report, commissioned by the Thatcher government, recommended a system of general managers, often brought in from the private sector, to take the helm in hospitals and heath authorities. An 'internal market' replaced the top-down system of resource allocation. Under New Labour the developments were taken further, with Strategic Health Authorities and Primary Care Trusts replacing the Regional and Area Health Authorities. The coalition government of 2010 opened yet a further phase of reform with controversial legislation to abolish the Primary Care Trusts and enable greater use of private health care providers.

# Accountability, secrecy and openness

## *Accountability*

The executive is constitutionally accountable to parliament through the conventions of collective individual responsibility. These are now defined in the *Ministerial Code: A Code of Conduct and Guidance on Procedures for Ministers*. Collective responsibility lays down that ministers must be able to argue freely within the cabinet and its committees while maintaining a united front before parliament and the public. Ministers must not disagree publicly with cabinet decisions, or suggest that the published minutes are not an accurate record of government discussions. If the desire to speak out becomes irrepressible then the only course of action is resignation and the indulgence of a resignation speech to a (usually packed) House of Commons. The 2003 departure of Robin Cook from the Blair cabinet over the invasion of Iraq was such a case.

Individual responsibility lays down that ministers, rather than civil servants, are held responsible to parliament for anything concerning their portfolios. Ministers can be held to account during Question Time when they appear, on a rota basis, before the House to answer questions. However, there is a weakening of the convention resulting from the agencification of the civil service. This can allow ministers to evade parliamentary questions on the grounds that a matter rests with an autonomous body. Quangos, the NHS, the police service and local government are similarly shielded.

Ministers can also appear before all-party select committees. With the power to call for persons and papers and to use expert witnesses, their role is the scrutiny of government departments. While not comparable with the formidable US congressional committees, they have achieved some notable results, particularly through the work of the oldest of them all, the Public Accounts Committee.

Accountability to parliament is generally weakened by party discipline. MPs of the governing party may put questions designed to show ministers in a favourable light, indeed, ministers themselves may plant such questions with a tame or ambitious MP. Similarly, MPs on select committees may take a party line and there have been reports of ministers and whips putting pressure on members and of members leaking early drafts of reports to ministers.

A traditional reading of the convention of individual ministerial responsibility suggests that, in cases of serious failure, ministers will resign. However, while they are frequently called upon to do so, the convention has been honoured more in the breach than the commission. The resignation of Foreign Secretary Lord Carrington in 1982 over the failure of his department to foresee the events leading to the Falklands war was a rare instance. More common are cases where ministers have successfully resisted calls for their resignation for departmental failure. For example, Northern Ireland Secretary James Prior did not go in 1983 after the Maze prison break out when 38 dangerous prisoners escaped. On 'Black Wednesday' of 16 September 1992, when sterling was forced to leave the ERM and parliament held an emergency debate on what was effectively a confidence motion, Chancellor Norman Lamont chose to remain on the grounds that the economic policy was that of the whole government.

However, resignations do occur where the ministers themselves have been personally culpable, as in the case of Edwina Currie who, in 1988, precipitated a political furore in speaking of salmonella and egg production. In 1988 Peter Mandelson resigned as Secretary of State for Trade and Industry, following revelations of a £373,000 loan from Geoffrey Robinson, the Paymaster General, whose own financial dealings were subject to oversight by Mandelson's department. Despite its limited power, the House of Lords can effectively assist accountability. With members less subject to party discipline and not dependent upon further executive patronage, the House can sometimes embarrass a government and even result in the Commons being forced to accept amendments.

At the level of local government, accountability of councillors was reduced with the rise of the 'new magistracy' with non-elected members. Although the Labour Party in opposition had criticised the loss of local accountability, the New Labour government saw no wholesale return of functions to elected councils. Indeed some areas, such as education, moved further from council control with schools coming under the control of faith groups and private businesses. This trend continued with the formation of the 2010 coalition.

### Secrecy and openness

Accountability in British government has long been inhibited by secrecy, an inheritance from a monarchical past, when state information belonged to the king. Yet a modern tendency to withhold information was replenished with legislation in the form of Official Secrets Acts. The most celebrated of these was that of 1911, with its notorious Section 2, which criminalised any Crown servant disclosing any information learned at work. It was also an offence to receive such information, making investigative journalism a hazardous profession. The claim that disclosure was in the public interest was no defence even though the government could withhold information on these grounds. In the 1985 Ponting case, where a civil servant leaked information concerning the sinking of Argentian battleship, the *General Belgrano*, during the Falklands war, the judge ruled that only the government could define the public interest. However, the jury rejected the judge's direction and acquitted the whistle-blower. Another case involved the unsuccessful attempt by government to prevent the publication of *Spycatcher*, the memoirs of ex-MI5 officer Peter Wright. These cases undermined the Section 2 principle and it was omitted in the 1989 Official Secrets Act.

Other measures towards greater openness followed with the publication in 1992 of two hitherto secret items: a list of cabinet committees and the guidance received by ministers, *Questions of Procedure for Ministers*. A 1993 White Paper on Open Government (Cm 2290) outlined a code of practice on access to official information. However, this suffered many limitations: governments could still use the defence of public interest to withhold and the access was to information rather than to actual documents. Furthermore, 15 areas were exempted.

The culture of secrecy went beyond Official Secrets Acts to various other means of criminalising disclosure. In the Arms-to-Iraq affair four directors of the British firm Matrix Churchill were put on trial for supplying an oil pipeline to Iraq that was suspected by Customs and Excise of being the barrel of a large weapon. The trial collapsed in 1992, when it was discovered that the company had been advised by the government in a manner not in keeping with official policy as declared to parliament. Public Interest Immunity Certificates had been issued to prevent the release of the information.

In 1997 the New Labour government incorporated the European Convention on Human Rights into British law. The Human Rights Act promised new rights and a White Paper on freedom of information appeared in December 1997. This introduced an independent Information Commissioner with the power to compel the release of information and made evasion of disclosure and the destroying of records a criminal offence. However, enthusiasm waned as the responsible minister became a casualty of Blair's first cabinet reshuffle. A Freedom of Information Act appeared in 2000, but it was a considerably watered-down version of the earlier promise. Criticised by the Campaign for the Freedom of Information, it was condemned by parliament's Public Administration Committee for its failure to create a presumption in favour of disclosure. A formidable list of absolute exemptions remained, including security matters, the economy, national security, defence, and anything judged to be prejudicial to effective conduct of public affairs. Yet, despite its limitations, journalists and others were able to use the Act to extract information and cause some inconvenience and even embarrassment to officials and government. A notable scandal was uncovered with the revelations of the ways MPs used the expenses system.

## Democracy and the administrative system

Democracy is enhanced by various mechanisms allowing citizens a voice and means of redress of grievance. While Britain lacks a body of administrative law such as the French *droit administratif* there are systems of administrative tribunals, public inquiries and the office of ombudsman operating at the levels of central and local government.

Administrative tribunals are non-judicial bodies adjudicating in cases where citizens feel aggrieved by official actions. They operate in areas such as social security, housing and the benefits system. Although offering the advantages of speed and informality, they are criticised for a lack of judicial professionalism. In addition, public inquiries are established to examine particular cases where the public concern is collective rather than individual, such as the planning of a new bypass or airport runway. These are conducted in the presence of interested parties and some can attract considerable media attention. However, their decisions are usually regarded are advisory only and can be rejected by ministers.

Since 1967, an ombudsman system has operated at central and local levels to deal with the ill-defined area of maladministration. A Northern Ireland Ombudsman was established in 1969. Originally termed the Parliamentary Commissioner for Administration, complainants were obliged to seek access through an MP. A Commissioner for the NHS was subsequently created in 1993 and here access was direct. However, as the same person fulfilled both roles the office became the Parliamentary and Health Service Ombudsman. Three local government ombudsmen covered England, Wales and Scotland respectively. However, unlike the Scandinavian prototype, the British version operates under a number of limitations. Although there are substantial legal powers to aid the process of investigation there are no coercive powers with respect to any findings or recommendations. There are also restrictions on the jurisdiction, with the armed forces, police and government contracting excluded. However, sometimes a case can hit the headlines, as when Ombudsman Ann Abrahams criticised the government rejection of her recommendation that an independent tribunal be set up to determine the compensation to be paid to over a million policy holders who lost money when the Equitable Life insurance company collapsed in 2001. Her report had found 10 instances of maladministration by regulators and Whitehall officials.

## Further developments and issues with the system

Changes in public administration tend to follow political changes. Much change came as a result of the nineteenth-century rise of the bourgeoisie. The early twentieth century saw the New Liberal reform in welfare provision and the House of Lords. The post-war era was a period of welfare statism including the creation of the NHS. Under Thatcher the neo-liberal agenda saw the many changes detailed above. Much of this continued under New Labour and the Conservative–Liberal Democrat coalition. This government's commitment to reducing the huge financial deficit left by the global banking crisis made much of the goal of reducing the size of the public sector.

The terrorism threat made more salient since 9/11 is by no means a new concern to Britain, which had endured the Northern Ireland troubles and more violent groups such as Animal Liberationists. However, the 9/11 attack and a heightened sense of fear following the London bombings, places challenges on traditional constitutional freedoms, posing the classic conundrum: how does a liberal society preserve its ideal while dealing with those who wish to threaten it from within? As Prime Minister Gordon Brown asserted, the new circumstances had 'changed the rules of the game' and had therefore 'changed how we need to protect ourselves against it' (Brown, 2006). The result is intense debate over police powers, civil liberties, the role of judges, surveillance of citizens, the monitoring of citizens' Internet use, the length of detention of suspects and the use of Control Orders. Moreover, the wide range of threats, including nuclear, biological, cyber attack and suicide bombing, calls for even greater attention within the machinery of government (see Wilkinson, 2007).

Reforms to the House of Lords, promoted by the Liberal Democrats, may continue. This may move towards the complete elimination of the hereditary element, leaving the problem of how to populate the House. Elections offer democratic representation democracy but, to critics, promise a House of failed MPs and party hacks. The alternative of appointment may bring in expertise not available to the Commons, but will open it up to charges of patronage. There is also a second question over the powers of a reformed House. An elected chamber may not be willing to accept the current subservient status.

Another area of reform that may not have reached its conclusion is devolution. In Scotland the SNP, which in 2007 became the largest party in the Scottish Parliament, called for the referendum on complete independence. From Wales comes the demand for increased legislative power. In Northern Ireland, violence has not been entirely eliminated and continuing segregation between communities leaves the future of the province in question.

Over-riding all specific reform debates is the constitution itself. There have been significant moves in the direction of a written constitution. These include the Freedom of Information (FOI) Act and the incorporation of the European Convention on Human Rights into British law. The formation of the coalition government in May 2010 suggested a time for some constitutional clarification and three documents were quickly published. A Ministerial Code set out the standards of conduct expected of ministers, a second document detailed a list of Cabinet Committees and a third was a Coalition Agreement, setting out the practical and operational arrangements for the parties involved. Just before this, in February 2010, Prime Minister Gordon Brown had asked Cabinet Secretary, Sir Gus O'Donnell, to draft a Cabinet Manual, detailing the relationships between the government, the monarchy, parliament, the civil service, local councils, Europe and the devolved administrations. After consideration by the Cabinet Home Affairs Committee this appeared in January 2011. The Cabinet Secretary considered that it could be seen as a starting point towards a written constitution. Graham Allen MP, chairman of the Commons' Political and Constitutional Reform Committee, appeared to agree: 'We don't have a written constitution and this is as close as we are likely to get' (*Daily Telegraph*, 13 December 2010).

Yet the parties, even the Labour Party, are decidedly cautious on the subject of constitutional reform (Dorey, 2008). Moreover, although Britain may be seen to be becoming a 'constitutional state' it may not be carrying the popular culture; it may not be becoming a 'popular constitutional state' (Bogdanor, 2009: i). It probably remains true that those seeking radical change to the Westminster system are doomed to disappointment, and further reform will continue to be incremental (Hazell, 2008: 297).

Finally, the global financial crisis had profound implications for the public sector. Although all the main political parties recognised a need for retrenchment, Labour favoured a more Keynesian approach while the Conservative–Liberal Democrat coalition came to power promising an immediate assault on the £156 billion budget deficit. The programme entailed a scaled-down public sector with a cull of quangos and a reduction in the size of the civil service. The cuts would also be felt keenly in local government with a possibility of more work going to the private sector. A ban on new public sector recruitment, announced in May, as part of a £6.2 billion package of spending cuts, would leave some 30,000 jobs unfilled in the next financial year. In a speech in August 2010 Prime Minister David Cameron asserted that cuts needed to be 'sustainable', meaning that funding levels would not be restored once the deficit was under control. While public sector unions opposed, there were suggestions from managers that the crisis could spawn more efficient ways of working. Hence, the opening of the second decade of the twenty-first century offered a future of considerable uncertainty for British public administration.

## Note

Thanks to Howard Elcock for helpful comments on an earlier draft.

## References

Adonis, A. and Pollard, S. (1997) *A Class Act: The Myth of Britain's Classless Society*, London and New York, NY: Hamish Hamilton.

Almond, G. A. and Verba, S. (1963) *The Civic Culture: Political Attitudes and Democracy in Five Nations*, London: Sage Publications.

Barber, M. (2007) *Instructions to Deliver: Tony Blair, Public Services and the Challenge of Achieving Targets*, London: Politico's.

Bogdanor, V. (2009) *The New British Constitution*, Oxford: Hart Publishing. Online, available at: www.treasury.gov.uk/press_72_06.htm (accessed 13 January 2010).

Burch, M. and Holliday, I. (1996) *The British Cabinet System*, Hemel Hempstead: Prentice Hall/Harvester Wheatsheaf.

Burnham, J. and Pyper, R. (2008) *Britain's Modernised Civil Service*, Basingstoke: Palgrave Macmillan.

Cassidy, S. (2010) 'Social inequality gap remains', *Independent*, 27 January.

Chandler, J. A. (2009) *Explaining Local Government*, Manchester: Manchester University Press.

Cowley, P. (2005) *The Rebels: How Blair Mislaid his Majority*, London: Politico's.

Devine, F. (1997) *Social Class in America and Britain*, Edinburgh: Edinburgh University Press.

Dodd, V. and Gentleman, A. (2010) 'UK lags behind on women in cabinet', *The Guardian*, 13 May. Online, available at: www.guardian.co.uk/politics/2010/may/13/cabinet-women-diversity (accessed 16 January 2011).

Dorey, P. (2008) *The Labour Party and Constitutional Reform: A History of Constitutional Conservatism*, Basingstoke: Palgrave Macmillan.

Elcock, H. J. (1991) *Change and Decay: Public Administration in the 1990s*, Harlow: Longman.

Evans, G. (1993) 'Class conflict and inequality', in Jowell, R., Brook, L. and Downs, L., *International Social Attitudes: The 10th British Social Attitudes Report*, Aldershot: Dartmouth, pp. 123–41.

Gifford, C. (2008) *The making of Euroscepticism in Britain: Identity and Economy in a Post-Imperial State*, Aldershot: Ashgate.

Hall, W. and Weir, S. (1996) *The Untouchables: Power and Accountability in the Quango State*, London: Democratic Audit/Charter 88.

Hazell, R. (ed.) (2008) *Constitutional Futures Revisited: Britain's Constitution to 2020*, Basingstoke: Palgrave Macmillan.

Hutton, W. (1996) *The State We're In*, London: Vintage.

James, O. (2003) *The Executive Agency Revolution in Whitehall*, Basingstoke: Palgrave.

Jarvis, R. (2002) *The UK Experience of Public Administration Reform*, London: Commonwealth Secretariat.

Kavanagh, D. (1980) 'Political culture in Britain: The decline of the civic culture', in Almond, G. A. and Verba, S. (eds), *The Civic Culture Revisited*, Boston, MA: Little Brown, pp. 124–76.

Lovenduski, J. (1996) 'Sex, gender and British politics', *Parliamentary Affairs, 49* (1), 1–16.

Macpherson Report (1999) *The Stephen Lawrence Inquiry*, London: The Stationery Office, Cm 4262-I.

Mitchell, J. (2009) *Devolution in the UK*, Manchester: Manchester University Press.

Norton, P. and Cowley, P. (1999) 'Rebels and rebellions: Conservative MPs in the 1992 parliament', *British Journal of Politics and International Relations, 1* (1), 84–105.

Parekh, A., MacInnes, T. and Kenway, P. (2010) *Monitoring Poverty and Social Exclusion 2010*, Joseph Rowntree Foundation and the New Policy Institute. Online, available at: www.jrf.org.uk/publications/monitoring-poverty-2010 (accessed 16 January 2011).

Phillips, T. (2004) 'Multiculturalism's legacy is "Have a nice day" racism', *The Guardian*. Online, available at: www.guardian.co.uk/society/2004/may/28/equality.racein theuk (accessed 15 January 2011).

Seymour-Ure, C. (2003) *Prime Ministers and the Media: Issues of Power and Control*, Oxford: Blackwell.

Stewart, J. (1992) 'The rebuilding of public accountability', *European Policy Forum*, December.

Stewart, J. (1995) 'Appointed boards and local government', *Parliamentary Affairs, 48* (2), 226–41.

Stewart, J. (2003) *Modernising British Local Government*, Basingstoke: Palgrave.

Wilkinson, P. (ed.) (2007) *Homeland Security in the UK: Future Preparedness for Terrorist Attack Since 9/11*, Abingdon: Routledge.

## Further reading

Burnham, J. and Pyper, R. (2008) *Britain's Modernised Civil Service*, Basingstoke: Palgrave Macmillan.

Chandler, J. A. (2009) *Explaining Local Government*, Manchester: Manchester University Press.

Greenwood, J., Pyper, R. and Wilson, D. (2002) *The New Public Administration in Britain*, London: Routledge.

Kingdom, J. E. and Fairclough, P. E. (2014) *Government and Politics in Britain* (4th edn), Cambridge: Polity Press.

Wilson, D. and Game, C. (2011) *Local Government in the United Kingdom* (5th edn), Basingstoke: Palgrave Macmillan.

# 3 The Republic of Ireland

*Neil Collins, Aodh Quinlivan and*
*Emmanuelle Schön-Quinlivan*

## Introduction

Ireland presents an important illustrative case of changing public administration in liberal democracies. Many of the major trends that have been seen elsewhere have affected Ireland in recent years. The Republic of Ireland, a small jurisdiction with an open economy, is particularly subject to the impact of globalisation. In the past, the major influence on Irish political thought and practice was Britain. Geography and history combine to make it so. Political independence from Britain, for the 26 counties that now form the Republic, came in 1922. It followed the ending of the War of Independence and the signing of the Anglo–Irish Treaty in 1921. The British legacy on Irish public administration is pervasive. The constitutional forms adopted have been those of British parliamentary democracy. Ireland's governmental practices are based on the Westminster model. The party system in Ireland differs from that of most European countries. It is not based as clearly as elsewhere on social cleavages such as class, religion or language. Such cleavages were relatively weak at the formation of the party system as the major issue after independence was the Anglo–Irish Treaty. The divisions created by the Treaty form the basis of the Irish party system, though the salience of the issue has faded to near irrelevance. The success of Irish parties now depends mainly on their economic policies, their perceived managerial ability and on the loyalty of their traditional supporters. See Table 3.1, Irish political parties in *Dáil Éireann*.

Since its foundation, the Republic has undergone many important changes of policy direction, especially since the late 1950s. A long period of protectionism in economic policy, parity between the Irish pound and sterling and almost total dependence on the British market have ended. Between 1973 and the early 2000s, Ireland was an enthusiastic member of the European Union. The Republic joined the European Monetary Union in 1998. However rejection of the Nice and Lisbon treaties respectively in 2000 and 2008, as well as Ireland's new status of net contributor to the EU budget from 2007, signalled the start of a 'growing anti-European feeling' (Laffan and O'Mahony 2008: 49). In November 2010, Ireland lost its economic sovereignty to a troïka

*Table 3.1* Irish political parties in *Dáil Éireann*

| Party name | Seats in Dáil | % vote 2011 | Leader | Comment |
|---|---|---|---|---|
| Fine Gael | 76 (+25) | 36.10 | Enda Kenny | Government party |
| Labour | 37 (+17) | 19.45 | Eamon Gilmore | Government party |
| Fianna Fáil | 20 (−58) | 17.45 | Micheál Martin | Opposition |
| Sinn Féin | 14 (+10) | 9.94 | Gerry Adams | Opposition |
| United Left Alliance* | 5 (+5) | 2.57 | Opposition | |
| Green Party | 0 (−6) | 1.85 | Eamon Ryan | No representation |
| Others | 14 (+7) | 12.41 | Five support govt | |

*The United Left Alliance (ULA) is an electoral alliance of left-wing political parties and independents. It ran 20 candidates at the 2011 general election, of which five were successful. As the ULA is not a registered political party, it did not appear on the ballot papers at the election. The five ULA TDs (an abbreviation for *Teachta Dála*, Member of Parliament) elected in 2011 were Clare Daly and Joe Higgins (both of the Socialist Party), Joan Collins and Richard Boyd-Barrett (both of the People Before Profit Alliance) and Séamus Healy (Workers and Unemployed Action Group).

Out of the 19 TDs (i.e. ULA and 'Others') 16 elected from outside the big parties have formed a technical group. This affords those TDs more speaking time and allows them to become part of *Oireachtas* committees.

Source: McCarthy, D. (ed.) (2011), *RTÉ The Week in Politics – Election 2011 and the 31st Dáil*, Dublin: RTE Publishing

composed of the EU, the International Monetary Fund and the European Central Bank as a result of the international financial crisis and a sharp domestic economic downturn. During the Celtic Tiger years, administrative reforms were aimed at promoting a viable economy and enhancing Ireland's status and competitiveness internationally. The impact of New Right economics was also marked (Collins and O' Raghallaigh 1996) and led Ireland to devise its own solution to the modernisation of its bureaucracy, namely the Strategic Management Initiative (SMI) (Collins et al. 2007).

In 2008, the OECD published a report into Ireland's public service. This was the first such country review undertaken by the OECD and the report stated that Ireland had been able to deliver effective public services despite having a public sector that was relatively small given the size of the economy and labour force. However, the OECD criticised Ireland's reform programme for being too inward orientated and argued that greater focus needed to be placed on citizens and their expectations, and on targeting delivery of service in such a way as to achieve broader societal goals. Following the economic recession, the government has had to adopt a Public Sector Reform Plan, which reconciles the OECD's suggestions with the financial pressures Ireland is undergoing. It focuses on 'customer service, innovative service delivery channels, implementation and delivery' while 'radically reducing [. . .] costs to drive better value for money' (Department of Public Expenditure and Reform 2011: 3)

# Political culture

The concept of political culture lacks precision but it is used here as shorthand to describe the major beliefs and attitudes that exert an influence on public policy and administration in the Republic. It was not always used in this simple heuristic way. The expectation was that it would transform the state into a 'modern' liberal democracy along lines that mirrored developments in the United States, Britain and elsewhere. As cultural attitudes changed, the Republic would gradually lose those features associated with democracies in transitional or developing economies. High on the list of perceived anachronisms was a party system that defied easy left–right categorisation, pervasive clientelism and high levels of church influence. The Republic has changed radically both politically and economically but few of the modernising theorists' predictions have been realised.

Though coalition governments are becoming the norm over the past 30 years, the party system has been dominated by the two large parties formed in the early years of the state, *Fianna Fáil* and *Fine Gael*, who traditionally commanded nearly 70 per cent of the vote in general elections. However, the political landscape changed dramatically at the 2011 general election when *Fianna Fáil* was relegated to the third largest party, dropping from 78 seats to a mere 20. The Labour Party emerged as the second biggest party and formed a coalition government with *Fine Gael*. Political rivalry remains very localised and voters continue to expect politicians to be consumer representatives first and foremost, rather than legislators. The Church, on the other hand, has declined as a political force especially in urban areas. Economically, the Republic was Europe's fastest growing economy until the property bubble on which its success rested burst in 2008. The underlying causes of the Republic's economic success were a complex mixture of global and local influences. They incorporated:

- more budgetary discipline since 1987;
- substantial receipts from EU;
- foreign investment in manufacturing, IT and financial services; and
- 'social partnership'.

The neo-corporatist agreements between the 'social partners' was an essential dimension of the policy process between 1987 and 2009. This bargained corporatism was formally tripartite, between government, unions and employers. Ireland, like other small European states, effectively changed the boundaries between politics and industrial relations to give a greater role to the so-called 'social partners', i.e. representatives of major interests such as business, unions, farmers and voluntary groups, across an increasingly wide range of public policy. The central aim of social partnership was usually to gain a trade union commitment to wage restraint in exchange for an input into public policy-making. The agreements were generally for three-year periods, beginning with the Programme for National Recovery in 1987, followed by seven agreements including the Programme for Prosperity and Fairness (2000–03) and Sustaining Progress (2003–05).

The latest social partnership agreement entitled *Towards 2016: Ten-Year Framework Social Partnership Agreement 2006–2015* aimed to produce 'a dynamic, internationalised and participatory Irish society and economy, founded on a commitment to social justice, and economic development that is both environmentally sustainable and internationally competitive' (Department of Taoiseach 2006: 6). Due to the unprecedented and unforeseen economic and fiscal crisis that Ireland is going through, the government reviewed the agreement for 2008–09. In December 2009, two decades of social partnership collapsed after the Irish government announced that talks with the public sector trade unions had failed to agree on the method to secure a €1 billion reduction in public pay.

## The consitutional framework

The Irish Free State inherited an almost complete administrative apparatus, together with several important state institutions at its formation in 1922. Indeed, in the period before independence, the British Treasury put extra effort into the organisation and staffing of Irish departments. Nevertheless, newly independent countries frequently experience an initial period of relatively rapid constitutional change. This was the case with Ireland, which has had three constitutions, one in 1919, another in 1922, and the present one in 1937. A further change of some constitutional importance was caused by the Republic of Ireland Act 1948, which, without requiring a constitutional amendment, formalised the status of the state as a republic.

*Bunreacht na hÉireann*, the 1937 Constitution, plainly mirrored the views of Eamon de Valera, its main sponsor and then *Taoiseach* (prime minister). It represented a significant constitutional break with Britain. De Valera's constitution was 'a profoundly democratic document' (Whelan 2011: 58). In opening the second stage debate in the *Dáil*, de Valera was keen to stress, 'If there is one thing more than another that is clear and shining through the constitution, it is the fact that the people are the masters' (Dáil Éireann 1937).

Following the Constitution Review Group's report in 1996, the All-party Oireachtas Committee on the Constitution 1997–2002 identified seven areas for constitutional change:

*   Northern Ireland;
*   European Union;
*   international human rights developments;
*   socio-economic change;
*   working experience of the constitution;
*   outmoding of some provisions;
*   inaccuracies in the text.

Amendment to the constitution needs the consent of the people. In October 2002, a constitutional amendment was passed enabling the state to ratify the Treaty of Nice. Since then, there have been three further constitutional amendments: in 2004 removing the automatic right to citizenship from children born on the island of Ireland, in 2010 facilitating the ratification of the Lisbon Treaty and in 2011 removing the ban on reducing judicial salaries in a context of widespread public sector wage cuts. For each referendum since 1995, a 'Referendum Commission' has been appointed by government to inform the public of the issues in an even-handed and impartial manner.

The Irish constitution is one of the oldest constitutions in Europe (Gallagher 2010a: 102). As adopted in 1937, *Bunreacht na hÉireann*, contained an inventory of positive social principles. It also guaranteed many fundamental rights. In the articles on the family and its protection, the constitution clearly reflected Catholic social teaching of the 1930s, though many of the principles enunciated would also be acceptable to other Christian churches. In recent decades, the Catholic gloss on the constitution has been substantially eroded, most notably the removal of the ban on divorce legislation, following the 1995 amendment. On the other hand, judicial activism has greatly increased the role of *Bunreacht na hÉireann* as a source of individual rights.

The constitution sets out the system of government that remains in place today. The national parliament is known as the *Oireachtas*. It consists of the president and the two Houses, *Dáil Éireann* and *Seanad Éireann*.

### President

The President of Ireland (*Uachtarán na hÉireann*) is the only office holder directly elected by the citizens of the Republic. The term of office is seven years, with a maximum of two terms. The main functions of the president are ceremonial. Most of the others are exercised on the advice of the government. The president's main functions are:

- as ceremonial Head of State;
- summoning and dissolving *Dáil Éireann*;
- signing bills into law following parliamentary assent;
- referring legislation to the Supreme Court to test its constitutionality.

The president has very few functions that may be exercised independently of government control. In the words of Clarke (2008) the president is 'a role model, not a ruler'. Nevertheless, it is an important part of the system of checks and balances on the power of the legislature. Since 1938, there have been nine presidents of Ireland (see Table 3.2).

There have been seven electoral contests and on five occasions the candidate was nominated following all-party agreement.

*Table 3.2* Presidents of Ireland

| | |
|---|---|
| Douglas Hyde | 25 June 1938 to 25 June 1945 |
| Seán T. Ó Ceallaigh | 25 June 1945 to 25 June 1959 |
| Eamon de Valera | 25 June 1959 to 25 June 1973 |
| Erskine Childers | 25 June 1973 to 17 November 1974 |
| Cearbhall Ó Dálaigh | 19 December 1974 to 22 October 1976 |
| Patrick Hillery | 3 December 1976 to 3 December 1990 |
| Mary Robinson | 3 December 1990 to 12 September 1997 |
| Mary McAleese | 11 November 1997 to 11 November 2011 |
| Michael D. Higgins | 11 November 2011 – |

Source: www.president.ie

## Dáil Éireann

The constitution establishes the framework for the central government system. The government is the chief executive organ of the state. It is the centre of the administrative system. There are 14 senior ministers and 15 ministers of state (junior ministers), who support the *Taoiseach* and assist in the management of departments. The following list shows the government departments in the Irish administrative system.

Department of Agriculture, Food and the Marine
Department of Arts, Heritage and the Gaeltacht
Department of Children and Youth Affairs
Department of Communications, Energy and Natural Resources
Department of Defence
Department of Education and Skills
Department of Environment, Community and Local Government
Department of Finance
Department of Foreign Affairs and Trade
Department of Health
Department of Jobs, Enterprise and Innovation
Department of Public Expenditure and Reform
Department of Social Protection
Department of the Taoiseach
Department of Transport, Tourism and Sport
Department of Justice and Equality

Source: www.irlgov.ie

The following constitutional provisions apply to the system of government:

- executive power of the state is exercised by or on the authority of the government;
- the government is responsible to *Dáil Éireann;* and
- the government acts as a collective authority, with collective responsibility.

Membership of *Dáil Éireann* is open to people over the age of 21, who are elected by citizens over the age of 18. Members of Parliament are referred to as deputies or TDs, an abbreviation for *Teachta Dála*. The 31st *Dáil*, elected in February 2011, has 166 members. The current *Taoiseach* (prime minister) is Enda Kenny who was elected by a historic margin of 117 votes to 27. Deputies represent constituencies of three, four or five seats. The electoral boundaries of constituencies must be revised at least every 12 years in the light of population change. In practice they are revised every four or five years on the basis of recommendations from a Statutory Constituencies Commission. Members are elected under a system of proportional representation by means of a single transferable vote. The work of the *Dáil* is as follows:

- considering proposals for legislation initiated by ministers or by private members;
- considering expenditure proposals presented by ministers;
- debating motions; and
- holding government ministers accountable through parliamentary questions.

## Seanad Éireann

Following the Westminster model of a bicameral legislature, *Seanad Éireann* is the Upper House. It consists of 60 members of whom 43 are elected from vocational panels, the *Taoiseach* nominates 11 and university graduates elect six. The *Seanad* may initiate legislation but the main function is to review legislation already passed by the *Dáil*. In practice, the *Seanad's* role in the legislative process is quite restricted. In the words of Basil Chubb (1992), it is a house for 'rising, falling or resting politicians'. It exerts little significant control on the business of the *Oireachtas* and is 'by far the weaker of the two houses' (Gallagher 2010b: 222). One of the *Fine Gael* manifesto promises for the 2011 general election was to put a referendum before the people to abolish the *Seanad*.

The committee system is a feature of parliamentary life in many countries. Committees provide greater opportunities for deputies and senators to become involved in all aspects of the parliamentary process. For many years, there had been calls for *Dáil* reform and for the development of a committee system that would improve the legislative process. The committee system promotes more incisive, yet less adversarial scrutiny of legislation. In a committee setting, government ministers are more likely to accept opposition or backbench amendments to bills, than in plenary sessions of parliament. Committees provide a forum for voluntary and other groups with an interest in a particular piece of legislation to make an oral presentation and/or written submission. Membership of committees encourages deputies and senators to develop a parliamentary competence in specific policy areas. Select committees typically parallel the government departments.

A significant element in the process of change reviewed here, has been by Ireland's membership of the European Union. The EU and its governing treaties represent an important new source of policies, laws and court rulings for Irish politics. Another factor that seems likely to hasten the pace of constitutional change is the consensus between the political parties on many aspects of constitutional reform.

### Ireland and the EU

The requirements of the EU membership on Ireland were met through an incremental process of Europeanisation of its administrative culture and policy-making rather than radical change (Laffan 1999; Laffan and O'Mahony 2008). For public administration purposes, it is probably helpful to regard the EU as an additional layer of government. Many public policies are driven from Brussels. Irish government ministers, civil servants, other public officials and representatives of interest groups are very active at all levels of the EU in the formulation and negotiation of policies. This is especially the case for four key government departments, Agriculture, Enterprise, Trade and Employment, Finance, and Foreign Affairs. The *Taoiseach's* department plays a key co-ordinating role. Among the policy areas most affected by Europe are financial and commercial policy, agriculture, trade, gender equality, health and safety and environment.

Membership of the EU changed the approach to economic governance in Ireland. First and foremost, Ireland benefitted significantly from the EU's structural funds, O'Donnell (2001) arguing that GNP increased by 2 percentage points between 1989 and 1999. Beyond financial support, EU membership also led to stricter financial discipline and low inflation. Ireland embarked on a path of rational planning of its development that crystallised in the form of National Development Plans. A series of independent regulatory agencies also flourished as a result of the Single European Market requirements and led to a transformation of the Irish regulatory system. Finally, in the early 1990s, Ireland made the commitment to join the Economic Monetary Union, which was the final step after joining the European Monetary System of fixed exchange rates in 1979 and cutting ties with the sterling pound. This decision shaped Ireland's fiscal policy, fostering more fiscal and budgetary discipline and therefore helping the country to turn around its economic fortune.

After 10 years of successful membership of the EMU and economic prosperity, Ireland faced a severe economic and fiscal crisis, which resulted in public deficit at 32.4 per cent of GDP and public debt at 96.2 per cent of GDP in 2010 (Eurostat 2011). The Irish crisis erupted when economic growth became increasingly fuelled by rising house prices and a rapid expansion of credit coupled by Irish households' indebtedness. When the international financial crisis emerged in 2007 and property prices dropped, Irish banks became very vulnerable and started experiencing losses on their loans. Despite quickly implementing austerity measures and giving a blanket guarantee of the banks' liabilities, the Irish government could not contain the loss of confidence in Ireland on international bond markets. In November 2010, the government reached an agreement with the IMF, the ECB and the European Commission regarding a financial assistance package of €85 billion in exchange for reforms of the banking sector, fiscal consolidation measures and structural reforms. The involvement of the Troïka has meant a loss in economic sovereignty for Ireland. At the same time, the crisis spread across several Eurozone countries and put the EMU at risk of explosion. This resulted in a European Financial Stability Facility being set up in June 2010 to provide financial assistance to the Eurozone member states that needed it. Between June and October 2010, the scope of activity of the EFSF was regularly increased to finally guarantee commitments up to €780 billion.

However, Ireland and the Eurozone were still in a difficult position by mid to late 2011. After several months of negotiations regarding the creation of a fiscal union, Germany and France led the way towards an intergovernmental Treaty on Stability, Coordination and Governance in the EMU – more regularly referred to as the Fiscal Compact. Despite Chancellor Merkel calling for an EU treaty, it was quickly agreed that a revision to the Lisbon Treaty in order to reform the Stability and Growth Pact would be lengthy and uncertain. This treaty contains, for the most part, provisions that were already included in the Stability and Growth Pact. However there is an obligation for governments ratifying the treaty to introduce a permanent golden rule regarding public debt and deficit as well as an automatic corrective mechanism that would be guaranteed at constitutional level. The European Commission will monitor compliance with the treaty rules, making recommendations for penalties in case of non-compliance. However, a qualified majority of Eurozone countries will be able to block the Commission's recommendation, which was not the case in the Stability and Growth Pact. This will allow for more flexibility 'only in exceptional circumstances'. In case of non-compliance, the European Court of Justice will have the power to impose financial penalties.

The Fiscal Compact will come into force on 1 January 2013 if at least 12 member states have ratified it. The UK and Czech Republic refused to sign the treaty. Despite very difficult ratifications of the last two European treaties, the 2000 Nice Treaty and the 2008 Lisbon Treaty, the Irish people look set to ratify this intergovernmental treaty. It might be explained by the fact that they do not feel pressurised to vote 'Yes' since the treaty can go ahead if a minimum of 12 countries approve it. Another factor that might explain the polls indicating a comfortable ratification by the Irish people is that there is an understanding of the drastic economic situation the country is in and the tight room for manoeuvre. Among the Eurozone periphery countries in economic difficulty such as Greece, Portugal and Spain, Ireland already appears as a success story, meeting all the targets set by the Troïka and returning to positive growth in 2011, thanks to strong Irish export levels and an increase in competitiveness. For Ireland, ratifying this treaty means the possibility to access the EFSF in case the country is not strong enough to go back to markets in 2013. Ratification is also seen as a way of not being left behind in a European integration process that could quickly descend into a two-tier Europe where Ireland would be geographically, economically and politically on the periphery.

## The civil service

After independence, the Free State bureaucracy retained the centralising features of its British predecessor but in the post-civil war period the Civil Service Commission and the Local Appointments Commission were established 'in order to maintain the impartial nature of the public administration' (MacCarthaigh 2008: 63). Up until 2004, the civil service was selected by the Civil Service Commission, to service the president, the *Oireachtas*, judiciary, *Taoiseach* and his ministers, the Attorney General and the Comptroller and Auditor General. In 2004, the Public Service (Recruitment and Appointments) Act established the Public Appointments Service to replace the Civil Service Commission and the Local Appointments Commission. According to MacCarthaigh (2008: 64), the Public Appointments Service

> acts as a centralized recruitment, assessment and selection body for departments and other public service bodies. It recruits new entrants to the civil service as normal, who will then be assigned to various departments and agencies.

The enormous importance of the civil service and local authorities and, to a lesser extent, the state-sponsored bodies was heightened by the dominance of the public sector in the rather underdeveloped post-independence economy. Because of its political indispensability, the civil service was able to retain its corporate integrity and identity, and to resist pressures towards politicisation. The establishment of the Civil Service Commission and the Local Appointments Commission in 1926 was a critical measure. The result was the creation and survival of a 'powerful bureaucracy', independent of the party machine.

Like all bureaucracies, the civil service is hierarchical and employs large numbers of people at the lower levels. Those in the general service grades, from assistant principal upward, constitute the higher civil service. Typically, the number of people employed in the civil service represents 10 per cent of the total number employed in the overall public service. The Government's Public Service Reform strategy (Department of Public Expenditure and Reform 2011), published in November 2011, refers to the 'peak' public sector employment level of 320,000 in 2008. The target, as part of the country's austerity measures, is to achieve a reduction of 37,500 staff to 282,500 by 2015. The strategy states (p. 2), 'when delivered, this will have reduced our gross pay bill by over €2.5 billion (or 15 per cent since 2008). Even at the aforementioned peak in 2008, the OECD (2008: 22) described Ireland's public service as 'relatively small given the size of its economy and labour force'. The OECD went on to state (ibid.), 'even when factoring in infrastructure investment, Ireland has the third smallest total public expenditure (among OECD countries) as a percentage of GDP, and this figure has actually decreased over the past 10 years'. Of course, as described earlier, the economic context in Ireland – including indicators such as GDP and the labour force – has changed dramatically since 2008.

The recruitment and promotion procedures of the Irish public service are formally and rigorously meritocratic. The majority are career officials who enter the service at an early age. The central tenet is that persons selected for posts in the public service must have the requisite skill and knowledge. Though public service recruitment is controversial elsewhere, particularly in newly independent states, Ireland has had no sustained challenge to the system, based as it is on the possession of prescribed qualifications, and selection by open competition. Canvassing on behalf of candidates is not permitted and this rule is respected. The Employment Equality Act, 1998 now precludes discrimination on nine grounds:

- gender;
- marital status;
- family status;
- age;
- disability;
- religion;
- sexual orientation;
- race;
- member of traveller community.

The Irish approach is that of creating a 'level playing field' to allow as many people as possible to apply for public service jobs with the best getting appointed, as opposed to operating a system of quotas or positive discrimination. The one exception here is the governmental target that at least 3 per cent of positions in the civil service should be filled by persons with a disability. O'Toole and Dooney (2009: 298) cite a survey published in 2002 that showed that 7 per cent of civil service staff had a disability.

Departmental Secretaries (now known as Secretaries General since the Public Management Act, 1997), Assistant Secretaries General and Principals are the most influential members of the bureaucracy. Their primary function is policy appraisal and formulation. Their ideas on economic and social policy and on the viability and acceptability of particular proposals can have an important bearing on the ultimate decisions taken by individual ministers or the government. The Secretaries General and senior management are the main channels of civil service advice to ministers and, though ministers frequently change, the officials do not. The well-established ethos of the civil service is to serve ministers of all parties with equal loyalty. When a general election is in progress, senior civil servants will study the various manifestos and prepare policy papers for presentation to the new minister on arrival in the department.

The main legislative framework for government departments dates from the Ministers and Secretaries Act, 1924, which adopted many of the essential features of British practice at the time. At its core is the notion of a minister as a 'corporation sole' responsible for all the acts and omissions of his/her department. All legal powers are exercised in the minister's name. Following a review of the Ministers and Secretaries Acts, 1924 to 1991, designed to bring about a greater focus on service delivery, performance and the achievement of results, the Public Service Management Act, 1997 was passed. While based on the principle of ministerial accountability to the *Dáil*, the 1997 Act provides that the traditional role of senior civil servants as policy advisers be complemented by an enhanced role as managers of the service. There is now more emphasis on delegation of functions, policy appraisal, strategic and performance management and ensuring that appropriate accountability procedures are in place. This Act is a key piece of the wider process of civil service modernisation, which commenced in 1994 with the SMI and which continues to the present day with the strategy of November 2011.

The SMI called for a strategic approach by civil servants based on the need for better planning and management. It set out a schedule of change starting with a strategy statement by each department, taking stock and preparing initial plans. The essential tasks are specifying government objectives and client needs. Each department then identifies what steps or strategies it should pursue. The strategy statement and subsequent policy document are meant to encourage a searching self-analysis. The remit should be a management process that ensures ongoing improvements in efficiency and effectiveness. It is too early to assess how meaningful it has been.

In its 2008 review of Ireland's public service, the OECD concluded that the SMI-led modernisation programme had been a qualified success with improvements in internal processes and structures. However, a key conclusion (2008: 13) was that 'the focus to date in Ireland has been on performance reporting, rather than managing for performance'. The 2011 Public Service Reform strategy calls for a modern public service, which is based on innovation, flexibility and the delivery of streamlined services.

Traditionally, the civil service has focused on equity, impartiality and integrity being their key assets. Today, these are still important but a number of other criteria have been identified as part of the 'New Public Management' (NPM) trend and the changing needs of the state and of the people. This is reflected in the five major commitments to change at the heart of the government's reform agenda:

1    placing customer services at the core of everything;
2    maximising new and innovative service delivery channels;

3   radically reducing costs to drive better value for money;
4   leading, organising and working in new ways; and
5   strong focus on implementation and delivery.

In all the discourse on reforming the public service, these central objectives are very much the dominant items on the agenda. It is widely recognised that the traditional management structure did not encourage individuals to take personal responsibility. There was a tendency to take the safe rather than the best option. A process of change has begun. Authority and accountability are shifting to the person making the decision or carrying out the decision. The Public Service Management Act, 1997 specifies that the responsibility for policy objectives and agreeing necessary results lies with ministers while Secretaries General advise ministers and ensure their department produces the necessary results. Secretaries also devolve responsibility down the line.

Up to recently, expenditure controls have been viewed as being over centralised and too short-term in planning. The principal budgetary change involves moving from a year-to-year financial planning process to a three-year planning cycle. As well as detailed budgets for the forthcoming year, departments and offices prepare outline expenditure plans for the two years following. Similarly, the budget contains forward projections of aggregate expenditure and revenue. In this way priorities should be better planned and departments should be able to make their own long-term plans with a greater degree of confidence.

Despite the failure of neo-liberalism to drive broad economic policy, current civil service reform remains heavily influenced by the paradigm of NPM. NPM recognises that the efficiency of the public sector is a vital part of national competitiveness in the global market. Although this perspective of public service may be relatively new in the Republic of Ireland, other liberal democracies with comparable traditions of public service have already embraced a similar consumer orientation. The public service – and specifically the civil service – is at the heart of daily political and administrative life and has been undergoing constant reorganisation since the mid-1990s. While the modernisation efforts have generally been successful, major challenges lie ahead in an era of austerity and cut-backs. The biggest challenge is to enhance service quality and demonstrate both innovation and flexibility with drastically reduced numbers that will, inevitably, impact on frontline services.

## Central government agencies and state-sponsored bodies

State sponsored bodies (SSBs), sometimes referred to as semi state bodies, form a large part of the public sector. They began with the Electricity Supply Board, the Dairy Disposal Company and the Agricultural Credit Corporation in 1927. They numbered about 130 at the end of 1998. Each SSB was established by statute. While SSBs are largely independent of control in their day-to-day operations, the exercise of some functions, particularly major financial ones, are subject to ministerial approval. They are also obliged to submit their annual reports and accounts to the minister for presentation to the *Dáil*.

There are two broad categories of SSB. These are commercial (trading), which correspond to nationalised enterprises, and non-commercial, which have promotional, regulatory and semi-judicial functions. In line with the internationally-dominant liberal economic agenda, the commercial bodies, often referred to as public enterprises, now operate like private companies in the market place. Where possible they are expected to make profits, pay dividends and finance new investment. The current fashionable belief is that business skills used in the private sector may be utilised to equal effect in the service of the state, thus combining public accountability and commercial success. This sector is being transformed particularly because of EU competition policy, directives on liberalisation and the elimination and/or regulation of monopolies.

Some SSBs were established as independent enterprises. In other cases, their activities were originally operated by a department of state. The boards of directors, mostly non-executive, are formally appointed by the minister with responsibility for the industry or service concerned. The basis of selection varies. In some cases, the statute prescribes no criteria, leaving selection entirely at the minister's discretion. In other cases, the minister may be obliged to select persons having special knowledge or experience, or representatives of designated interests, or, occasionally, nominees of a statutory selection committee. The major commercial bodies also have worker directors. As noted by Collins and Quinlivan (2010: 369), the chief executives of large SSBs have a clear and direct role in public policy, with ready links to ministers and senior civil servants in their 'parent' departments.

Examples of SSBs engaged in regulatory or semi-judicial functions are the Environmental Protection Agency and *An Bord Pleanala*. These agencies have been used to take controversial decisions out of the party political framework. The Environmental Protection Agency (EPA) was set up in 1993. Ireland was among the leaders in Europe in establishing such an agency with a wide range of functions. The EPA is different from most other semi-state bodies in having a full-time executive board consisting of the director general and four other directors. The function of the EPA is to protect the environment while ensuring also that development can take place but in a manner that is sustainable. The EPA is an independent body with a wide range of regulatory and enforcement powers to promote a clean and healthy environment.

The recession of the 1980s adversely affected the financial performance of many SSBs. It coincided with a swing to the right in political and economic thinking and a strong backlash against public enterprise. Further, the competition policy of the European Union is strongly opposed to monopolies and state subventions. These factors lead to large-scale liberalisation and deregulation across Europe. Unlike in the United Kingdom, Ireland has not

had a radical privatisation programme but, nonetheless, privatisation has proceeded on a pragmatic, case-by-case basis as shown in the following list:

*   Irish Sugar; Irish Life Assurance Company (1991);
*   B&I Line (sold to Irish Continental Group 1992);
*   Irish Steel (sold to Ispat International Group for £1, 1996);
*   Telecom Eircann (1999);
*   ICC Bank (sold to Bank of Scotland, 2001);
*   ACC Bank (sold to Rabobank Nederland, 2002);
*   Aer Lingus (2006).

Privatisation is likely to feature highly in the current government's austerity
programme with the sale of some assets in the Electricity Supply Board
(ESB) and Bord Gais already announced. In addition, the government will
look to raise money through the sale of Coillte's trees (but not its land) and
the 25 per cent stake in Aer Lingus.

MacCarthaigh (2008: 97) correctly states that 'today, many state enterprises
compete with privately owned companies to provide energy, transport services
such as buses, and television and radio services in both English and Irish'.
With this competition between former state monopolies and private companies
now in place it has been necessary to set up several regulators. Chief among
these (date of establishment in brackets) are: the Competition Authority (1991),
the Commission for Energy Regulation (1999), the Commission for Aviation
Regulation (2001), the Commission for Communications Regulation or
ComReg (2002), the Financial Services Regulator (2003) and the Commission
for Taxi Regulation (2004). Regulation cannot always be achieved and 'the
balance between regulation and commercial freedom for state enterprises
continues to be contested' (MacCarthaigh 2008: 97). The Irish Financial
Services Regulator, in particular, has been severely criticised for its failure to
control the property bubble that subsequently contributed to Ireland's
economic crash and consumer wealth losses. Collins et al (2007: 134) asserts
that Ireland's regulators 'are even less popularly accountable than civil servants'
and that, in time, they will require stronger democratic underpinning.

Ireland has also created a host of 'stand-alone' bodies or agencies that exist
outside the traditional structures of government. The number of state agencies
has more than doubled since the 1990s. The OECD (2008: 294) is critical of
Ireland's approach in this regard, referring to the 'proliferation of agencies'
leading to 'a decrease in accountability, and a fragmentation of purpose and
scale of public sector activity'. Worryingly, the OECD concludes (2008:
296–7), 'It is unclear how much public funding they use for their own
functioning, for further distribution or investment. Neither is it known exactly
how many staff they employ.' The government's Public Service Reform plan
of November 2011 (2011: 9) pledges to rationalise the number of state agencies
and departmental bodies 'to streamline service delivery, increase democratic
accountability and secure €20 million in enhanced service efficiencies and

value-for-money'. There is also a commitment to implement a new governance and performance management approach for agencies with 'more meaningful performance indicators' and 'robust service delivery agreements between parent departments and agencies'.

In January 2005 the government created a 'super-agency' with the Health Services Executive (HSE) replacing a system comprised of 11 decentralised regional health boards. The HSE now manages delivery of health and social services in Ireland. Collins et al. note that this reform represented 'what is said to be the largest programme of change ever undertaken in the Irish public service'. They describe the HSE as 'a highly complex organisation with over 100,000 employees and an annual budget of €12 billion' (2007: 72). The HSE has received much criticism, not least because it is outside the realm of *Oireachtas* scrutiny in terms of parliamentary questions and it does not have elected local authority representation as existed with the health boards. O'Toole and Dooney (2009: 331) concede that health service reform is a long and difficult process and that 'Ireland's health transformation programme is on a larger scale than any other public service redesign programme in the history of the state.' The OECD review commented (2008: 12), 'there are difficulties involved in leading system-level change, and in pursuing system-wide coherence'. Undoubtedly, health service reform remains one of the major challenges facing government today.

## Local government

The Republic is a unitary state. There is, therefore, no federal government but, as will be discussed below, the EU has a substantial impact on public administration. Local government is less powerful and provides fewer services in Ireland than in most other European countries and there is no recent tradition of local autonomy (Quinlivan and Schön-Quinlivan 2009).

There are 114 local authorities in the Republic of Ireland, divided between county councils (29), city councils (5), borough councils (5) and town councils (75). Apart from *Dáil Éireann* and the presidency, local government is the only Irish institution whose members are directly elected by all of the people. The scheduling of local elections has been guaranteed by Article 28A of the constitution (passed by referendum in 1999), which requires that elections are held no later than the fifth year after which they were last held. Between the 114 local authorities, there are a total of 1,627 councillors with 883 at county and city level and 774 at town and borough level (Weeks and Quinlivan 2010). Voter turnout at the last two sets of elections, 2004 and 2009, was steady at 59 per cent.

The functions of local authorities are divided into the following eight categories.

- Housing and building;
- Road transport and safety;

- Water supply and sewerage;
- Development incentives and controls;
- Environmental protection;
- Recreation and amenity;
- Agriculture, education, health and welfare; and
- Miscellaneous services (financial management, elections, consumer protection, etc.).

Currently housing, roads, water supply, planning and development, and environmental protection dominate the list of local authority functions.

Local government experience is very important in terms of getting elected to the *Oireachtas*. Politically, the functions carried out by local authorities are significant in the context of clientelism. A study by Weeks and Quinlivan in 2009 (with responses by 505 local election candidates) indicated the presence of a number of different types of local election candidates.

- *Aspirant*: someone not that interested in local office, but who sees it as a useful route to national politics.
- *Local broker*: someone looking to represent and fight for the interests of his/her local community.
- *Policy-maker*: someone whose primary focus is policy development.
- *Lobbyist*: someone running or promote the cause of an interest group.
- *Activist*: someone who enjoys politics and likes to devote time to it.
- *Loyalist*: someone not particularly keen on electoral politics but who runs because of a party request.
- *Protector*: someone who runs because of family links to a politician, either to maintain a tradition of family representation or to 'protect' a local seat when a relative transfers to the national arena.
- *Dissident*: someone whose motivation stems from having fallen out with an organisation over an issue, be it a party or a local community group.

Outside of these eight categories is the *maverick* whose presence in the electoral contest is unpredictable and can be a product of idiosyncratic factors.

The Local Government Act, 2003 introduced a significant change in the relationship between national and local politics. The legislation abolished the dual mandate that had heretofore allowed people to simultaneously hold local authority and *Oireachtas* seats. Before 2003, approximately two-thirds of general election candidates for both *Fianna Fáil* and *Fine Gael* had run at the previous local elections and almost all had been elected as a councillor. The main result to date of the dual mandate abolition is the creation of even more councillors who aspire to national office. Weeks and Quinlivan (2009: 158) note, 'Not only is local office a springboard to launch national careers but, in keeping with the water-based metaphor, it has also been used as a lighthouse by TDs to keep a watchful eye on their constituencies.'

A defining feature of the Irish local government system is city and county management. The management system divides the functions of local authorities into two classes, reserved functions (authorised by resolution of the elected members) and the executive function (authorised by the city or county manager). The reserved functions relate to the determination of policy, within limits prescribed by legislation, including financial policy, development plans and making bye-laws (Quinlivan 2006). Other reserved functions include the appointment of members to various bodies and nomination of a person for the office of President of Ireland. All other functions are called 'executive functions' and are performed by the manager.

While the law makes an exact division of functions, the elected members and the manager do not operate independently. Managers and councillors have established a *modus operandi* that successfully balances the needs of local democracy and administrative efficiency (Collins 1987). A system of partnership has evolved where the county manager consults regularly with members on the executive functions, while at the same time advising members on the performance of their reserved functions. Quinlivan (2008: 619) argues that some Irish local authority managers have grown accustomed to being 'the primary instigators of policy proposals'.

Since the late 1960s successive governments have promised reform of local government, but little has happened. Central to any reform is the system for financing local government. Unless the problem of local authority finance is tackled successfully, the independence and viability of local government must be seriously called into question and any benefits from other re-organisation proposals seriously diminished.

A review of local government finance was conducted by Indecon International Economic Consultants in 2006 (see Collins and Quinlivan 2010: 366) and it stated that a significant increase in the level of resources should be made available to local authorities to simply maintain service provision levels. The report also called for a considerable change in the system of local government financing, with a move towards more locally based sources of funding. The OECD report on Ireland (OECD 2008: 69) repeated this call and added that 'from an international perspective, there is little fiscal autonomy in Ireland'.

Partly as a result of Ireland's obligations under the EU/IMF agreement, the introduction of locally based charges is beginning to happen. In Budget 2012, the Minister for Finance announced a flat €100 household charge which will, in time, be replaced by a full property tax requiring a property valuation system. Furthermore, domestic water charges will be introduced, with a meter installation programme commencing in 2012.

The current Minister for the Environment, Community and Local Government has yet to unveil his broader reform plans for local government. At the moment, the focus is very much on rationalisation, cost-cutting and reductionism. In line with this, the minister has announced the merging of

Limerick County Council and City Council into one authority. The same is planned for Waterford and Tipperary (where currently there are two county council jurisdictions). We are also likely to see the abolition of a large number of town councils.

## Financing the system

The Department of Finance has responsibility under statute for the administration of the public finances of Ireland as well as for the promotion of economic and social planning. Its main functions are to act as economic adviser to the government and co-ordinate and regulate the financial and administrative system as a whole. It is responsible for public expenditure, taxation, the budget, economic policy and the management of the public service. The department is always referred to in the context of the dominant nature of central control in the Irish administrative system.

The taxation base in Ireland is very narrow, with revenue from four taxes predominating:

- income taxes: €12.47 billion (36.26 per cent);
- Value Added Tax: €11.42 billion (33.2 per cent);
- excise duties: €4.63 billion (13.47 per cent);
- corporation tax: €3.74 billion (10.87 per cent).

These four taxes contribute over 90 per cent of the total revenue. The major discussion point in terms of sources of revenue in the Irish context is the dependence of local authorities on funding from the exchequer and the absence of a local tax base, particularly a property tax. Until 1978, domestic rates were paid on private dwellings but *Fianna Fáil* in the 1977 general election removed this local source of revenue, following an election commitment. Various efforts to introduce a property tax have been abandoned as politically unpalatable.

As highlighted above, Ireland has been under the monitoring of the EU-ECB-IMF since the end of 2010. This led to the adoption by the *Fianna Fáil* government of a National Recovery Plan 2011–14 in order to return to economic growth. It includes measures to bring public finances back in line and outlines the reforms and sectoral policies that the government will implement in order to boost growth and employment. From a taxation viewpoint, the *Fine Gael*/Labour government elected in 2011 decided in the 2012 budget to increase the rate of VAT to 23 per cent but left the corporation tax untouched at 12.5 per cent. A household charge of €100 was introduced to fund essential local services. The Carbon Tax and Motor Tax rates were both increased as well.

On the current spending issue, four main spending areas can be identified in 2011 (Department of Finance 2012):

- social welfare: €13.3 billion (29.1 per cent);
- health: €12.89 billion (28.21 per cent);
- education and skills: €8.25 billion (18.06 per cent);
- service of national debt: €4.77 billion (10.44 per cent).

These four categories account for over 85 per cent of government expenditure. After a decade in 2000s of budget surpluses, the state of the public finances has deteriorated dramatically since 2007 leading to a budget deficit snowballing from just over €1.5 billion in 2007 to over €24 billion in 2009 before the government introduced drastic austerity measures.

Until 2004, Ireland had relied heavily on the EU to provide resources for major infrastructural developments. At that date, the EU enlarged to 10 Central and Eastern European countries, with Romania and Bulgaria joining in 2007. Those countries' standard of living was much lower than the EU's average, which meant that the EU re-directed infrastructural and regional policy budgets towards them. As a result, in 2011, the receipts from the EU budget totalled just over €56 billion and are as follows:

- Cohesion fund: €8.93 billion;
- European regional fund: €33.05 billion;
- Trans-European network: €1.11 billion;
- EU Solidarity fund contribution: €13.02 billion.

Despite Ireland being part of the Eurozone, it has not been able to comply with the terms of the EMU since 2009 when the government gross debt reached 66 per cent of GDP. In 2011, the debt–GDP ratio soared to climb above 100 per cent after having been as low as 25 per cent in 2007. Similarly public deficits increased dramatically to reach over 11 per cent of GDP. This has led to the involvement of the IMF, the EU and the ECB in bailing out Ireland in exchange for a series of austerity measures that reduce public expenditure. Before the tightening of public spending imposed by the Troïka, an agreement has already been reached with the public services organisations in the Irish Congress of Trade Unions as well as the representative Garda and Defence Force Associations, known as the 2010 Cork Park Agreement covering the period 2010–14. It involves cutting down on the number of public servants, introducing reforms in order to deliver services more efficiently and economically as well as a guarantee given to public servants that there will be no compulsory redundancies and no further reductions in their wages.

The IMF believed that Ireland would be able to go back to the markets by the end of 2012 and that it would be able to afford to borrow money in order to repay its debt. This was not achieved until 2014. A ratification of the European Fiscal Treaty would give Ireland a safety net in terms of accessing the EFSF and keep financing the system at a sustainable rate.

## Accountability, secrecy and openness

The tradition of secrecy associated with the working of government was very prevalent in the Republic. People often speak of a culture of secrecy. Ironically, Ireland remained 'true' to the British model it adopted, long after the United Kingdom itself had changed. Indeed, in 1997, a constitutional referendum reaffirmed and modified a stricter rule on cabinet confidentiality than applies in Britain from where it was originally taken. Conversely, the Freedom of Information (FOI) Act, 1997, is regarded as being liberal in comparison to similar legislation in other countries. The FOI Act came into effect for central government, many public bodies, local authorities and health boards in 1998. It gives the public access to official records, files and reports of government departments and public bodies. The legislation effectively overturns the presumption that all official information is secret. Some data, especially commercially sensitive or legally privileged material, are excluded from the scope of the Act. Nevertheless, a Supreme Court decision, also in April 1998, widened the right of the media to report court cases and clarified the public's rights to information.

For its advocates, the FOI legislation marks a radical departure from a public service culture of secrecy to one of public service openness and transparency. The Act is clearly and deliberately predisposed in favour of achieving the greatest possible access to official information subject only to necessary exceptions to safeguard the public interest and the right to privacy. The long title of the Act sets out its aim 'to enable the public to obtain access to official information to the greatest extent possible consistent with the public interest and the right to privacy'.

The FOI Act 1997 established three new statutory rights as follows:

- a legal right for each person to access information held by public bodies;
- a legal right for each person to have official information relating to him/herself amended where it is incomplete, incorrect or misleading;
- a legal right to obtain reasons for decisions affecting oneself.

Significantly, the Act places the burden of proof firmly on the body or person opposing disclosure. Section 34(12) provides that a decision to refuse to grant a request shall be presumed not to have been justified unless the head of the public body concerned shows to the satisfaction of the Information Commissioner that the decision was justified. The Information Commissioner is an independent person who reviews decisions made by public bodies under the Act.

The FOI Act has changed the culture within the Irish public service, with O'Toole and Dooney (2009: 482) contending:

This legislation was seen as a milestone on the road to good governance and best practice in terms of accountability. It was grounded in the belief that public bodies must be accountable to the ordinary public they are there to serve and that accountability requires openness.

International experience in countries where FOI legislation has been passed is that it has led to an improvement in the quality of reporting, advice and decision-making. Conversely, condensed or deficient recording of decisions may circumvent the law. O'Malley and Martin (2010: 321) develop the point that public service culture may have evolved in response to FOI in less positive ways. They note,

> It seems plausible to suggest that decisions are being taken but not minuted on paper, and that written communication more generally has declined within public bodies. Employees in bodies subject to FOI are likely to be more aware that what they write could be subject to a FOI request.
>
> (O'Malley and Martin, 2010: 321)

In 2003, the government amended the FOI Act and curtailed access to information. The then Information Commissioner, Kevin Murphy, who outlined his fears in his 2002 annual report, that some elements of officialdom were showing signs of fatigue towards the legislation. The 2003 amendment Act 'increased the exemption period for Cabinet papers from five to ten years, introduced measures to ensure "protection" of communications between ministers on government business and documents relating to parliamentary questions, tribunals and international relations' (Collins et al. 2007: 62). Fees for FOI requests for non-personal information were introduced as follows:

- €15   initial request;
- €75   internal appeal;
- €150  final appeal to Information Commissioner.

The combined total of €240 is one of the highest fee levels in the world and has led to a reduction in the number of FOI requests. The current Information Commissioner, Emily O'Reilly, is an outspoken critic of the 2003 amendment Act and of the introduction of fees. She observed in 2003 that 'the original Freedom of Information Act may have been winded but hasn't yet been stretchered off the pitch'. The Information Commissioner has also challenged the continued omission of certain bodies from FOI, including the Vocational Education Committees (VECs), the Central Applications Office (CAO), the State Examinations Commission, the Adoption Board, *An Garda Síochána*, those bodies dealing with asylum applicants, the Central Bank and Financial Services Authority and the State Claims Agency.

The FOI Acts must not be seen in isolation. They are but one aspect, though perhaps the most central one, of a wider process of reform in the area of government and public service generally. As well as the Information Commissioner, Ireland now also has the Standards in Public Office Commission, the Children's Ombudsman, the Data Protection Commissioner, the Garda Síochána Ombudsman Commission and the Financial Services Ombudsman, to name but a few. The two such bodies that most complement the Information Commissioner are the Comptroller and Auditor General (C&AG) and the Ombudsman.

Article 33 of the constitution states that 'there should be a C&AG to control (on behalf of the state) all disbursements and to audit all accounts of monies administered by or under the authority of the *Oireachtas*'. In other words, the job of the C&AG is to report to *Dáil Éireann* on whether public funds have been spent appropriately and to good effect. He does this by providing reports on audits and examinations to the Public Accounts Committee and by investigating whether value for money has been achieved by state organisations.

The Office of Ombudsman was established under legislation enacted in 1980. The Ombudsman investigates complaints from members of the public who feel they have been subjected to unfair treatment by public bodies. The Ombudsman can also prepare special investigation reports; most notably this happened in 2001 with a report on nursing home subventions. This report 'highlighted the practice of the state illegally charging some long-term residents in nursing homes' (O'Malley and Martin 2010: 319). The report pointed to defective relationships between the executive and parliament, within the government, and between government departments and agencies such as the HSE.

## Conclusion: further developments and issues within the system

Ireland faces many challenges in terms of its finances, *Oireachtas* reform and public service reform. Since the middle of the 1990s in particular – with the introduction of the SMI – the country has been on a path of piecemeal and incremental change. Traditionally, departmental rivalry and civil service conservatism have acted as barriers to the establishment of radically new public policies. Accordingly, despite the rhetoric of party policies, in Ireland as elsewhere, public policies are more notable for continuity than for change. New ideas take time to find acceptance among politicians, bureaucrats and the public, and even longer to effect state provision. Small countries like Ireland often wait to learn from experiment and innovation elsewhere, and, in Ireland's case, the example of the United Kingdom is inevitably a powerful influence.

Despite the somewhat laggardly approach to reform, Ireland has been well served by its political and administrative institutions. However, a certain complacency set in during the latter years of the so called 'Celtic Tiger' and, more often than not, mediocrity was accepted. The current Information Commissioner and Ombudsman, Emily O'Reilly, has referred to Ireland being content with 'a bog standard C grade in every area in which the state is charged with a duty of care' (O'Reilly 2011). She notes,

And in my work I have often observed that things go bad when institutions, whether public or private, stop doing what they're supposed to do. The last Financial Regulator did not regulate the banks. The banks themselves stopped banking and became the enablers instead of a decade of pyramid selling that crippled the country and cued at least a further decade of misery and desperation for thousands if not tens of thousands of families throughout the country. Parliament, sidelined through long years of largely self-imposed impotence, allowed the Government to cheerlead its way through a period of what has since emerged was economic lunacy.

Administrative modernisation is harder to achieve than any other reform because the benefits are long term. Few politicians see any electoral gain from radically changing public administration. In contrast, they may anticipate resistance from public servants themselves. Nurturing and sustaining a political commitment to such a project is very difficult. Nonetheless, the Public Service Reform plan of 2011, following the 2008 independent review by the OECD, offers some cause for optimism. A number of cost-cutting initiatives have been announced and it is hoped that a renewed focus on value for money, shared services, rationalisation of agencies and the introduction of a government-level performance management system (GovStat) will drive a reform process with the twin objectives of improving customer service and reducing costs. The government has also committed to restoring the FOI Act to its status before the 2003 amendments in which its scope was limited.

Reform is also needed at a political level. In Lincoln's words democracy is 'government of the people, by the people and for the people'. The people are, according to this popular model, the real guardians of democracy. Their role is centred on the assessments that are made at elections. Nevertheless, the rate of participation in Irish general elections in the last 20 years has overall exhibited a downward trend. In 1997, only 67 per cent of the electorate voted at the general election and this decreased by a further four points in 2002 before returning to 67 per cent again in 2007. At the most recent general election in February 2011, there were some encouraging signs as turnout rose to 69.9 per cent and a record number of candidates (566) put themselves before the electorate.

The government has proposed the abolition of *Seanad Éireann* and a referendum will be held to decide on its future. This cannot be described as a reform, however, and will do nothing to improve *Dáil Éireann* or make it more relevant and significant. Gallagher correctly argues (2010b: 226) that

> Parliament would become more powerful if TDs of the government parties ceased to see their main role as supporting the government and became, instead, quasi-neutral observers of the political process, ready to back or oppose the government depending on their view of the issue at hand.

It is further hoped that any reform of Ireland's political institutions will not ignore the rich potential of local authorities as a driver of change and innovation that has never been explored.

## References

Chubb, B. (1992) *The Government and Politics of Ireland*, London: Longman.

Clarke, V. M. (2008) 'Tea and a Nice Taste of Grace and True Nobility with the President', *Sunday Independent*, 16 November.

Coakley, J. and Gallagher, M. (2010) *Politics in the Republic of Ireland*, 5th edn, London and New York: Routledge.

Collins, N. (1987) *Local Government Managers at Work*, Dublin: Institution of Public Administration.

Collins, N., Cradden, T. and Butler, P. (2007) *Modernising Irish Government: The Politics of Administrative Reform*, Dublin: Gill & Macmillan.

Collins, N. and O'Raghallaigh, C. (1996) 'Ireland', in F. F. Ridley and A. Doig (eds) *Sleaze: Politicians, Private Interests and Public Reaction*, Oxford: Oxford University Press, pp. 149–63.

Collins, N. and Quinlivan, A. (2010) 'Multi-level Governance', in J. Coakley and M. Gallagher (eds) *Politics in the Republic of Ireland*, New York: Routledge, pp. 384–405.

Dáil Éireann (1937) *Parliamentary Debates*, 11 May, 67 (1).

Department of Finance (2012) 'End of December Exchequer Statement', Dublin. Online, available at: http://finance.gov.ie/documents/exchequerstatements/2011/enddecexcheqstat.pdf (accessed 17 September 2013).

Department of Public Expenditure and Reform (2011) *Public Service Reform*, 17 November 2011, Dublin. Online, available at: http://per.gov.ie/wp-content/uploads/Public-Service-Reform-pdf.pdf (accessed 17 September 2013).

Department of the Taoiseach (2006) *Towards 2016: Ten-Year Framework Social Partnership Agreement 2006–2015*, Dublin: Stationery Office.

Eurostat (2011) 'Provision of Deficit and Debt Data for 2010 – First Notification', *Newsrelease euroindicators*, 60/2011, 26 April 2011. Online, available at: http://epp.eurostat.ec.europa.eu/cache/ITY_PUBLIC/2–26042011-AP/EN/2–26042011-AP-EN.PDF (accessed 17 September 2013).

Gallagher, M. (2010a) 'The Changing Constitution', in J. Coakley and M. Gallagher (eds) *Politics in the Republic of Ireland*, 5th edn, London and New York: Routledge, pp. 72–108.

Gallagher, M. (2010b) 'The Oireachtas: President and Parliament', in J. Coakley and M. Gallagher (eds) *Politics in the Republic of Ireland*, 5th edn, London and New York: Routledge. pp. 198–229.

Laffan B. (1999) 'The European Union and Ireland', in N. Collins (ed) *Political Issues in Ireland Today*, Manchester: Manchester University Press.

Laffan, B. and O'Mahony, J. (2008) *Ireland and the European Union*, Basingstoke: Palgrave Macmillan.

MacCarthaigh, M. (2008) *Public Service Values*, Dublin: Institute of Public Administration.

National Recovery Plan (2010). Online, available at: http://budget.gov.ie/The%20National%20Recovery%20Plan%202011–2014.pdf (accessed 17 September 2013).

O'Donnell, R. (2001) 'To Be a Member State: The Experience of Ireland', Public Lecture (Dublin European Institute) UCD, 26 September.

OECD (2008) Ireland: Towards an Integrated Public Service, Paris: OECD.

O'Malley, E. and Martin, S. (2010) 'The Government and the Taoiseach,' in J. Coakley and M. Gallagher (eds) *Politics in the Republic of Ireland*, 5th edn, London: PAI Press and Routledge, pp. 295–326.

O'Reilly, E. (2011) 'The Perfect State', Ombudsman's address to UCC Annual Philip Monahan Memorial Lecture, Department of Government, Cork, 17 November. Online, available at: http://ombudsman.gov.ie/en/SpeechesArticlesandPresentations/Ombudsmansspeeches/Name,14783,en.htm

O'Toole, J. and Dooney, S. (2009) *Irish Government Today*, 3rd edn, Dublin: Gill & Macmillan.

Quinlivan, A. (2006) *Philip Monahan, A Man Apart – The Life and Times of Ireland's First Local Authority Manager*, Dublin: Institute of Public Administration.

Quinlivan, A. (2008) 'Reconsidering Directly Elected Mayors in Ireland: Experiences from the United Kingdom and America', *Local Government Studies*, *34*, 5: 609–23.

Quinlivan, A. and Schön-Quinlivan, E. (2009) *Innovation and Best Practice in Irish Local Government*, Dublin: Chambers Ireland and SIPTU.

Weeks, L. and Quinlivan, A. (2010) *All Politics is Local: A Guide to Local Elections in Ireland*, Cork: Collins Press.

Whelan, N. (2011) *Fianna Fáil: A Biography of the Party*, Dublin: Gill & Macmillan.

## Further reading

### Websites

www.irlgov.ie
www.environ.ie
http://ucd.ie/~politics/irpols (a useful source of basic information on Ireland)
http://irish-times.com

# 4 France

*J. A. Chandler*

## Political culture

French political culture generates considerable controversy. At one extreme it is regarded as a regime in which a measure of democracy has been grafted onto an administrative structure that had been highly centralized in the seventeenth century. During his long reign Louis XIV built a court around his Palace of Versailles to keep the aristocracy in impotent subservience to the monarchy but ensured that he was aided in political and economic matters by intelligent and loyal advisors drawn from the lesser nobility or middle classes such as Colbert and Cardinal Richelieu. Such practice initiated a cultural reliance on a centralized technocratic civil service as support for a strong political leader. The French Revolution that began in 1789 succeeded in removing the hereditary monarchy and even more firmly the influence of the aristocracy, but did not dissipate a predisposition for government domination by a single leader relying on the influence of middle-class technocrats. Indeed, the dominant figure who emerged from the maelstrom of the revolution, Napoleon, was not only a skilled general but a highly competent technocratic administrator from a middle-class family.

However, most modern historians have argued that in reality France has always had a pluralistic system of government in which local values and opinions are influential and respected. D. E Ashford (1981) compared France with Britain's pretence towards liberalism, in relation to local government under the title of *British Dogmatism and French Pragmatism*. Arguably neither of the extreme views is fully valid and in reality, under its administrative system, France evolved a system of government that can balance a capacity for central leadership with a respect for local values and opinion. As a large country with differing geographical environments and local economies, France had a culturally diverse population. In the late nineteenth century a quarter of its mainland citizens were still speaking languages other than French (Stevens 2003: 3). Despite the trend to strong personalized government from the centre and reliance on well-educated meritocratic technocrats, a parallel trend, that was fostered in the pre-1789 *Ancien Régime* and continued after the revolution, off-set centralization through a patron–client system that ensured local regions and communities could be kept within the central political system by giving concessions to local powerful leaders. The revolution demonstrated to politicians in Paris that without some concessions to the provinces France could divide into separate political units. Much of the violence of the revolution was meted out not just in Paris but by revolutionary armies attempting to suppress local pro-monarchist or separatist rebellions in Brittany and the Vendé.

The 1789 revolution also differentiated French administrative practice by establishing a separate branch of administrative law along side the codes for civil and criminal law. This was developed partly to ensure that the state and some of its more totalitarian leaders such as Robespierre could not be prosecuted through the courts. However, this apparently self-serving position had a moral justification in the writings of some pre-revolutionary theorists such as Rousseau who argued that once society had consented to legal rules it was the duty of the state to ensure that every citizen of France kept to laws that benefited society in general. During the early nineteenth century, under the leadership of lawyers and politicians who had no wish to return to the terrorism of an uncontrolled executive, the idea of a system of administrative law determining the powers and duties of the state was established in the French legal code and became the bulwark to ensure that would-be demagogues remained accountable to the laws and precedents of the state.

Following the fall of Napoleon Bonaparte France experienced a succession of autocratic regimes punctuated by violent revolutions. The humiliating defeat of Napoleon III in 1870 at the hands of the Prussian military created some stability with the constitution of the Third Republic. During the following 70 years French political history was divided between loosely connected Catholic conservative parties and liberal parties that detested the dominance of the Catholic Church in domestic politics. After the First World War the expansion of socialist and communist parties added further complexity to the party system. The multi-party divisions within a dominant legislature ensured France was subject to frequent changes of government. The weakness of the political executive was shored up by the creation of a technocratic civil service. The political system was, until its downfall at the hands of Nazi Germany in 1940, workable, but never popular, as it failed to bring forward stable and politically effective governments that could industrially modernize the nation as had happened in Britain or Germany. After 1945, General Charles de Gaulle, who had led the Free French against the German occupation, became head of an interim government with the task of drawing up a new constitution for France. De Gaulle had little time for party politics and hankered after a return to more authoritarian government. Elections, however, returned strong support for communist and socialist governments opposed to the conservatism of the weakened right. The parliamentary system returned as the Fourth Republic and the General returned to private life hoping that some day he would receive the call to once again lead his country. The ineffectiveness of the Fourth Republic in establishing stable governments that could resolve serious economic problems and the long running colonial wars in the French colonies led in 1958 to a *coup d'état* by generals based in Algeria that paved the way for de Gaulle's return. The General threw out the Fourth Republic's constitution and established the Fifth Republic with the aim of ensuring a stronger executive that could create more stable governments that would be less susceptible to defeat within the more decentralized and divided legislative arm of the state.

## The constitutional arrangement

The constitution of the Fifth Republic has lasted with the help of a number of significant changes following its promulgation in 1958 and yet it is far from a perfect document. Its success has to a large extent been a reflection of the concern of political parties after the troubles of 1958 to avoid the problem of frequent changes of coalition governments that made long-term policy development difficult in the Third and Fourth Republics. De Gaulle was concerned to establish an executive under the control of a powerful president who could expect to serve a substantial seven-year term of office and be able to stand on further occasions for re-election. The president was originally elected indirectly by the legislature and mayors but in 1962 the constitution was changed to ensure the position was chosen through direct election by all French citizens under a two-ballot system in which, as is likely, if no candidate receives an overall majority of votes in the first round, the two candidates with the highest vote contest a further round of voting. In 2000 the electoral term for the president was reduced to five years. Normally the candidates who contest presidential elections with any hope of success are the leaders of the major parties. However, the party system is rather fluid. On the left the socialists and communists have endured since the early twentieth century but on the right parties have tended to congregate around specific political leaders. The parties of the centre right tend to acknowledge the legacy of de Gaulle, although he, himself, did not strongly endorse loyalty to the parties that supported him. On the far right, following amalgamations of smaller parties, there is considerable cohesion around the *Front National* led until 2011 by Jean-Marie le Pen and subsequently by his daughter.

The president is not only head of the executive but also the head of state and it was expected by de Gaulle that the holder of the office would have a major role in determining foreign policy. The president has the power to dissolve the lower house of the legislature, the Assembly, and appoint a prime minister. However, the prime minister has the task of choosing members of the government but only subject to the president's approval. In practice the constitution allows the president to determine the principle decisions of the executive provided he or she has the support of the legislature. This crucial check is secured by the prime minister who must countersign most decisions of the president for them to be enacted. As the prime minister is required to resign his office if he loses a vote of confidence in the Assembly, it became apparent that a president could get few of his policies accepted if he did not have the support of the majority of Assembly members. When the president enjoys firm support from the legislature he has selected a close party lieutenant who will normally defer to his policies in cases of conflict. However, a vital test of the robustness of the constitution took place in 1986 when, during the socialist President Mitterand's term of office, Assembly elections returned a right-wing majority. Mitterand appointed Jacques Chirac, the leader of the largest right-wing party in the Assembly, as prime minister and, while a restraining influence on the prime minister, he conceded most policy initiatives particularly on domestic matters to Chirac. Subsequent occasions when the president does not enjoy majority support in the Assembly, termed periods of cohabitation, have continued to give the initiative to the prime minister as leader of the majority party. The probability of cohabitation has been reduced following a constitutional change that set both Assembly, Senate and the president's term of office at five years.

Government ministers are chosen by the prime minister and normally are leading politicians in his or her party. The most senior are members of a Council of Ministers, often termed the Cabinet. Junior ministers may also be involved in cabinet discussions affecting their responsibilities. There is, unlike Britain or the USA, little sense of a ministerial team as junior ministers are given clear areas of responsibility by the prime minister rather than serving as deputies to a cabinet minister. The names and number of ministries have changed during the Fifth Republic but the key and enduring departments are those for Foreign Policy, Justice, Defence, Agriculture and Interior. Finance is also a key position but under a divide-and-rule strategy responsibility for economic issues has at times been divided between at least two ministerial departments. Ministers are usually chosen as senior members of the prime minister's party and, usually, therefore, the president's party, and normally are Assembly members. However, while ministers can sit in the Assembly and address the chamber they must resign their seat and cannot vote as an Assembly member.

The legislature consists of two houses. The most important chamber is the Assembly, whose members, known as deputies, are elected to represent a constituency using a two-ballot system. The second chamber, the Senate, consists of representatives selected for a nine-year term of office representing local authorities with a third of its members subject to re-selection every three years. Legislation must normally pass both houses to be accepted and hence the Senate has considerable powers to hold up or amend bills but in the event of disagreement between the two chambers joint committees are established to thrash out an agreed version of the bill and if this fails then the Assembly's view can prevail over that of the Senate. The Senate, nevertheless, can have sufficient amending and delaying powers to ensure that the results of local elections have importance as this can greatly change the overall balance of party control in the legislature. The 1958 Constitution was designed to give fewer powers to the legislature and allow the president greater authority through a number of provisions such as stipulating a relatively short period for its meetings and decreasing the capacity for non-government measures to take precedence over government legislation and policy statements. Under the framework for cohabitation the length of time for the legislature to meet has, however, increased and governments are less insistent on dominating parliamentary proceedings.

## The civil service

At one level the French Civil Service is a huge organisation encompassing all employees, except the military, in the centralized public services and hence includes all teachers, police, tax officers and social security workers. Anyone employed directly by the state is officially a civil servant. However, there is a much smaller core to such a sprawling bureaucracy that is often seen to exert huge authority and respect in the nation. Many senior politicians in France have risen to ministerial and presidential eminence through earlier work within the civil service and, in contrast to Max Weber's ideal of political neutrality, it is possible for a civil servant to gain election to the Assembly or engage in some other party political role, and later return to his former bureaucratic post.

The French Civil Service can trace its origins to at least the early eighteenth century when successive kings recognized the professionalism of civil engineers concerned with highways and bridges as a specific self-governing group of state servants. This development opened up the creation of a permanent government service built on professional groups termed *corps* that determine the entry qualifications, training and, subject to government acceptance, have reserved to them specific functions. There are within the French Civil Service some 1,300 *corps* (Elgie and Griggs 2000: 53), the largest being the *corps* of primary school teachers. Within this framework a small number of *corps* are collectively categorized as *grands corps* and are respected as the most prestigious elements within the civil service with, generally, the most powerful positions. The *grands corps* consists of engineers, the prefects who supervize devolved regional and local government, diplomats, financial and economic advisors and inspectors and those involved with the Council of State whose members deal with the legal regulation of the constitution and the administrative machinery of the state. Members of the engineering *corps* are normally graduates who have been trained in the *École Polytechnique* founded in 1794. A parallel body the *École Nationale d'Administration* (ENA) was established at the beginning of the Fourth Republic to provide postgraduate training for the administrative, diplomatic and financial *grands corps*. Competition to enter the ENA is intense with a half to a third of entrants from lower civil service *corps* and the majority from high achievers in leading universities. Graduation from the institution is seen as a route to the most prestigious offices in France and numbers three presidents, including the present incumbent François Hollande and six prime ministers among its alumni. Training standards for the two-year course are high and in the final exams students are ranked in order of their success. Those with the highest grades get first preference in choosing the positions open to them in the civil service. Most of the leading graduates choose to enter financial or administrative *grands corps*. Although prestigious, the system is open to considerable criticism as a means of ensuring that the sons and some daughters of France's political and economic elite are most favoured as entrants to ENA and hence retain positions of power within a small ruling elite.

The structure of government departments do not lend themselves to the Weberian hierarchy of a pyramidal structure led by a single dominant bureaucrat. The structure at ministerial level is highly fragmented (Ridley and Blondel 1964) and is formed into truncated pyramids within particular departments and also horizontally divided by the loyalties of civil servants to their *corps* rather than to the civil service as a whole. The civil service in each ministry is arranged in separate *bureaux* each under a head who reports directly to the minister. The concern that the minister can divide and rule has ensured that there is no exact equivalent to the position of the permanent secretary in Britain who is the final line manager for all civil servants in a department, let alone a figure such as the cabinet secretary who is regarded as the head of the civil service (Hayward 1983: 127). Co-ordination is secured through the ministers personal cabinet composed of around 10 advisors many of whom are drawn from the ranks of the civil service. The minister is free to select the members of his personal cabinet and ensures that many of its members are familiar with the *bureaux* under his authority and can communicate his or her ideas to their senior civil servants. In practice, with judicious informal appointments, a minister's cabinet may extend to at least 30 personnel. The cabinet is co-ordinated by a *directeur de cabinet*, who is normally the principle advisor to the minister and is usually a senior civil servant seconded for his or her time in the office from his former post. Senior members of ministerial cabinets are selected on political grounds and therefore reflect the position of their minister's party.

There is considerable division among academic commentators on the French Civil Service as to how it may best be categorized (See Elgie and Griggs 2000: 72 for a tabulated summary). During the 1970s it was fashionable to describe the civil service as technocratic (Meynaud 1968) but this is misleading in that, while civil servants may have had specialist training in law, public finance and politics in the *ENA*, or engineering in the *Polytechnique*, they must also have generalist understanding of the eclectic environment of public policy. Many civil servants have their eyes on political positions or a senior post in the private sector as their final goal rather than reaching the highest possible position as a politically neutral bureaucrat. While the core civil service has prestige it is, nevertheless, often regarded as remote from the general public and forms a power elite at the centre of French government regardless of whether the centre right or centre left occupies the presidency or has a majority in the Assembly.

# Central government agencies

The tradition of centralization that was engineered by Louis XIV and continued under more proletarian rule by the Jacobin traditions of the revolution, in theory gives relatively little scope for the formation of government agencies that are neither subsumed into the civil service nor are a branch of local or regional government. Nevertheless, the growth of state involvement in the business life of an industrial country, the demands for liberalization of business from the European Union and the need for the government to be subject to its own administrative laws has created pressure to further decentralize decision-making and policy implementation.

The doctrine of *service public* that evolved in the early twentieth century maintained that certain activities – whether they be delivered directly by the state or on the state's behalf by private sector organizations – must adhere to norms that would be of benefit to society as a whole. These require equality of access for the public to the services offered by the organization, continuity in the provision of the service and it also requires that the service adapts to changing needs (Cole 2000: 167). The direction of nationalized industry and the health service are indicative of the ambiguity concerning direct state control. In 1945 there was pressure from both the then more dominant Communist Party and also the nationalist values of de Gaulle to ensure that the French economy was strengthened. Several sectors of the economy were consolidated into nationalized services including the banks, insurance, gas, electricity and coal between 1946 and 1947 (Maclean 2002: 28). State control of industry and finance was briefly further deepened in 1982 when Mitterrand inaugurated the first socialist governments of the Fifth Republic in the face of very different enthusiasm for privatization and reliance on market forces within Britain and the United States. After two years he was obliged to retrench this policy when confronted with the fiscal problems entailed in paying for the purchase of formally privatized businesses and difficulties created by the more laissez faire values of many other European Union (EU) members. Mitterrand conducted an adroit 'U' turn and began after 1986 a policy of privatization that accelerated after Chirac assumed the presidency. Nevertheless, France still retains a much larger swathe of nationalized firms than most EU member states and the ideological if not legal status of privatized firms from the state is not that distinctive. Chirac's prime minister, Édouard Balladur, although privatizing banks such as Paribas and manufacturers such as Saint-Gobain, ensured that control passed into the hands of established businessmen, many of whom had been graduates of the ENA or the *Polytechnique* and served in one of the *grands corps* (Maclean 2002: 159). The links between government and business elites are, therefore, far closer than in the United States or Britain and many of the captains of French industry and finance are highly knowledgeable about the needs and workings of the state.

In addition, the state initiated an effective system of economic planning issuing every four years both national and later regional economic development plans that, especially in their earlier years, enjoyed widespread popular and elite support among business and political interests. Responsibility for planning lies with a commission that has undergone several transformations and attachments to government ministries. Until the 1980s the plans issued by the government, while never mandatory, were highly influential and supported by the private sector as much as being a blueprint for longer-term national economic policy. The emergence of New Right laissez faire values in the later 1980s has, however, greatly attenuated the planning process, but compared with the United States or Britain there remains a view in France of a *dirigiste* State that should have a significant voice in the development of long-term industrial and commercial growth.

The health service in France was regarded in 2000 as the best in the world by a UNESCO study, although it is far from the cheapest. The service is in theory largely under state control but in practice about a third of hospitals usually referred to as *cliniques*, are privately owned, mainly by voluntary and church organizations, and most primary health care doctors are self-employed. Public sector hospitals have a measure of autonomy in that they can set their own budgets although their income is largely dependent on the cost per patient for a days stay in hospital that is set by the Ministry of Health. The chair of the hospital boards is usually the local mayor who may not be without political influence although in the 1990s greater authority was also given to the senior doctors and administrators. However, in 1995 under plans developed by Prime Minister Alain Juppé hospitals were placed in 22 regions under the control of senior civil servants, known as health prefects, with greater powers to determine health care budgets and to close more inefficient hospitals (Griggs 2000: 190–1). The extent to which hospitals are agencies of the state with a measure of independence or directly under state control has therefore varied during the Fifth Republic but, in general, hospitals like other state agencies have found it difficult to assert significant independence from central control unless they have the protection of a powerful politician.

## Local governance

French local government seems on the surface a rather uncomplicated three-tier system dominated by central government. The informal reality ensures it is a far more complex system of power based in part on counter-balancing community interest and the needs of efficiency through a system of patron–clientelism that secures, for the well-connected locality, the benefits of central control. The system is moreover undergoing, at the time of writing, considerable restructuring following the Balladur Report and subsequent legislation in 2010 under the Sarkozy Presidency that is yet to be fully implemented.

Local governance is founded at the community level on some 36,000 communes, the largest number of lower tier governments in any EU country. On average this amounts to 1,500 citizens per commune but the population of a commune varies hugely from encompassing the major cities of Paris, Lyon or Marseille to the smallest hamlets and rural communities. The communes evolved over centuries to encompass organically forming centres of population and by the twelfth century most villages and towns had their own elected communal assemblies or assemblies of local worthies who succeeded each other by self-selection (Schmidt 1990: 13). The second substantive level of sub-government consists of the 96 departments plus four overseas territories that were developed by central governments as the means of ensuring control over the communities and regions of France. While there were attempts by the eighteenth-century monarchy to exert more control over localities and regions, little progress was made until the 1789 revolution that shepherded in the idea of departments. These only took a permanent shape under the consulate of Napoleon Bonaparte who had a highly centralist view of the nation and established senior government officials, the prefects, to be the head of each department with powers to appoint or remove mayors of communes (Schmidt 1990: 20–3). The third tier of 22 regions is a much more recent creation and emerged in response to the demand for large-scale national economic planning and the creation of the European Community. They were formed in the 1950s by the planning commission but gained a constitutional presence in 1964 with the creation of a regional planning agency and the appointment of advisory councils for each of the regions to draw up their economic plans. It was not until 1982, however, that the regional councils were elected bodies that could be said to form part of the sub-governmental structure rather than a state agency. In addition to the three tiers there remain remnants of former divisions. Large cities are divided into *arrondisements* for administrative purposes and in rural areas these have been electoral divisions as are the cantons, which are smaller sub-divisions of the department set up in the revolutionary period. In recent years, a more substantive division is developing in rural areas of communities of communes (*communauté de communes*) through the voluntary grouping of neighbouring small communes into groups that can, for example, tender more effectively for refuse collection services or develop tourism.

The communes are governed by a council elected by local citizens every six years through a two-ballot system for those with a population of over 3,500

*Table 4.1* The French sub-government structure

|  | Number | Created |
|---|---|---|
| Regions | 22 | 1950s–1964 |
| Departments | 96 | 1799 |
| Communities of communes | Approx 2,500 | 1960s onwards |
| Communes | 36,000 | Circa twelfth century |

and a single ballot for the many smaller communes. The number of councillors elected ranges from a minimum of nine in the least populated communes and increases in number depending on population. Paris elects 163 councillors for the city as a whole but is also divided into 20 *arrondisements* that have their own council and mayor. The electoral system is arranged so that in councils with over 3,500 citizens electors choose between party lists and the outcome will award at least half the seats to the party with either over half the votes in the first round of voting or the largest support in the second round. Parties with less than 5 per cent of the vote in the second round get no seats at all. The system was initiated in 1982 under a major reform of the local government system to ensure that most councils had a clear majority party in control rather than being 'hung'. Following the election the councillors vote one of their members as the mayor of the commune who is not only the leading representative of the town but also the head of the executive for the commune. The mayor has a dual and potentially conflicting role as being also the representative of the central state within the commune. In larger communes the mayor is in effect a professional politician and is normally the local leader of their party.

The functions of the communes in practice vary according to their size and, for the smaller communities, may be shared with neighbouring communes under local agreements acceptable to the prefect of the department often through their membership of a *communauté de communes*. The tasks include responsibility for local infrastructure including, primary schools, minor roads and refuse collection and the maintenance of communal buildings such as the town hall (*hôtel de ville*). They also promote the commune to attract tourists or new businesses into their area. The commune may also participate in ventures with other public or private agencies for larger-scale urban re-development and the construction of public housing. In the larger cities such as Paris or Lyon these tasks can amount to major undertakings. Following the Balladur Report the 11 largest cities are to be encouraged to establish larger metropolitan authorities in co-operation with their suburban communes and their department and region.

Above the level of the communes the departments were until 1871 purely administrative divisions of central government controlled by a senior civil servant, the prefect. Under the Third Republic prefects had to report to an elected departmental council but under the principle of *tutelage* they remained as a chief executive and had the power to set the departmental budget and to strike down any proposals that they deemed were unlawful. It was not until the 1982 reforms that the council and its president became the legal decision-making and budget-setting authority. Prefects still have powers to refer any action they consider unlawful to an administrative court, are chief executive of their department's bureaucracy and represent the national government's views to the council, but they do not legally dominate the departmental government as was formerly the case. The power of the prefect, like that of the mayor, is also dependent on political connections as much as their legal powers. The departmental councillors are elected for six-year terms of office with half of the council standing for election every three years. Voting is through the two-ballot system similar to that used for national elections. Once elected, the council votes for its president who is the head of the political policy-making executive of the department. The office is likely to be held by a mayor of a larger commune in the department and can be seen as a step towards becoming a professional politician.

The role of the departments was until the late twentieth century more concerned with ensuring that the communes conducted their affairs in accord with state policy rather than themselves undertaking tasks directly. They have had, however, responsibility for major roads in their area, apart from the national network of motorways, public housing and promotion of tourism. In 1982 they also acquired direct responsibility for social work and some secondary schools. The department and its prefect is, outside the influence of its elected council, also a division for the out-reach activities of many central government departments and hence the prefect will also be co-ordinating decentralized government offices concerned with, for example, education, health and social service.

The role of regions initially was to plan and steer economic policy for their area but since 1982 they have slowly accrued further powers such as control over the upper secondary schools (*lycées*) and the promotion of work opportunities such as apprenticeships. Although the regions have relatively few tasks, they have significant economic importance as the route through which EU development funds are channelled. As with the departments, the regions are under the administrative direction of a prefect who was formally recognized in 2010 as being superior to their colleagues in the departments. Each region is, currently, governed rather like the departments through a council elected every six years that in turn elects a president as the political executive leader for council. Legislation passed in 2010 and due to come into effect in 2014 will, however, radically reshape the elected representation to departments and regions by merging the role of regional and departmental councillors, as territorial councillors with a seat at both levels. This will also substantially cut the number of councillors at this level and there is considerable debate as to whether this will result in the departments dominating the regions or the regional interest absorbing for departmental concerns (Cole 2012: 346).

Despite the role of the prefects as representatives in the localities of central government, the balance between central and local government is characterized by networking and joint office-holding among politicians. In contrast to Britain, local mayors and departmental presidents may not only be powerful local figures but also retain positions of power as either deputies and senators or even as government ministers at the heart of the French political system. In many cities the leader of the dominant political party will not only take on the role of the city's mayor but also be elected to the Assembly or Senate. Government ministers may also often retain the position of mayor.

Gaston Defferre the socialist party leader for many years in Marseilles was at the same time both mayor of the city and Minister of the Interior from which position he steered through the 1982 restructuring of the local government system. Prior to his reforms powerful local politicians often piled up an array of local and state offices including both mayor, departmental president and membership of the state legislature under a framework termed the *cumul des mandats*. Following the 1982 legislation politicians may only hold two elective offices simultaneously. Senators, as representatives of local governments, also generally take an unsympathetic view to any attempts to lessen the discretion enjoyed by sub-national governments, and they ensured that the suggestions for streamlining the system proposed by the Balludur Commission were much watered down in the Act of 2010.

The basis of holding office at the centre and locally is argued by Ashford (1982) to lie in the patron–client structure of central local relations in France. Localities will elect politicians who can gain national prominence and as a result through a formally centralized administrative system, ensure they get the government and civil service to allocate resources and powers for them to benefit their locality. Despite their formal authority, prefects always realized that they must work closely with, rather than in opposition to, a mayor or departmental president who may be able to pull strings at the centre, that could deprive them of their position. The tensions and costs of legal review of local actions also ensures close and co-ordinated working between the centre and periphery. Following recent political theory many French commentators on the relationship now model the system by applying network theory. The many actors in the system are now so dependent upon one another to implement their policies that they form local networks in which they forge the compromises needed to satisfy the interests of central government and the locality (Elgie and Griggs 2000: 73–96).

## Finance

As Table 4.2 indicates France has relatively higher levels of public expenditure and taxation and is far more partial to state control and investment in essential infrastructure such as the railways.

Control of financial resources has, in France, been a central element in the state's armoury for steering field administration and the potentially divisive

*Table 4.2* Public expenditure as a percentage of GDP in 2011

| | |
|---|---|
| France | 56 |
| United Kingdom | 48 |
| Germany | 45 |
| United States | 41 |

Source: Eurostat and www.USgovernmentsSpending.com

power of local political interests. Management of the budget, auditing spending and planning for growth are regarded as central and prestigious positions of power and the most sought after offices for ambitions graduates from the ENA.

The budget is determined formally in early October but is the product of an almost continuous process of making forward estimates of expenditure three years into the future and then refining these projections for the immediate forthcoming year (Burns and Goglio 2004: 11–12). The process is steered by the budgetary directorate of the Ministry of Finance but, given the inevitable tendency of ministers in spending departments to challenge their allocation of funds, the overall framework of the budget is determined by negotiations between the prime minister and departmental ministers. Provided France is not in a period of cohabitation the overall policy for the budget will lie with the president who will demand austerity or growth dependent on his or her reading of the state of the economy. The president will also be, on most issues of financial policy, the final court of appeal for contending ministers (Hayward 1983: 172–7).

Spending within the budget is tightly controlled and monitored. Civil servants who authorize spending must have their decision verified by civil servants from the Ministry of Finance implanted within their department. The accountability of the bureaucracy concerning finance is overseen by a quasi-judicial service, the *Cour des Comptes*, the Court of Accounts, which was established in 1807 in order to report on the management of public spending. The Court's modern role is to comment on the effectiveness and efficiency of public spending rather than the investigating cases of corruption. An Inspectorate of Finance, created in 1831, largely to deal with this element of the audit process, examining not only central government accounts but those of all public sectors including local authorities. Despite these restraints France is not immune to financial scandals involving public monies.

The financial autonomy of decentralized government units are even more tightly constrained since local governments must, unlike the national government, ensure that they are in surplus at the end of each financial year and cannot exceed pre-determined levels of taxation. Nevertheless, communes, departments and regions have considerable discretion over how much they may raise from the taxes that they are legally allowed to use. Approximately one-third of revenues for communes come from direct subsidies from central government while the remainder is raised through several taxation streams of which the most significant are taxes on undeveloped land and built-on land, housing, and through a smaller 'professional' tax falling largely on the self-employed. There are also many minor taxes at the disposal of local authorities and they may also charge for services such as refuse collection. However, the Sarkozy Presidency in 2009 placed a cap on many of the local taxes falling on businesses (Cole 2012: 344).

In addition to the state and local funding arrangements lies the complex but costly framework for funding social security, which is determined in consultation with the Ministry of Finance by the Ministry of Health and remains largely separate from the budget for all other state activities. Funding for health care substantially derives from a compulsory welfare insurance scheme run by a small number of 'not for profit' insurance agencies that are subject to government regulation. Patients initially pay doctors and hospitals for their service but then can claim back most of the cost from the state insurance scheme. However, the system is often under financial stress and frequently bailed out by direct funding from central government. Income to support social care is also derived from taxes related to the payrolls of businesses and to a much lesser extent on personal incomes and capital gains.

## Co-ordinating the system

In theory co-ordination of the political system was traditionally secured in the Fifth Republic through the president and prime minister setting out broad policy outlines to be accepted by ministers and, through ministerial cabinets, communicated and monitored in the directorates of the ministries. At sub-national level, the prefects are the heads of national field agencies within their departments and also network with departmental presidents and communal mayors on how they should implement central edicts. In addition are the links that cut across party animosity, binding party leaders and bureaucrats representing particular regions, and, finally, there are the networks that have grown up through membership of one of the *grand corps* and for many politicians education at elite Universities and the ENA and *Polytechnique*.

The development of public–private partnerships has had deep roots in French municipal life since local authorities continued to deliver productive services such as gas, electricity and water services and, given the size of many communes, could only deliver services efficiently in co-operation with nationalized businesses or private corporations. Thus, when local governments in Britain were obliged to contract out services such as refuse collection, the major beneficiaries have been multinational French enterpises, such as Veolia, which were experienced in the delivery of services to French communes. Similarly, central government in France has been able to influence social change largely through encouraging networking between bureaucrats, professionals and decentralized governments (Griggs 2000: 185). Links with industry have also benefited from the success of state planning and the interconnected careers of politicians, civil servants and heads of major businesses. There is, therefore, little reflection within French political reformism in the last 20 years for ensuring 'joined-up' government in order to resolve problems such as urban deprivation or crime, which are the result of several dimensions of social and economic issues. Within French local government the development of public–private partnerships has been secured with far less central government legislation and local opposition than in Britain, with most cities operating a range of interactive schemes (Cole and John 2001).

## Managing the system

Barry Owen (2000: 66) observed that

> What is sometimes called the New Public Management is present in
> France, but its impact has been less than in, say, Britain. In part this might
> simply be an expression of anti-Americanism; alternatively, the greater
> legal content of French public administration renders it less flexible. In
> other words, managerialisation, 'fits' the French public sector and its way
> of doing things less easily than is the case in Britain.

This view of the management style of French public administrations has not
substantially changed. As Ridley (1996) suggests, one of the most important
factors that differentiates the French from the British system is the importance
of a separate body of administrative law, which determines not only the scope
of what a civil servant should undertake but also their method of resolving
problems through adjudicating on differing decisions. While the Council of
State, the supreme law court that adjudicates on administrative law, ensures
that the framework of administrative judgements is not set in stone, there is
in France a stronger tradition of how administration is to be determined
and implemented and thus far less concern to restructure the shape of the
administrative framework or how decisions are reached.

## Accountability, secrecy and openness

The Council of State is the supreme court that adjudicates on administrative law and also has an influential role in advising the government on legal
issues. New legislation is referred to the Council and its views are seriously
considered by both the legislature and executive. The membership of the
Council is chosen by the president and members are usually leading politicians
and former civil servants, as opposed to lawyers and judges. Servicing the
Council and presiding over its lower courts are civil servants who are members
of the appropriate *grand corps*. Presidents such as Pompidou and prime ministers
such as Debre or Fabius, have served on the Council (Wright 2000: 102). While
the Council of State will consider the legality of major administrative disputes,
the system of lower administrative courts that report to it, can be used by
French citizens to resolve their grievances against their treatment by the State.
The courts will adjudicate, for example, on complaints concerning planning
decisions or unfair discrimination against government employers. Although
the administrative courts are accessible to most French citizens, they can be
slow to reach a judgement and are often argued to be insufficient in numbers
and too traditional and aloof from the concerns of ordinary citizens. The
Courts are also unable to deal with complaints about poor administrative
practice as opposed to complaints over illegal treatment. To remedy these
defects an ombudsman-style office, the *Mediateur de la republique*, was established

in 1973. This body was merged in 2011 with several smaller organisations concerned with complaints against the state, for example the police and children, to create the office of *Defenseur des droits*, the defender of rights.

France can also be considered to be a relatively open society although perhaps not in the first league of nations concerning access to government information. Legislation of 1978 gave the public the right of access to all documents held by public bodies, with a few exceptions, but the agency that oversees this right lacks binding powers to compel public agents to release information and its activities are not well known by many citizens. The right of access may also be countered by very strict laws on the right to privacy for individuals that, while preventing unwarranted intrusion by the press in the private lives of political activists, can also be used to shield more corrupt politicians from exposure. With the growth of the Internet, where France was a world leader in embracing cutting-edge communications technology, there have, however, been considerable advances in opening up sections of government to public scrutiny.

## Democracy and public administration

In 2010 the Intelligence Unit of the *The Economist* journal saw fit to downgrade France from the status of full democracy to that of a flawed democracy. The concern probably related more to the rather heavy-handed approach of President Sarkozy's social policy, especially on immigration and community relations, and a series of scandals largely related to party funding (Drake 2011: 973). The infrastructure of the French public administration system in respect to democratic issues is, in contrast to policy and practice prior to the election of Hollande as president, generally sound as far as liberal democracies can exhibit effective personalized democracy. Besides providing free and fair elections the state has effective legal means for citizens to gain redress against the government, relatively open government and a strong community basis for local policy-making and administration. However, concerns may still underlie the structures that maintain elitism within the French political and administrative system. Government and bureaucratic officers are open to all but there remains a system of education that socializes the dominant members of the government bureaucracy to harbour similar lifestyles and interests.

## Further developments and issues

Alasdair Cole and David Hanley (2006: 41) have observed that since the 1970s France has faced as many pressures for change as other European nations but 'there is also much evidence of French resistance to unwelcome external ideas such as "neo-liberalism"'. This observation remains valid despite the traumas of the economic recession following the crash of world banking in 2008. The response of the Sarkozy Presidency to the economic downturn was less austere than the response of the British government of Cameron and had a much more Keynesian flavour geared to priming strategic industries and providing support for the short-term unemployed. Some emphasis was, however, placed on efficiency savings, and financial transfers to local governments were frozen (Miller 2011: 188–9). The first budget of Hollande adopted an even more pronounced Keynesian attempt to balance the resultant deficit by raising individual taxation especially among the rich far more sharply than initiating cuts to the public services and health and social security payments.

France is not, however, a wholly conservative and outdated nation in respect to its government and public administration. In the past, frequent revolutionary changes in the constitutional arrangements might suggest it is a nation typified by what Baumgartner and Jones (1993) have described as punctuated equilibrium in which rapid change ushered in periods of stability that were shaken up by new revolutions. However, the comparative longevity of the Fifth Republic, which by 2028 will exceed the Third Republic as the most stable constitution of France since 1789, suggests that France has achieved the capacity of countries such as Britain and the USA, where a flexible interpretation of the constitution enables more gradual evolutionary change and modernization of its political and administrative system. The Fifth Republic became, as christened by J. E. S. Hayward (1964: 27), the Five-and-Half Republic, as politicians facilitated, with little acrimony, the periods of co-habitation of a president from a different party to that of a prime minister with the backing of an Assembly majority by convention rather than consitutional change. The public administrative system has similarly changed significantly since 1958 especially as regards the decentralization of power. French local government is not so much a confused and unco-ordinated system of small communes under the domination of the prefect. The power of central tutelage has become more of a central–local partnership. Regions have increasingly accrued powers and the communal system has responded to social and economic growth by the formation communities of communes.

Enthusiasts for the French system of public administration may well argue that it has reformed during the last 50 years the elements of the system that needed to respond to change. France has, however, largely kept intact the systems that have worked effectively, such as the technocratic competence of the civil service the capacity to ensure politicians can utilize and adjudicate on civil service advice rather than be led by the bureaucrats. The system provides a flexible but effective system of state regulation over utilities and the banking system even at the expense of a rather slow if, in the long run, effective means of redress against insensitive bureaucracy.

## References

Ashford, D. E. (1982) *British Dogmatism and French Pragmatism*, London: George Allen and Unwin.

Baumgartner, F. R. and Jones, B. D. (1993) *Agendas and Instability in American Politics*, Chicago, Illinois: Chicago University Press.

Burns, A. and Goglio, A. (2004) 'Public Expenditure Management in France', *OECD Economics Working Papers*, No. 404, Paris, OECD.

Cole, A. (2000) 'The Service Public under Stress' in Elgie, R. (ed.) *The Changing French Political System*, London: Frank Cass, pp. 166–84.

Cole, A. (2012) 'The French State and its Territorial Challenges', *Public Administration*, *90*, 2: 335–50.

Cole, A. and Hanley, D. (2006) 'French Politics in the Twenty First Century' in Cole, A. and Raymond, G. (eds) *Redefining the French Republic*, Manchester: Manchester University Press, pp, 25–43.

Cole, A. and John, P. (2001) *Local Governance in England and France*, London: Routledge.

Drake, H. (2011) 'France', *European Journal of Political Research*, *50*: 970–9.

Elgie, R. and Griggs, S. (2000) *French Politics: Debates and Controversies*, London: Routledge.

Griggs, R. (2000) 'Restructuring Health Policy Networks: A French Policy Style' in Elgie, R. (ed.) *The Changing French Political System*, London: Frank Cass, pp. 155–204.

Hayward, J. E. S (1964) 'Presidentialism and French Politics', *Parliamentary Affairs*, *18*, 1: 23–39.

Hayward, J. E. S (1983) *Governing France: The One and Indivisible Republic*, 2nd edn, London: Weidenfeld and Nicolson.

Maclean, M. (2002) *Economic Management and French Business*, Basingstoke: Palgrave.

Meynaud, J. (1968) *Technocracy*, London: Faber and Faber.

Miller, S. (2011) 'France: Steering Out of Crisis?' in Della Poste, P. and Taloni, L. S. (eds) *Europe and the Financial Crisis*, Basingstoke: Palgrave, pp. 183–97.

Owen, B. (2000) 'France', in J. A. Chandler (ed.) *Comparative Public Administration*, 1st edn, London: Routledge, pp. 50–74.

Ridley, F. (1996) 'The New Public Management in Europe: Comparative Perspectives', *Public Policy and Administration'*, *11*: 16–29.

Ridley, F. and Blondel, J. (1964) *Public Administration in France*, London: Routledge and Kegan Paul.

Schmidt, V. (1990) *Democratizing France: The Political and Administrative History of Decentralization*, Cambridge: Cambridge University Press.

Stevens, A. (2003) *Government and Politics of France*, 3rd edn, Basingstoke: Palgrave.

Wright, V. (2000) 'The Fifth Republic, From the Droit de l'Etat to the Etat de droit' in Elgie, R. (ed.) *The Changing French Political System*, London: Frank Cass, pp. 96–119.

# 5 Greece

*Howard Elcock*

## Political culture

Ancient Athens was the birthplace of western liberal democracy. Since her heyday then, Greece has been repeatedly conquered and occupied, first by Alexander the Great, then the Romans, followed in turn by the Franks, various marauding Crusader bands, including the Grand Catalan Company, and finally the Ottoman Turks after the fall of Constantinople in 1453. She remained under Ottoman rule until her War of Independence was won in 1827 with the European Great Powers' help. A parliamentary democracy was established by her first prime minister, Ioannis Kapodistrias, before he was assassinated in 1831. At this time an administrative system based on the Napoleonic model adopted throughout continental Europe, with a meritocratic civil service as its central feature (*la carrière ouvert aux talens*) was introduced but 'the formal structures introduced then experienced an uneven and fortuitous development having to adjust to a different socio-political and cultural environment and they never really achieved the efficiency and prestige of the French prototype' (Spanou 2008: 152). Southern European cultures have a different approach to work to their northern neighbours – a difference dictated in part by their hot climates.

From the beginning, 'the whole system had a markedly centralist character with a minimal decentralisation in favour of the organs of regional administration and very few decision-making competences for the organs of local government' (Spiliatopoulos 2001). Furthermore, 'the Greek Civil Service bore the costs of clientelistic networks, mainly around powerful local notables' (Spanou 2008: 162). Its development over the next century was disrupted by further dictatorships, instability and occupations including the more autocratic periods of the long reign of King Otho in the nineteenth century, the Metaxa dictatorship in the 1930s, the Nazi occupation and the subsequent civil war in the 1940s and most recently the colonels' CIA inspired coup in 1967. This military regime ruled tyrannically and often brutally until it lost a war with Turkey in Cyprus and was consequently overthrown in 1974. One lasting consequence of this regime is that both the police and the military are held in low esteem by the general citizenry. There is a strong tradition, as in France, of *incivisme*: 'bureaucratic inefficiency and red tape discredit state action' (Spanou 2008: 152). Political apathy and alienation have increased in recent years as the parties' policies have converged. Another legacy of the military regime is hostility to the United States because of the Greek people's awareness of the part the CIA played in bringing about the 1967 coup. More generally, a consequence of Greece's turbulent history is its still relatively weak civil society, although both the extended family and the Orthodox Church still have considerable influence over Greek morals and customs. The latter has a powerful influence on legislation, which has resulted in the banning of cremation and strict Sunday trading hours.

Only after the colonels' regime fell was the Third Hellenic Republic, the present democratic regime, established under the presidency of a veteran conservative politician and former prime minister, Constantinos Karamanlis. Since then Greece has been a parliamentary democracy whose politics were dominated until recently by two main party federations, PASOK (the Pan-Hellenic Socialist Party) on the left and Nea Demokratia (ND) on the centre right. A number of smaller parties are represented in the *Vouli* (parliament), including the Greek Communist Party, and sometimes they emerge as coalition government-makers when neither main bloc gains an overall majority. The party system has been a powerful influence on the administrative system because there is a long-standing tradition of appointments being made on a partisan basis by successive governments. The economic crisis triggered by the bank collapse of 2007–08 has severely disrupted this system, however. The PASOK majority government elected in 2009 was forced to resign in April 2012 because it could not enforce the severe terms imposed by the European Union (EU), the International Monetary Fund (IMF) and the European Central Bank (ECB), the 'Troika', in return for two successive 'bailouts' of Greece's bankrupt economy. Acceptance and implementation of the terms has been fiercely resisted by the trades unions in a series of general strikes. The first election resulted in an indecisive result and no party was able to form a government. A second election was therefore called in June, as a result of which PASOK, ND and the smaller Democratic Left Party (DIMAR) formed a coalition government under the ND leader, Antonin Samaras. However, the most important result of these elections was the rapid increase in the number of seats won by the new left-wing party, Syriza, led by 38-year-old Alexis Tzipas, which is opposed to accepting the bailout terms and is now the major opposition party. The other gainer is the far right party New Dawn, which is demanding a harsh line on immigration, largely from south-east Europe.

Modern Greece, in geographic terms, was mostly established by Eleftherios Venizelos, prime minister before and after the First World War, who presented the case for Greece's recognition and territorial boundaries at the Paris Peace Conference in 1919 in the face of conflicting and competing Italian, Turkish, Bulgarian and other territorial claims. He was determined that Greece should be accepted by the Great Powers as a modern western democratic state. Margaret Macmillan sums up his work at the Conference as follows:

Venizelos was Greece's greatest asset and in the long run, its greatest liability. Without him, Greece would never have won what it did at the conference table; without him it would not have tried to swallow so much of Asia Minor (2001: 358).

Lloyd George regarded Venizelos as 'the greatest statesman Greece has thrown up since the days of Pericles' (Macmillan 2001: 164). However, his achievements at Paris were to lead Greece into a major conflict with Turkey within two years of the signing of the Peace Treaty of Sèvres with Turkey in 1920. This treaty was soon overtaken by events. Greece was ultimately forced to cede a large area of Thrace to the Turkish Republic created by Kemal Ataturk in 1920. The inhabitants of many Greek communities that had lived in Turkey for centuries were in consequence forced to move to their Greek homeland in a population exchange with Muslim Turks living in the remaining Greek part of Thrace. A lasting reminder of this crisis is the district of Athens named Nea Smyrna because a large number of refugees from that city settled there after being driven out of their homes in Turkish Izmir (for a fictional account of these events, see Louis de Bernière's novel, *Birds Without Wings*). Greece has no significant ethnic minorities concentrated in any area, hence she does not have stateless nations within her borders making demands for autonomy or independence like those in other European nation states, including the United Kingdom. The ethnic minorities that live in Greece are more or less evenly spread across the country, hence it is ethnically homogeneous, except for a small Muslim minority in Thrace who were not moved to Turkey in the 1920s. This small group suffered discrimination for many years but is now protected by the constitution and the European Convention on Human Rights. The social stresses imposed by the financial crisis that has hit Greece in recent years is stimulating hostility towards immigrants, expressed by the growing strength of the New Dawn Party in parliament.

The result of this turbulent history has been the development of a unitary and highly centralised state, with a relatively stable constitution since the end of the military dictatorship in 1974, although it is amended from time to time. The present constitution was drawn up in 1975 but underwent amendments in 1986, 2001 and 2008. The central government has long tried to control Greece's local authorities and in particular their clientelistic relations with local interests. The major political parties play a strong role in the government and governance of the country both nationally and locally. They maintain clientelist and corporatist relations with major interest groups. The central government has long attempted to maintain firm control over the country's local authorities, which are often also dominated by clientelist and sometimes corrupt relations with local interests. A spoils system is thus an established part of the governmental system nationally and locally (Chondroleou *et al.* 2004).

Greece first applied for an Association Agreement with the European Community (EC) in 1959 but the negotiations were suspended when the colonels' regime seized power in April 1967. Since the existence of a multi-party democracy is a fundamental requirement for EC/EU membership, no negotiations could take place between then until the collapse of the military regime in 1974. Greece resumed talks with the European Union (EU) when democracy was restored and finally became a full member of the EC/EU in 1980. However, her relations with her European partners have often been uneasy. For 10 years after her accession Greece was 'an awkward partner' but more recently there has been 'a smooth but clear shift . . . from a defensive, Greek-centred and financial perception to a more open and politically pro-European one' (Dimitrakopoulos and Passas 2004: 3–4). However, Greek application of EU laws and policies is still hindered by her lack of strategic leadership capacity, a 'highly ineffective, centralized and politicized' public administration and a weak civil society unable to challenge 'state corporatism' (Dimitrakopoulos and Passas 2004). Greece is still seriously in default of her EU obligations, for example, in her laggardly development of policies to deal with environmental pollution and degradation (Giannakourou 2004), which has resulted in the Greek government being repeatedly fined by the European Commission. Antony Makridimitris (2001: 19) argues that Greece is now securely a member of the European democratic community: the rule of law, representative democracy, the market economy and public services constitute fundamental elements of the social and political reality of Greece, as in the rest of the countries of Europe that make up the European Union. However, the application of stern bailout terms by the EU, the IMF and the ECB is generating increasing hostility, especially towards Germany, whose chancellor, Angela Merkel has taken a tough line on imposing spending cuts, redundancies and higher taxes on the Greeks.

## The constitutional framework

Under the constitution adopted in 1975, Greece is a parliamentary democracy with a unicameral legislature, the 300 member *Vouli*. The constitution can only be amended by two votes in the *Vouli*, held each side of a general election. At least one of these votes must be by a three-fifths majority. The electoral system is defined by the *Vouli*. It uses a party list system with multi-member constituencies: 250 of the 300 MPs are elected in 48 constituencies electing on average five members to the *Vouli* but the actual numbers elected per con-stituency vary widely according to the area's population. Thus the largest constituencies elect more members, for instance Athens B elects 42 members and Attica 12. The remaining 50 seats are allocated to the party or coalition of parties achieving an absolute majority in the *Vouli*, thus providing an enhanced majority for the ruling party and guaranteeing the stability of governments. Any party must gain 3 per cent of the votes cast to gain seats in the *Vouli*. The *Vouli* elects the President of the Republic by a two-thirds majority for a five-year term. Although this is a largely ceremonial office the need for an enhanced majority forces the parties to agree a candidate, an agreement not always easily achieved. It has produced major cross-party conflicts and the threat of deadlock on some occasions.

The prime minister is the leader and the government is formed by the largest party in the *Vouli*, with or without the support of minor parties. The leadership of the two main parties and hence the holding of the post of prime minister is extraordinarily dynastic. At least three generations of the Karamanlis family have led *Nea Demokratia*, most recently the last prime minister, Kostas Karamanlis, while four generations of the Papandreou family have led PASOK and its predecessor parties of the left and served as socialist prime ministers, leading to the previous prime minister, George Papandreou – the third George to lead the Socialist party.

The government is responsible to the *Vouli* and can be unseated by the passage of a 'No confidence' resolution. In recent times control of the government has oscillated fairly frequently between PASOK and *Nea Demokratia*, if necessary with smaller parties giving support to one or other major party. Until 2012 the two major parties got over 80 per cent of the votes cast. The Communist Party gets about 6 per cent and the smaller left party federation, Synaspismos, gets about 3 per cent. The contest between the major parties for office and control over policy is vigorous. Caliope Spanou (2008: 153) states that the 'parties tend to overstress disagreement and down-play converging approaches and objectives. This is particularly important for administrative reform policies, which were heavily affected by alternation in government'. Policies are changed frequently, which 'undermines their legitimation and render them vulnerable to opportunistic forms of pressure and circumvention on the part of vested interests' (Spanou 2001: 163). Weak policy-making and planning are also the result of frequent changes of personnel, especially party nominees. Hence, the administration is 'fragmented and compartmentalized; staff structures and functions and co-ordination appear undervalued' (Spanou 2001: 166). Such administrative weakness hinders the implementation of EU directives.

The government is dependent on retaining the confidence of parliament but it is regarded as a strong executive. 'The Greek political system manifests the signs of the "strong state", chiefly through the reinforcement of the executive power as a whole and particularly of the most representative and politically answerable part of it' (Makridimitris 2001: 21). The prime minister appoints all other ministers and chairs the Council of Ministers (the Cabinet), the supreme collegiate government organ, which consists of all senior ministers, currently 19, and other invited attendees. Minsters are bound by collective responsibility to support government decisions. The prime minister is '*primus solus* and not *primus inter pares*' (Makridimitris 2001: 28) in contrast to the formal position of his British counterpart. He 'exercises a sum of powers and competences the conjunction of which not only sets him apart from other ministers but renders manifest the superiority of his legal and political position over that of the other members of the Government' (Makridimitris 2001: 30). The extent of the prime minister's powers depends whether his party has an overall parliamentary majority or is dependent on the support of coalition partners. However, until 2012 the two major parties were strong enough to govern singly.

## The civil service

The Greek Civil Service can best be described as being the product of a tension between western, particularly Napoleonic, administrative norms of meritocratic recruitment and impartiality, with the long-standing tradition of clientelism that dominates both the Greek political parties and public administration. This tension is reflected in the changing balance between career civil servants recruited on meritocratic grounds and required to observe political neutrality and temporary or contract appointees who are avowedly partisan and maintain clientelist relations with commercial firms and other organised interests, including the powerful trades union movement, with which successive governments are thus compelled to maintain corporatist relations. A further problem is that the civil service is unduly large, a problem exacerbated in the early 1980s, when 'the policies of nationalisation of over-indebted, ailing enterprises . . . mostly as a job-saving effort' (Spanou 2008: 156) resulted in an undue expansion of the bureaucracy. At the same time Greece was establishing its welfare state, which further boosted civil service numbers.

Modern administrative virtues reflect Max Weber's account of bureaucracy. They include meritocratic recruitment, transparency, political neutrality together with effectiveness and efficiency. These values are reflected in the Civil Service Code enacted in 1999, which ensures 'the establishment of consolidated and uniform rules which govern the engagement and in-service status of civil administrative servants in accordance with the principles of meritocracy and of social solidarity and the ensuring of their optimum performance in their work' (Chryssenthakis 2001: 82). Civil servants are selected by an independent agency, the Supreme Staff Selection Council. They are required to be impartial and are prohibited from undertaking political activities except at the local level, where they can serve as a mayor or local council member. Their tenure is assured as long as their posts exist and apart from redundancy, the terms on which they can be dismissed are limited. The retirement age is 65 but civil servants can retire after 30 years' service, hence many of them are able to retire in their mid to late fifties. Demands for large-scale redundancies, extending the working week and raising the pension age imposed by the 'Troika' are being fiercely resisted by the trades unions, who are calling a series of protest strikes that command substantial support from public sector workers.

The departments tend to operate largely as separate fiefdoms and co-ordination among them is poor. There is also no very effective mechanism for policy planning. For example, in agricultural policy, 'the Ministry shapes policy virtually on its own' (Spanou 2001: 167), especially as relations with farmers' organisations are close and clientelistic. More generally,

Decisions tend to be spasmodic and co-ordination faulty. In the Greek context compartmentalisation is reinforced by the clientelistic and corporatist tendencies of the political personnel and the simultaneous undervaluing of the planning and co-ordination functions.

(Spanou 2001:166)

Furthermore, 'organised social groups succeed in influencing the course of policies by means of a defensive behaviour and parallel ties with the government party of the day' (Spanou 2001:169). As a result, public policies tend to be reactive rather than proactive. However, the increasing importance of EU policies and laws may in the longer term produce some improvement in the planning, co-ordination and consistency of government policies.

The constitution permits the employment of non-tenured advisers for specific posts, who are able to be explicitly partisan. These non-tenured appointments include the General Secretaries of the Departments. Such advisers are people who 'enjoy the Minister's political and personal trust' (Spanou 2008: 163). Such appointees, as well as ministers, 'occupy themselves with ensuring their own self-protection at a personal and/or party level and seem incapable of playing the guiding role in the application of an integrated policy' (Spanou 2001: 166). Such political appointees commonly aspire to achieve tenured civil service status. The reform of this system is 'the most recalcitrant reform area in Greece' (Spanou 2008: 162). Control and evaluation are both weak, 'their absence encourages diffusion and confusion of responsibility', and also 'introversion militates against transparency' (Spanou 2008: 162). This is an accusation that could at least until recently have equally well have been applied to the British Senior Civil Service, sometimes with equally undesirable results (Dunleavy 1995). The governmental machinery is heavily politicised by the making of temporary appointments of party supporters, often on a patronage basis, which ensures the domination of policy-making by the party in office. Thus Calliope Spanou (2001: 170) refers to 'the hegemonic position of political parties'. A related problem is the awarding of government contracts. 'Thousands of contracts are awarded through non-transparent procedures, enhancing the misallocation of human resources' (Spanou 2008: 165). The Troika has demanded the introduction of performance appraisal for civil servants, a demand that the coalition government elected in 2012 is moving reluctantly to accept.

## Departments and agencies

There are 19 government departments each headed by a minister who is a member of the Council of Ministers. These include, as one might expect, the Ministry of Finance and the Ministry of Foreign Affairs. Other ministries are concerned with specific sectors, such as the Ministry of Agriculture, others with major public services, such as the Ministries of Health and Welfare and that of Labour and Social Security. Another important Ministry, because of Greece's huge archaeological legacy, is the Ministry of Culture. Then there are two territorial Ministries, one concerned with Macedonia and Thrace, the other with the Aegean islands, these being the problematical or border regions. This large range of ministries is 'both indicative of the wide range of public policy, which extends into almost all areas of social action and of the importance of state intervention in the social sphere. It also reflects the corresponding need for control of public bureaucracy by an equally complex and extensive political structure' (Makridimitris 2001: 39).

There are seven Independent Administrative Agencies (IAAs), which are regarded as the equivalent of British quasi-government agencies, although this comparison is not exact. They include Capital Market Committees, a Competition Commission, the National Radio and Television Council, the Postal and Telecommunications Commission and the Citizens' Advocate – the Ombudsman. Their members are mostly selected by the prime minister or the Council of Ministers but the Competition Commission's members must be nominated by agencies independent of the government. Nominees can be scrutinised by parliamentary committees before they are appointed. Some of these IAAs are subject to ministerial oversight but others, notably the Citizens' Advocate, are not. The Citizens' Advocate is also guaranteed immunity from prosecution for acts 'carried out in the performance of their duties' (Koulouris 2001: 101). All these agencies are subject to the judicial review of their actions. They are all guaranteed a greater or lesser degree of independence. One of their functions is to ensure public confidence because of citizens' chronic distrust of the state. The IAAs are also expected to ensure the protection of citizens' rights, 'the effective protection of which is not consistent with the bureaucracy, lack of transparency, partiality, inflexibility and delay in taking action which have characterized the State's classic intervention mechanisms' (Koulouris 2001: 144).

As in other developed democracies, the public–private sector divide has become blurred by the creation of national and local agencies of various kinds: 'the concept of the public sector occurs in the law in a scattered and fragmentary manner', although EU laws 'inhibit to a significant degree . . . state expansionism' (Fortsakis 2001: 140–2). Privatisation has been attempted in recent years but progress has been generally slow because of resistance by trades unions and other interested parties. The *Nea Demokratia* government elected in 2004 made a particularly determined effort to carry through privatisation measures but the attempt to privatise the bankrupt national airline, Olympic Airways, was a failure. Significantly, the Council of State has ruled that private companies providing public services are still subject to public sector laws, including restrictions on the right to strike in essential services. An extensive privatisation programme has been demanded by the Troika but progress is still small, although the national telephone company, OTE, has been privatised. Railway privatisation has yet to be achieved.

# Local and regional government

## *Local government*

A local government system was established in 1833 after independence had been achieved. The areas were based on traditional communities and the former local administration of the Ottoman regime. It was reformed in 1912. From the beginning, local authorities were given executive mayors as well as elected councils. Many of the primary local government units were very small and were of two types, the Demos and the Koinotita. Most were *Demoi* but smaller, rural areas were *Koinotitoi*, with somewhat fewer powers. Above them was a secondary level of local government; the *Nomoi* (prefectures) were originally headed by civil servants who were 'individuals enjoying the confidence of the Government of the day' (Sioutis 2001: 45), exercising competences delegated by ministers. They later acquired elected councils and leaders.

Councils and mayors are elected using a party list system. An enhanced majority of three-fifths of council members is awarded to the winning party but that winning party must gain an absolute majority of the vote and to achieve this, a run-off election may have to be held if the initial poll does not produce such a majority. The first person named on the winning party list becomes the mayor for a four-year term. The effect of this electoral system,

> taken in conjunction with that of the mayor . . . does not need the declared confidence of the majority of the municipal council [which] gives rise to the conditions for a 'monocracy' of the mayor in the municipality, particularly in cases where he or she has a strong personality.
>
> (Hlepas 2001: 67)

The issue of the power of local leaders, the *toparxes*, addressed by successive governments since that of Kapodistrias, remains a problem because many mayors engage in clientelism and other forms of corruption.

Local authorities are subject to control by the national government and the Courts, hence 'local government . . . is regarded as something less than the State' (Sioutis 2001: 55). They have a power of general competence but specific powers are allocated to them by the central government and local authorities are subject to central government supervision. Central–local government relations are characterised by mutual distrust: it is a top-down process that 'ignores or undervalues the contribution of inferior administrative levels' (Spanou 2001:159). The local councils' competences include 'the promotion of the social and economic interests and of the cultural and intellectual interests of the residents' (Hlepas 2001: 73) and are quite wide-ranging, including education, culture, town planning, water, electricity supply and social welfare. However, the problem of unfunded mandates has reared its ugly head for Greek local governments. 'During the past 20 years, numerous responsibilities have been transferred to municipal government, though often without adequate financial and organisational resources' (Spanou 2008: 159). The *Nomoi* had a general competence to secure 'the economic, social and cultural development of their region' (Hlepas 2001: 76), while the peripheries (regional councils – see next section) created in 1993 were given strategic planning responsibilities.

Local authorities were also granted the power to establish autonomous agencies, notably Local Development Companies (LDC), but many of these have run into trouble because they employed too many local people, with the result that they have got more or less heavily into debt. The municipality of Megara, for example, created a multi-purpose LDC to speed up regeneration and development in the municipality. 'It is a private sector body but taxed and governed by the rules of free enterprise and works within the LA framework . . . We are an open door to the private world' (Chondroleou *et al.* 2005). The LDC also 'operates as a mediator between local society (individuals and private organisations) and the European and national authorities with excellent results, the chief one being the decline of suspicion' (Chondroleou *et al.* 2005). The Megara LDC has concrete achievements to its credit, including two motorway service stations that sell local products and advertise the facilities available in the area. However, other LDCs have been less successful, especially in failing to avoid corruption and over-staffing. In consequence, the power of local councils to create them has now been restricted by the central government (Oikonomopoulos, n.d. see also Chondroleou *et al.* 2005).

Local authorities' resources are drawn from a number of local sources of income, including local charges and taxes plus a share of the state budget that is determined by the amount of motor and property taxes and Value Added Tax collected by each council. Local authorities are required by law to prepare annual budgets and balance sheets for approval by higher level authorities and the central government. Their activities are subject to scrutiny by higher level authorities and the judges of cassation, up to the highest administrative court, the Council of State.

The Greeks have now caught the British addiction to local government reorganisation. The former pattern of some 6,000 *Demoi* and *Koinotitoi*, was radically reorganised in 1997 by the Kapodistrias Reform, which reduced the number of primary local governments from 5,825 to 1,033 units. This reform was justified by the increasing urbanisation that was resulting in small communities literally dying out as the young people left them for the towns and cities. There were 54 secondary local government units, the *Nomoi* (prefectures), with their own elected councils and presidents. Their duties mainly concerned strategic planning and regional development. As in England one reorganisation has led to another and in 2010, under the Kallikratis Programme, the number of primary local government units was further reduced to 369, the *Nomoi* were abolished and the thirteen *Peripheries* were granted elected assemblies to replace the previous *Nomoi* councils. The *Nomoi* had to be abolished if the *Peripheries* were to be given elected assemblies because the constitution only provides for two layers of sub-national government. One difference from the English case, however, is that the Greek reform programmes have been incremental, carried out by merging existing local government units rather than creating radically different new units, as the English did in 1973, causing much discontent at the transgression of traditional local loyalties (Leach 1998; Elcock 1998).

## *Regionalisation*

Greece is a homogeneous state that does not have any linguistic or ethnic minorities concentrated in particular parts of the country, with the minor exception of a small Muslim community in Western Thrace. In recent times multiculturalism has developed because of increased immigration from other EU countries and from Eastern Europe after the collapse of communism in 1989. However, this immigration is more or less evenly spread across the country, so responses have been xenophobic (on the part of the Greeks) rather than giving rise to territorial demands from new immigrants. This xenophobia has increased because of the financial crisis that has hit the country. Hence there has been no pressure from regions or stateless nations for the creation of regional government structures. However, in recent times Greece has developed functional regional institutions (Parks and Elcock 2000), mainly in order to maximise her chances (as one of the poorest nations in the EU) of gaining grants from the European Regional Development Fund and its other Structural Funds.

The first such process of regionalisation was commenced in 1986, following the EU's creation of the Integrated Mediterranean Programmes (IMPs) as 'a tool aiming to strengthen poor regions against the competitive challenges of an expanding common market' (Andrikopoulou and Kaftalas 2004: 39). Hence, 'at the European level the introduction of the IMP signified a change of view on the importance of regional development and the recognition of the EC's responsibility for the balanced development of the entire European territory' (Andrikopoulou and Kaftalas 2004: 39). This increasing importance of EU regional policies led to the establishment in 1986 of six regional agencies established for the purpose of bidding for funds from the IMPs. In 1993 these were replaced by thirteen *Peripheries*, which would be better placed to be able to bid for grants from the Structural Funds, which after the 1989 reforms of the EC's regional policy had to be made on the basis of regional development plans (see Elcock 1997, 2008), hence Greece needed regional authorities capable of preparing regional strategies. Their role was upgraded in 1997 as they grew to manage 'regional development programmes and the corresponding EU funds' (Spanou 2008: 160). Thus the driving force towards regionalisation in Greece, as in other countries (see Elcock 2003, 2008), is the cash nexus – the need to access the EU's regional development funds.

Initially these regions were administrative units with no political representative assemblies, only indirectly elected councils appointed by local authorities and social partner organisations but in 2010 they gained elected assemblies under the Kallikratis reform of local and regional government. The process of regionalisation has been driven by Greece's need to attract and administer EU development funds, a purely functional motive that was not driven by any regionalist cultural or ethnic demands. In 2001 the state structure was described as 'a concentric local-district-regional structure . . . the Greek state is an individual unity, characterized by the integrity of Greek territory and does not have the nature of a federation' (Sioutis 2001: 54). It has now been simplified by the Kallikratis reform, which abolished the *Nomoi* councils and governments, gave the *Peripheries* elected institutions and reduced further the number of primary local government units.

## Finance and budgeting

The government prepares the annual budget, which must be approved by the *Vouli*. This budgetary process is a traditional one (Elcock, Jordan and Midwinter 1989) that focuses mainly on allocating funds to the competing departments. Modern managerial reforms have not been adopted to improve budgeting: 'the budget system has not been at the centre of modernisation reforms. It is input based and lacks both a programme structure and performance orientation' (Spanou 2008: 168). In addition, external audit by the Court of Accounts is confined to legalistic issues of fiscal rather than process or programme accountability (Elcock 1991: 110–12), thus 'output and performance oriented management is not yet in place' (Spanou 2008:168). The weak central co-ordinating capacity of the Greek government machine, together with the clientelistic and corporatist relations that prevail between its departments and the major interest groups in their sectors, ensure that budgeting is an incremental process driven by departmental bids, rather than developing any sort of budgetary strategy. Greece's current financial problems are the result in part of the creation of an excessive number of civil service posts, partly in order to absorb unemployed workers, partly as a result of setting up its welfare state and lastly as a consequence of corruption and nepotism. In this respect Greece's administrative system recalls that of the American cities that were dominated by 'machine' politics (see Banfield and Wilson 1963).

A significant and long-standing problem is the extent of tax avoidance and evasion by the richer sections of society, which significantly reduces the government's income and hence its ability to pay for the public services it provides. The PASOK government elected in 2009 promised to crack down on such avoidance and evasion. The need to do so has been increased by Greece's parlous financial position and the consequent EU and IMF bailout loan it received in 2010, which has imposed burdensome requirements for the country's future financial management but the wealthy will not easily be persuaded to pay their proper dues to the state. One consequence of the financial crisis and low government revenues is that Greece now has a Value Added Tax rate of 23 per cent, one of the highest in the EU.

## Public management

Attempts by successive Greek governments over the last two decades at public management reform have been stimulated, first, by the fashion for New Public Management (NPM) that has developed since the early 1980s and, second, by the need to come into line with the practices of the European Union, including accepting the *acquis communautaire*. A major aim has been to reduce clientelism and corruption but these attempts have had limited success because of the entrenched power of vested interests, including the trades unions. Kevin Featherstone (2006: 15) states that

> Structural reform is heavily circumscribed by opposition within the system of disjointed corporatism. Rent-seeking behaviour and mistrust are central attributes of policy-making. The power of the party over the policy process and much of civil society continues . . . The Constitution is reformed but the underlying philosophy of the power of the majority remains intact, with a resistance to the notion of power being exercised through 'checks and balances'.

Also, Greek perceptions of NPM 'seem to have been largely confined to improving citizens' attitudes towards the administration: the core of its (NPM) logic is an improvement in the relations between the state and the citizen' (Michaelopoulos 2001: 178) The citizen is seen as 'the final judge of the services with which he is provided', hence in sum, 'it could be said that New Public Management expresses a model of administration which is oriented towards the citizen' (Michaelopoulos 2001: 179–80). So limited a view of NPM would not be accepted in those countries like the United Kingdom, Australia and New Zealand where it has been most enthusiastically adopted over the last three decades and where it extends to privatisation, the contracting out of state functions, efficiency reviews and much else besides. The demands of the Troika are resulting in the reluctant adoption of performance appraisal for civil servants.

In recent years privatisation has been embarked on by successive governments but with limited success. The state airline, Olympic Airways, has been the subject of several attempts at privatisation, for example. By 2001 16 public enterprises had been wholly or partially privatised (Fortsakis 2001: 143), as part of a wider 'State shrinkage' that has occurred 'with the transfer of state competences or activities in every direction: to the European Communities, local government agencies and now to private persons' (Fortsakis 2001: 144). However, where essential services are privatised, they may be subject to restrictive regulations resulting from their continuing status as providers of public services, including restriction of their employees' right to strike (the Public Petroleum Organisation) and wider guarantees of 'the principle of continuous operation', which requires the uninterrupted provision of services such as water supply, energy and communications, where those public enterprises which provide goods of vital public importance regardless of the legal form with which they are invested, that is even if they are private, are always dependent upon and under the supervision of the State, from which they can never withdraw'

(Fortsakis 2001: 147)

These obligations have been enforced by the Council of State (the highest administrative court) and impose restrictions on the extent to which such privatised industries can behave commercially. This must restrict the extent to which the nostrums of NPM can be applied to them. Increasingly privatisation is also regulated by the laws of the EU. Generally, Greece has been 'a latecomer to NPM (if at all)' (Spanou 2008: 169). The *Nea Demokratia* government elected in 2004 made determined efforts to introduce NPM style reforms but its success was limited: 'administrative modernisation remains closer to strengthening a Weberian type administration and closing the gap between formal rules and structures and informal practices model . . . In other words, NPM methods were often inappropriate to the Greek case' (Spanou 2008: 169). Even where NPM reforms were legislated for, 'many were never actually put into operation' (Spanou 2008: 169). Managerially, therefore, Greek public administration remains backward. The strongest impetus to reform comes from external pressures, particularly the EU and in recent times from the IMF too but so far their impact has been limited.

## Accountability, secrecy, openness

The Greek government system is heavily legalistic. Government can be held to account by the *Vouli* and the courts, through civil and administrative law. Pavlos Eleftheriades (2005: 110) states that 'courts and independent agencies must have the means and the prestige to stand up to power of all kinds, if this is necessary to protect fundamental principles of good government and the long term interests of the body politic'. Like all EU member states Greece is bound by the requirements of the European Convention on Human Rights, which is enforced by the European Court of Human Rights and by the transparency legislation of the EU. Other bodies concerned with transparency and citizens' rights include the Hellenic Data Protection Agency, the Hellenic Authority for Information and Communication Security and Privacy and the National Broadcasting Council. 'Most of these concern the improved protection of citizens' rights or the regulation of politically sensitive areas' (Spanou 2008: 161).

As in many other countries, Greece has had to deal with increasing demands for transparency in its governments' policies and procedures, as well as reductions in administrative delays and securing increasing trust between the state and the citizenry. These demands have been assisted by the development and application of new information and communications technologies. A strategic plan to achieve these objectives was drawn up in 1977 and subsequently amended. However, 'The improvement of relations between the public services and citizens is an on-going issue . . . Reports . . . and empirical research confirm the unsatisfactory nature of these relations' (Michaelopoulos 2001: 184–5) but Greece is not alone in facing this problem. Reforms have included the imposition of time limits for public servants to respond to citizens' requests, now 60 days, the creation of a Centre for Administrative Information to promote openness and the creation of similar bodies at local levels together with provisions for the payment of compensation for administrative errors or misdeeds.

An interesting development was the establishment nationwide of local Citizens' Service Centres early in the 2000s that 'provide administrative information and process cases of citizens in co-operation with responsible services' (Spanou 2008: 166). These 'one-stop-shop' centres make extensive use of e-government, which is particularly valuable in a country whose administration is scattered not only over many mainland communities but also across its numerous island communities. Consumers' charters have also been introduced. However, securing transparency in the face of officialdom's reluctance remains in Greece, as elsewhere, a continuing struggle in which the reiteration and extension of regulations is insufficient on its own to bring about satisfactory outcomes: 'there is still a long way to go until service is citizen (i.e. client) centred' (Spanou 2008: 166). Overall, the Greek citizen remains an *administré* rather than a participant in government.

## Democracy and the administrative system

The judicial review of administration is available to enable citizens to challenge the legality of actions by government departments and the IAAs, as well as their compliance with the public interest, which is 'determined by legal norms that regulate their activity' (Spiliotopoulos 2001: 121). Administrative laws are enforced by specialised administrative courts up to the Council of State, a system that was modelled on the French system of administrative courts with the *Conseil d'État* at their head. There is also an Ombudsman, the Citizens' Advocate who provides an alternative form of redress for citizens aggrieved by state actions or inactions. The Citizens' Advocate is empowered to investigate both illegal acts and inaction by public servants and maladministration, thus possessing a relatively wide remit. However, the Office has no power to impose sanctions, in common with many other European ombudsmen.

The judges can also ensure the protection of individual citizens' rights as defined by the constitution and legislation. The specialised system of administrative courts and the Council of State enables citizens to carry out this control function. The courts can annul administrative acts or failures to act and award compensation. However, these courts, like all Greek courts are overloaded with cases, resulting in delays in hearing cases. Also the means of enforcing their decisions may be inadequate. The other major means of citizen redress is the Citizen's Advocate, the Ombudsman.

**Further development and future issues**

Relations with the EU are developing and with Greece's entry to the Euro single currency, the EU's influence over the Greek government has become greater; like all the other member states Greece has had to come to terms with the notion that national sovereignty is now relative, not absolute. This realisation has been reinforced by Greece's need to apply for loans from the EU and the International Monetary Fund in 2010 to prevent her having to default on her international financial obligations and leave the Eurozone. However, the austerity measures taken by the PASOK government in order to secure these loans resulted in extensive social unrest, including demonstrations, a series of general strikes and occasional violence, including the torching of a bank in Athens that resulted in three deaths among its employees. Demonstrations and violence are confined to the centre of Athens and to a lesser extent the second city, Thessaloniki, but the frequent strikes affect the whole country.

Agricultural reform is likely to follow the review of the Common Agricultural Policy currently being conducted in Brussels. Since Greece is still quite largely an agrarian society, this will have major implications for its farmers and hence large parts of its economy and society. EU influences are bound to encourage the continuing effort to reduce and overcome the traditions of clientelism and corruption. In recent years, both *Nea Demokratia* and PASOK have pledged to tackle inefficiency and corruption in their election programmes but so far neither has succeeded in doing so to any extent. After the election of *Nea Demokratia* to power in 2004, a political commentator remarked that

> in the matter of honest governance, Karamanlis says what he means. Why is it so difficult for some to accept that he also means what he says? The problem is that being honest is not enough. Abolishing nepotism and corruption is but a first step. The next one is abolishing the thousands of utterly superfluous posts that nepotism and corruption have created over the years.
>
> (Dragoumis 2004: 13)

The obstacles in the way of reform are vividly illustrated by civil servants' determined resistance to attempts to reform their generous pension scheme – a resistance carried out in common with their French colleagues.

PASOK's determination to reform the public sector was overwhelmed by the financial crisis and the need to negotiate the EU and IMF financial bailout. The future of Greece's government and public administration remains, therefore both turbulent and uncertain. The consequences of the bailout terms for the citizenry are severe. Unemployment has risen to around 25 per cent, pensions have been halved with the result that increasing numbers of old people are committing suicide because they cannot survive on their reduced pensions. The Pelopponnese Railway has been closed down to save on its subsidy, after millions of Euros had been spent on re-laying the track and improving its level crossings. The government announced that it does not have the money to print road fund duty discs for 2013. This pressure has led to increasing divisions in the coalition government: the PASOK leader, Evangelos Venizelos, has declared that 'the Greek people have made too many sacrifices and are too proud to be treated patronisingly'. In the small DIMAR party, dissention among its MPs is rife (*Kathimerini*, English edition, 21 September 2012).

The question in the immediate term, therefore, is how long the present coalition government can survive the increasing pressure imposed by the Memorandum (the bailout terms), especially on salaries, pensions and redundancies. In the longer term the result could be a disastrous increase in social unrest. General strikes have already resulted in violence on several occasions. Greece's future is uncertain.

# References

Andrikopoulou, E. and Kaftalas, G. (2004) 'Greek regional policy and the process of Europeanisation 1961–2000' in D. G. Dimitrakopoulos and A. G. Passas (eds), *Greece in the European Union*, London: Routledge, pp. 35–48.

Banfield, E. C. and Wilson J. Q. (1963) *City Politics*, Boston, Mass. USA: Harvard and MIT Press.

Chondroleou, G., Elcock, H., Liddle, J. and Oikonomopoulos, I. (2004) 'Reorganisation: panacea or delusion? Local government reform in England and Greece', paper read to the Political Studies Association Annual Conference, University of Lincoln, April.

Chondroleou, G., Elcock, H., Liddle, J. and Oikonomopoulos, I. (2005) 'A comparison of local management of regeneration in England and Greece', *International Journal of Public Sector Management*, 38: 114–27.

Chrysebthakis, C. (2001) 'The civil service' in A. Makridimitris and E. Spiliotopoulos (eds), *Public Administration in Greece*, Athens: A. N, Sakkaloulas Publishers, pp. 81–94.

Dimitriakopoulos, D. G. and Passas, A.G. (eds) (2004) *Greece in the European Union*, London: Routledge.

Dimitrakopouolos, D. G. and Passas, A. G. (2004) 'Conclusion: Europeanisation and the Greek policy style: national or sectoral?' in D. G. Dimitrakopoulos and A. G. Passass (eds), *Greece in the European Union*, London: Routledge, pp. 139–47.

Dragoumis, M. (2004) 'So far so good but there is a need for speed', *Athens News*, 8 October, p. 13.

Dunleavy, P. (1995) 'Policy disasters', *Public Policy & Administration*, 10 (2): 52–70.

Elcock, H. (1991) *Change and decay? Public Administration in the 1990s*, Harlow: Longman.

Elcock, H. (1997) 'The North-East as a European region: Or when is a region not a region?' in M. Keating and S. Loughlin (eds), *The Political Economy of Regionalism*, London: Frank Cass, pp. 432–55.

Elcock, H. (1998) 'Territorial issues in local government. Don't reorganize! Don't! Don't!! Don't!!!' in M. Keating and H. Elcock (eds), *Remaking the Union*, London: Frank Cass, pp. 176–94.

Elcock, H. (2003) 'Networks, centres and peripheries: Strategic planning in a European region', *Regional and Federal Studies*, 13 (3): 44–65.

Elcock, H. (2008) 'Regional futures and strategic planning', *Regional and Federal Studies*, 18 (1): 77–92.

Elcock, H., Jordan, A. G. and Midwinter, A. F. (1989) *Budgeting in Local Government: Managing the Margins*, Harlow: Longman.

Eleftheriades, P. (2005) 'Constitutional reform and the rule of law', *West European Politics*, 28 (2): 317–34.

Featherstone, K. (2006) 'Introduction' in K. Featherstone (ed.), *Politics and policy in Greece*, London: Routledge, pp.1–19.

Fortsakis, T. (2001) 'The public sector: Contexts, limits, privatisations' in E. Spiliotopoulos and A. Makridimitris (eds), *Public Administration in Greece*, Athens: A. N. Sakkoulas Publishers, pp. 135–56.

Giannakourou, G. (2004) 'The implementation of EU environmental policies in Greece: Europeanisation and mechanisms of change' in D. G. Dimitrakopoulis and A. G. Passas (eds), *Greece in the European Union*, London: Routledge, pp. 51–60.

Hlepas, N.-K. (2001) 'Local government' in E. Spiliotopoulos and A. Makridimitris (eds), *Public Administration in Greece*, Athens: A. N. Sakkoulas Publishers, pp. 61–80.

Koulouris, N. (2001) 'The Independent Administrative Authorities' in E. Spiliotopoulos and A. Makridimitris (eds), *Public Administration in Greece*, Athens: A. N. Sakkoulas Publishers, pp. 95–118.

Leach, S. (1998) 'The local government review: A policy process perspective' in S. Leach (ed.), *Local Government Re-organisation: The Review and its Aftermath*, London: Frank Cass, pp. 18–38.

Macmillan, M. (2001) *Peacemakers*, London: John Murray.

Makridimitris, A. (2001) 'Public administration in the political system. The government, the prime minister, the ministers' in E. Spiliotopoulos and A. Makridimitris (eds), *Public Administration in Greece*, Athens: A. N. Sakkoulas Publishers, pp. 19–44.

Michaelopoulos, N. (2001) 'Methods of management and organisation of state-citizen relations' in E. Spiliotopoulos and A. Makridimitris (eds), *Public Administration in Greece*, Athens: A. N. Sakkoulas Publishers, pp. 177–92.

Oikonomopoulos I.(n.d) *Notes on Local Development Companies*.

Parks, J. and Elcock, H. (2000) 'Why do regions demand autonomy?', *Regional and Federal Studies*, 10: 87–106.

Sioutis, G. (2001) 'Decentralisation' in E. Spiliotopoulos and A. Makridimitris (eds.), *Public Administration in Greece*, Athens: A. N. Sakkoulas Publishers, pp. 45–60.

Spanou, C. (2001) 'Public administration and public policy' in E. Spiliotopoulos and A. Makridimitris (eds) (2004), *Public Administration in Greece*, Athens: A. N. Sakkoulas Publishers, pp. 157–76.

Spanou, C. (2008) 'State reform in Greece: Responding to old and new challenges', *International Journal of Public Sector Management*, 21 (2): 150–73.

Spiliotopoulos, E. (2001) 'The judicial review of administration' in E. Spiliotopoulos and A. Makridimitris (eds), *Public Administration in Greece*, Athens: A. N. Sakkoulas Publishers, pp. 119–34.

Spiliotopoulos, E. and A. Makridimitris (eds) (2001) *Public Administration in Greece*, Athens: A. N. Sakkoulas Publishers.

# 6  Italy

*R. E. Spence*

In July 2011 Italians celebrated the hundred and fiftieth anniversary of the foundation of the unified Italian state. The anniversary should have been a cause for a great deal of national pride and rejoicing. Unfortunately, the anniversary coincided with one of Italy's many economic and political crises.

The financial crisis, which engulfed the world economy following the banking crash of 2008, laid bare the fragility of the Italian economy. One indicator of the size of the problem facing Italy is its debt-to-GDP ratio, which currently exceeds 120 per cent. Though very large when measured against the public debt of the other Eurozone members (with the exception of Greece with a ratio in excess of 150 per cent), the figure was not historically significant in Italy. It has managed to survive with a debt ratio over 100 per cent of its GDP ever since 1991 and despite the Maastricht Treaty with its stipulation that government debt should not exceed 60 per cent of GDP, Italy's debt has remained around the 120 per cent mark.

Italy was able to live with such a high public debt for so long because a good portion of the debt was owed to Italians themselves. Successive governments also managed to ensure just enough growth in GDP to prevent the debt getting any larger and to pay the interest rates on the money it already owed. In the wake of the global financial crisis markets began to look more closely at the economic fundamentals of the weaker members of the Eurozone, Portugal, Ireland, Greece, Spain and Italy. The financial press, with their love of acronyms, gave these economies the unflattering name of the PIGS, often substituting Ireland for Italy and vice versa to maintain the acronym's precision. All these countries, at one time or another during the three-year period 2009 to 2012 had to offer 10-year government bonds at interests rates at or above 7 per cent, a figure that economists consider to be unsustainable. The yield on German bonds in the same period was 1.9 per cent.

Many reasons have been proffered as to why Italy's economic performance has been so poor in recent years. There is no doubt that the Italian economy has been slow in responding to the challenges thrown down by the emerging economies. Many of the industrial districts, which were believed to be the engine of Italian capitalism, have seen their lifeblood drain away to the so-called BRIC economies of Brazil, Russia, India and China. Italy, perhaps more than the other leading economies of the EU, has appeared singularly unprepared to cope with the competitive pressures resulting from globalization.

High on any list of contributory factors to the Italian crisis must be the problem of governance. The instability of Italian governments is usually the starting point for any analysis of the failure of the Italian political system to provide sound governance. For most of the post-war period the life expectancy of governments could be measured in months rather than years. The second government of Enrico Berlusconi, which lasted nearly four years between 2001 and 2005 was, by a large margin, the longest serving government in the post-war period.

Twice in the last 20 years the political class has had to turn to non-elected experts in order to respond to economic and political crises. The first occasion was in April 1993 when a technocratic government under the leadership of Carlo Azeglio Ciampi, a former governor of the Bank of Italy, was formed in the wake of the *tangentopoli* corruption scandals. The technocratic government, or government of experts, was necessitated by the fact that much of the old political class was under investigation by magistrates conducting the so-called *mani puliti* or clean hands investigation. At one point during the investigations, more than a third of the parliamentarians were either under investigation or under arrest for corruption. To these could be added politicians at regional and local level and numerous business leaders.

The second occasion in which the political class failed in its duty to the electorate is of more recent origin and followed the collapse of the third Berlusconi-led government 2011. Silvio Berlusconi, the Italian media tycoon turned politician successfully exploited his command of the media to become the prime minister of Italy on three separate occasions: from 1994 to 1995, 2001 to 2005 and again from 2008 to 2011. Apart from presiding over the economic decline in his last two administrations, he was personally involved in a large number of financial and sexual scandals. His sole *raison d'etre* for entering politics appeared to be to promote his vast media and publishing empire and to protect himself from being jailed for corruption. The resignation of his government became a fait accompli in November 2011 when the international financial markets along with the leaders of the global and regional financial institutions lost confidence in the ability of his government to restore economic stability and to service its growing public debt. The government that replaced Berlusconi's in November 2011 again consisted of non-political technocrats and was headed by Mario Monti, a former finance minister, European commissioner and rector of Bocconi University in Milan. The rest of the government consisted of rather unknown figures drawn from finance and the universities.

The parliamentary elections held in February 2013 once again threw the Italian political system into a state of crisis. The Italian electorate demonstrated its dislike and distrust of mainstream politicians and the austerity programme imposed upon them by the global financial institutions by voting for a movement that did not exist before 2008. *Il Movimento Cinque Stelle* – M5S

(The Five Star Movement) was launched by the stand-up comedian Beppe Grillo who describes himself as a popular activist and political blogger. If *Forza Italia*, the movement that propelled Berlusconi to power in the early 1990s was the product of the television age, Grillo and the M5S are the product of the Internet age. The movement's website characterizes itself as a free association of citizens. It is not a political party and does not intend to be one in the future. It wishes to locate itself outside the traditional divide between right and left, leaving it free to embrace new ideas. Its insistence on being a movement rather than a political party in the traditional sense leaves it free from the influence of party organization and intervening associations. In short, it is a form of direct democracy through the web. Many supporters on the M5S like to compare their movement to the movements that brought about the Arab Spring, being as they were the product of the Internet and the Facebook and Twitter generation.

What the long-term effects on government stability in Italy will be it is too early to tell. The immediate effect is one of crisis and instability. The M5S holds the balance of power in both the Senate and the Assembly where it is the single largest party. At the time of writing, the leadership is refusing to enter into a coalition of any description. Unless this situation changes, Italy is once again facing a political crisis that could very quickly turn into an economic crisis if the financial markets take fright.

Though the success of the M5S was due to a widespread belief that the political system was incapable of generating the changes necessary for the modernization of the political and administrative system, governments of both right and left had introduced a large number of measures designed to address some of the worst failings of the political and administrative system in Italy. The disappearance of the old political parties 'liberated' the Italian electorate from their traditional loyalties and focused its attention on the performance of public institutions, which they judged to be too large, over-centralized, too costly, too bureaucratic, self-serving and trampling on the rights of the citizen.

The crisis gave rise to new political forces that have dominated the Italian parliament following the post-crisis election in 1994. After the election, of the 630 deputies elected, 452 were elected for the first time, as were 213 of the 315 senators. The new members of parliament were elected under changed political banners as new parties arose to fill the political vacuum left by the collapse of the old political parties. Some, like *Forza Italia*, were completely new movements. Others were the remnants of the old political parties fighting the election under new names. The *Lega Nord* (Northern League) formed in 1991 was the oldest political party to fight the 1994 election.

It may be stretching the idea somewhat but the political crisis, which engulfed Italy in the wake of the bribery scandals in the early 1990s, provided an example of Naomi Klein's (2007) 'shock doctrine'. While there might have been no tanks on the streets or midnight disappearances of political opponents, the implosion of the party system, which had dominated Italian politics for two generations, gave the new political leadership the ability to do what had proved so difficult to do in the past – to change things. In order to seek a solution to the perennial problem of governance in Italy, legislators began a period of reform unparalleled elsewhere in the developed world. The measures taken were destined to have a profound impact upon the architecture of the state and the structure and culture of the entire administrative system.

The reforms, whether affecting the nature of the political or administrative system, were inspired by the methods and techniques, which can be subsumed under the umbrella of the New Public Management (NPM) theories and approaches. The reforms to the political system, like those designed to change the voting system or to directly elect a chief executive in the sub-national organs of government, may not, at first sight, appear relevant in a discussion of NPM. Both, however, were key steps in the attempt to generate greater accountability on the part of decision-makers to their electorates.

NPM reforms were late in arriving in Italy due to a combination of ideological resistance and a lack of political will and/or the authority to introduce them. The whole process, of injecting private sector values and instruments into the public services, was seen by Italian policy-makers and administrators, not just on the left, as a conspiracy, engineered by international organizations like the OECD and the IMF, to undermine the welfare state. The New Public Sector Paradigm was denounced as an Anglo-Saxon approach to public management that was alien to the law-centred continental European approach to government and public service (Klickert 1997). Whether we also include the EU as part of a perceived conspiracy, there is no doubt that in many respects, the need to conform to the treaty provisions of the EU, particularly with regard to Monetary Union, became a key resource of those wishing to transform the nature of Italian politics and society (Quaglia and Radaelli 2007).

## Political culture

Italy has long been viewed as a country rich in paradoxes and contradictions and a cause of puzzlement to foreign observers (Negri and Sciola 1996). The 'economic miracle' of the late 1960s produced the rapid increase in living standards that was considered not to have been matched by a similar miracle in the politico-administrative system. The dynamism of the economic system and the 'political lag' in the political system has given rise to a rich lexicon of terms to describe, what the Italian themselves refer to as, '*il caso italiano*' (Graubard 1974). The term literally means 'the Italian case', but its meaning is best encapsulated in the term 'Italian exceptionalism'. The term is intended to demonstrate how the Italian politico-administrative system differs from the more 'advanced' countries of the USA, Britain, France and Scandinavia. The ever present concept in much of the literature on the nature of Italian exceptionalism is that of backwardness. Manifestations of the backwardness of the Italian political system were perceived to be everywhere. The political system as a whole had been doomed to stagnation due to what Sartori (1966) and others have termed the system of polarized pluralism. Polarized pluralism describes a pluralist party system defined as one in which there were more than five parties represented in parliament. The parties are separated by a high degree of ideological polarization as represented by the existence of anti-system parties, the fascist MSI on the right and the communist PCI of the left. This polarization of the electorate led to the haemorrhaging away of votes from the centre to the extremes of both right and left producing what Sartori described as the dominance of centrifugal over centripetal forces.

Alongside the extremes of right and left were political cleavages based upon the conflict between lay and clerical traditions. The lay/clerical divide meant that it was difficult to hold the centre together when contentious issues like divorce, abortion and the demands for a modernization of the welfare system, in which the Church had played a leading role, became the focus of political debate. While the other advanced capitalist countries were said to be experiencing the 'end of ideology', Italian backwardness appeared to condemn the country to endure a political culture deeply divided on ideological and religious grounds.

This perceived backwardness of Italian political culture has become a common theme in much foreign literature on Italy. Joseph La Palombara, in a sympathetic study, *Democracy Italian Style*, comments that 'for forty years outsiders have thought about Italy, if at all, as a nation tottering on the brink of disaster'. La Palombara's book was an attempt to rescue the study of Italian democracy from the kind of opinions expressed by Tulio-Altan (1986) who saw contemporary Italy as an example of failed modernization, a country by-passed by modernization and which suffered from a socio-economic backwardness that encouraged endemic corruption, patronage politics, clientalism, organized crime and a lack of civic trust. Like many other observers of modern Italy, Tulio-Altan (1986) traced the roots of Italy's failed modernization to the failure of the leaders of the 'Risorgimento' to solve the problem created by the divide between the developing, industrial north and the backward, agrarian south.

Perhaps the most influential work in this genre was Banfield's (1958) study entitled *The Moral Basis of Backward Society*. Banfield's thesis has become the starting point for almost all discussions of the perceived backwardness of Italian political culture. Banfield coined the term 'amoral familism' as a short-hand for what he perceived to be the failure of the inhabitants of a southern Italian village and, by implication, the whole of the south, to participate in any form of collective action. It created an image of the typical southerner as one who looked after the short-term good of the family at the expense of any consideration of the common good. In other words, southerners were unable to develop the kind of social attitudes that were the essential building blocks for the creation of civil consciousness and modern democracy. Published in Italy in 1976, many Italians viewed the study as little more than latent racism and American ethnocentrism. Despite this, its central theme remained the dominant paradigm for understanding the failures of Italian democracy by most outside observers. The American political scientist Robert Putman (1993) in his book *Making Democracy Work*, sought to demonstrate a link between the varying performances of the regional governments between 1972, and 1990, and the concept of 'civic republicanism'. Putman identifies four attributes of civic republicanism that form the basis of stable democratic government. These are, civic engagement, political equality, solidarity, trust and tolerance, and social structures of co-operation. Civil engagement, relates to the extent to which citizens are interested in public affairs and are willing to participate in politics. The greater the level of interest and participation, the more stable will be the democratic process. Political equality relates to the extent to which citizens treat each other as equals or, to put the idea in slightly different terms, the extent to which citizens are able to relate to each other on a basis of reciprocity and co-operation rather than through relationships of hierarchy and authority. Solidarity, trust and tolerance denote the extent to which citizens respect one another, accept difference in lifestyles and trust each other. Finally, the presence of social structures of co-operation measures the extent to which citizens are willing to join clubs, organizations and political associations and, by so doing, learn the habits of trust and tolerance. Putman's conclusion was that the cultural heritage of many of the 20 regional governments had had a profound and lasting impact upon their performance. The northern and central regions of Italy performed better than their southern counterparts precisely because they had a much stronger heritage of civic republicanism than their southern counterparts.

Another prevailing theme in the study of Italian political culture has been an analysis of the causes and consequences of the kind of corruption that brought about the crisis of the early 1990s. According to figures provided by the Audit Court, corruption siphons €60 billion out of government finances every year. Figures provided by the IMF suggest that corruption in Italy is the equivalent of the GDP of Serbia, which means that if the costs of corruption were counted as if it were a state, it would rank about 76th in the world. Corruption is not the only problem faced by state finances. To continue with the country comparisons, the loss of tax revenue as a result of tax evasion and the hidden or black economy is estimated to cost the Italian exchequer about €260 billion a year. This is the equivalent to the GDP of the Ukraine.

The prevalence of corruption in Italy appears to provide confirmation of the assumptions of those seeking to demonstrate the absence of civic republicanism in Italy. Their view is that those in positions of power use the resources available to them to favour family and friends above any notion of civic republicanism. What came as a surprise to many, however, was the extent to which the *tangentopoli* corruption scandals engulfed the whole of the Italian state and business community and not just the south.

The question of corruption in Italy has been linked by a number of authors to the central concern of this chapter, the need to reform the structure and culture of public administration in Italy. Cassese (1983), Cavazza and Cazzola (1992) and della Porta (1992) sought to locate part of the explanation for corruption in Italian public affairs to a paradox at the heart of the administrative system itself. The paradox being that the administrative system with its rigorous detailed laws and procedures aimed at excluding the intervention of personal and clientelistic interests produced precisely the kinds of practices that the regulations were designed to exclude. Both authors provide a convincing argument to suggest that an over-regulated administrative system almost necessitates particularistic and corrupt practices if anything was ever to get done. Anyone coming into contact with the state administrative system, at whatever level, became involved in what appeared as a pointless paper chase. The citizen had to collect a large number of documents from offices spread throughout the town or city; these had to be stamped with the appropriate stamp and signed by the appropriate official, only then to be rejected for some minor irregularity. Gert Hofstede's (1991) cultural dimension of 'uncertainty avoidance' as much as any notion of amoral familism appears to capture the essence of such behaviour. The rigidity of the administrative system appeared above all to be born of a desire to avoid situations of uncertainty through extremely detailed rules and regulations that encourage a culture of conformity even when it is obvious to the officials themselves that the outcome of the procedures appeared unreasonable and dysfunctional.

## The constitutional framework

Had the founding fathers of the modern Italian state been able to return to join in the 2011 celebrations, the constitutional framework they would have found would not have been far removed from the one they established some 150 earlier. Nor would the ideas and proposals, which have dominated the debates concerning the architecture of the modern Italian state, be unfamiliar to the constitutional designers of the 1860s. The task faced by the early constitution builders was summed up in the famous words of Massimo D'Azeglio, 'Now we have made Italy we must make Italians.' The task of the Risorgimento was not just one of bringing together Italians who for hundreds of years had lived in separate political units under the tutelage of foreign powers. It was to create a citizenry wedded to the principles of democracy and this could only be done through a state apparatus that was based upon representative and responsible government and equality before the law. The question of how to render the government of the new state both representative and responsible was the major preoccupation of the constitution builders. In anticipation of a future unified state, Italian scholars had long debated whether a unitary or a federal governmental design would be more likely to create the kind of Italian citizen they desired. On the one side of the debate were those firmly committed to the belief that only some form of federal system capable of building upon the long-established traditions of self-government could provide the necessary cement to hold the new Italian state together. For these thinkers, only a state that builds upon and nurtures local institutions could successfully provide the foundations for stable government.

On the other side of the argument, the views that eventually prevailed, were from those who firmly believed that the only constitutional framework that would provide the necessary stability would be one firmly based around a central political authority with a parliament at its centre and a highly centralized system of public administration that enjoyed a monopoly in the provision of public services. A ready blueprint for the constitutional designers was to be found in the French administrative system, which had been imposed on much of Italy during the Napoleonic invasion. The administrative system that emerged in Italy was, in many respects, one of the most Napoleonic outside France. These constitutional arrangements appeared to serve Italy well providing a period of political stability and rapid economic growth until Italy's entry into the First World War. Despite emerging from the war as one of the victorious powers, the constitution did not survive the turmoil that came with the peace. Critics of the constitution who continued to adhere to principles of the federal constitutional design appeared to have their worst fears confirmed when the centralized political system proved to be a ready instrument of fascist control following Mussolini's rise to power in 1922. The centralized nature of the state was strengthened under fascism with the creation of new state bureaucracies to bring the economy and the institutions of civil society under direct fascist control.

## The structure of the modern state

The 1948 constitution was an attempt to remove the authoritarian aspects of the state apparatus created during the fascist period and to build the new republic based firmly on the principles that had guided the constitution builders some 80 years before. Their major concern was to create a system that contained enough checks and balances to hinder the easy takeover of power by a powerful minority, as had occurred in 1922. The constitutional designers created a bicameral assembly, the Senate and House of Representatives, which had identical powers; a constitutional court the task of which was to ensure that legislation was in conformity with the letter and spirit of the constitution; and a system of 20 autonomous regions, which, while falling well short of full federalism, provided the opportunity to create a significant degree of regional autonomy. The constitutional provision of abrogative referenda, that is, referenda the object of which is to modify or remove existing law, meant that even laws passed or approved by parliament could be challenged by popular vote in a referendum. Finally, constitutional guarantees of judicial autonomy were designed to provide checks on the behaviour of administrators and politicians.

## Central government agencies

In formal terms, central government in Italy is conducted through structures that are not dissimilar to those found in the other chapters of this book. The president of the republic is the formal head of state and acts as a guarantor of the constitution. He (there has never been a she) signs government acts into law, is head of the armed forces and has the power to declare war. His most high profile role in recent times has been the calling of elections and the choice of president of the Council of Ministers (the prime minister) after the electorate has made its choice.

The Council of Ministers (the cabinet), which constitutes the political heads of each of the departments of state, is presided over by the president of the council. In formal terms the ministers are individually responsible for his or her office and take collective responsibility for the actions of the council. In practice, for most of the post-war period, Italian governments were often coalitions of not very co-operative political partners to whom notions of collective cabinet responsibility were completely alien. Governing coalitions were essentially coalitions of convenience rather than coalitions with coherent policy agendas or ideologies. Before the corruption scandals of the early 1990s swept away the traditional political parties, the coalitions that governed Italy were dominated by the Christian Democratic Party, which formed coalitions with centre or right of centre parties up until the early 1960s, and then with the Socialist Party when the so-called opening to the left brought about a series of left of centre coalitions. It was not just the fragile coalition with other parties that generated the instability of Italian governments. The Christian Democratic Party itself was little more than an uneasy coalition of party factions or currents (*correnti*) led by larger-than-life political figures who dominated the Italian political scene for a whole generation. These senior party figures often remained outside the government, being content to leave the ministerial posts to lesser figures and to manipulate them like grand puppeteers. Whichever party faction was dominant in any period determined who controlled the government and the choice of party allies.

At the national level, government is currently conducted through 12 ministerial departments and six ministers without portfolio. In the past there were often 20 or more such departments, but these were steadily reduced as the reform process of the 1990s sought to regroup ministries under 'homogeneous missions'.

Alongside the formal ministries there are a number of 'para-state' organizations created to provide services of a particularly technical nature. In the past, large parts of the Italian economy were run by such para-state organizations. Until the privatization programme in the 1990s removed their *raison d'etre*, the economy was effectively run through the state participation system that involved entities such as the *Istituto per la Ricostruzione Statale*, the *Istituto Nazionale Idrocarburi* and the *Enti Finanziamento Industria Manifatturiera*. These formed part of the State Holding Enterprises that administered the majority of shares in Italy's leading companies following the banking crisis of the early 1930s. To these one can add major institutions like the *Ente Nazionale per l'Energia Electrica*, the railways, the post office, the central bank and a plethora of organizations managing the distribution of social welfare services.

The most important bodies among the current agencies are those responsible for administering the pensions system and the worker's compensation scheme. The pension scheme is managed by *Istituto Nazionale della Previdenza Sociale*, that has been in existence in one form or another since 1898 and, is the main social security organization, issuing pensions to 16.5 million people annually. The Institute also provides other services, such as unemployment benefits and many types of aid administered by the Ministry of Welfare, making the total number of constituents served around 35 million. The *Istituto Nazionale Assicurazione contro gli Infortuni sul Lavoro*, is the Italian Workers' Compensation Authority, and is responsible for protecting and insuring workers against injuries caused by work-related accidents and occupational diseases. Other significant agencies include, The National Roads Board (*Azienda Nazionale Autonoma delle Strade Statali*), The State Monopolies Board (*Amministraz-ione Autonoma dei Monopoli di Stato*) and the Italian Space Agency. In the past there were many more organizations (*enti pubblici*), which delivered health and social care and financial assistance and as such were key instruments for clientalism, patronage and corruption. Recent welfare reforms have seen their roles being taken over by the regions and communes.

## The civil service

The dominant themes in the literature concerning the Italian Civil Service in the post-war period focused on the nature of the service as being one that sought to pursue the general interest according to the law but with little regard to questions of efficiency and effectiveness. Its salient characteristics were considered to be: the highly legalistic nature of conditions of employment, the dominance of public administrators of southern extraction and the lack of mobility within the service and between the service and the outside world (Cassese 1983).

Employment in the civil service was, until the recent reforms, governed by administrative law in contrast to the civil law regulations that governed employment relations in the private sector. Employment disputes in the civil service would be resolved in administrative courts with the Consiglio di Stato at the apex of the system. Following the creation of the regional governments, the Regional Administrative Tribunals (*Tribunale Amministrative Regionale –* TAR) have played an increasingly important role in the process. The administrative court system itself has been blamed for the slow progress in introducing management reforms in the public sector. Given the fact that lawyers and officials working in the tribunals were themselves drawn from administrative ranks their judgments tended to favour the personnel and the status quo (Cassese 1983).

Recruitment to the public bureaucracy was a typical example of the impact of the administrative law tradition on employment conditions. Recruitment was surrounded by a large number of highly complex legal regulations stemming from Article 97 of the constitution. The article states that all appointments of public administrators must be made on the basis of competitive examinations (*concorsi*). The constitutional guarantees were inspired by the noblest of motives – to ensure the appointment of the most able candidates and to insulate the process from political interference. Reality, however, fell well short of the ideal. It has been estimated, for example, that between 1973 and 1990 some 350,000 employees out of a total of 600,000 were recruited without having taken any competitive examination whatsoever. Most of these would have been recruited on a temporary basis and then later made permanent through special measures (Cassese 1983). There were also many defects in the style and conduct of the examinations themselves. They were often extremely cumbersome, expensive and did not constitute a real test of the candidate's abilities. Once in post, the employee's career development was based on automatic mechanisms for advancement, which were focused largely on time served rather than achievement or merit. In order to reach the higher echelons of the service, the employee would have to serve anything from 15 to 20 years. Despite some movement in the direction of gender equality the executive post in the civil service were largely a male preserve. In the years leading up to the reforms of the early 1990s, female employment in the civil service amounted to about 50 per cent of the total. However, since career development was based upon time served, the number of females in top executive positions declined to about 2 per cent of the total. The typical director general was therefore over 60, male, of southern extraction and, in all likelihood, the son of a civil servant.

Part of the explanation for the contravention of the regulations has been the practice in both central and local governments of using the system of public employment as a kind of social shock absorber to resolve problems of the wider labour market. Once employed, public officials enjoyed a security of tenure through a complex system of legal guarantees. Italian public officials were also notoriously badly paid when compared to their near European neighbours. Much of the literature dealing with public employment in Italy has emphasized the trade-off that employees and unions have made between remuneration and job security. However, the resulting low pay should be set against the fact that pensions for state employees were the most generous in the developed world, both in terms of their relationship to the final salary and the length of time needed to qualify. Also, many public officials in the lower ranks of the bureaucracy were able to supplement their income in the 'black economy' as a result of short working hours and, often, uncontrolled absenteeism. It has been estimated as recently as 2002 that paid activities of public employees outside their regular contracted hours could add more than 10 per cent to their earnings (Ministry of Public Administration).

Italy, unlike Britain, France and Germany, has never successfully created a distinct, classical professional elite (Chapman 1959). The French, famously, have their *grands corps* that embraces all the senior civil service positions and to which access is gained through one of the *grand écoles*, such as the *École Nationale d'Administration*. The success of the French Civil Service has been its ability to dominate not just the state apparatus but the prevailing heights of the nationalized industries and the private business and commercial sector as well (Owen 2000; see also Chapter 4 in this volume, 'France').

In contrast, the Italian system has been described as a 'headless administration'. Italy's top civil servants remained separate and segregated not just from each other, but from the elected politicians and the wider community. While Italy did set up the *Scuola Superiore della Pubblica Amministrazione* (SSPA) in 1957 to recruit and train top civil servants its impact has been marginal compared to its near neighbours' experience. The SSPA's role has, in recent years, become more important as it plays a key role in the education and training of the new generation of managers through the introduction of the Fast Stream Programme. Entry onto the programme is very selective and success ensures immediate insertion into the executive levels of the service.

This preponderance of public officials drawn from the south of the country is often cited as a cause of many of the problems associated with the system of public administration. Even today, the south of Italy lags behind the north in terms of job opportunities. The vast bulk of wealth creation still takes place in the regions of the north and in the centre of the country. For much of the post-war period advancement for most southerners meant either migration to the industrial and commercial centres of the north, emigration abroad or employment in the public sector. The phenomenon of 'meridionalisation' of the public bureaucracy is demonstrated by the fact that in 1995, 73 per cent of state civil servants (1.2 million employees) had their origins in the centre and south of the country. This geographical bias becomes more extreme with increasing rank. In 1995 the centre and south produced 93 per cent of all the directors general.

Over the last 20 years or so a great deal of legislation has been enacted in an attempt to find a remedy for the worst features of the administrative system. The Italian bureaucratic tradition was, as we have already noted, based firmly on the principle that detailed control of inputs was more important than the evaluation of outputs. An ambitious series of reforms beginning in 1993 and continuing up to the present day have been introduced to bring about a kind of 'cultural revolution', by replacing legal formalism with the culture of performance, results, attention to the quality of services, advancement on merit and professionalism.

The process of reforming the administrative culture began to take shape after the passage of a series of measures in 1993 that sought to privatize employee relations in the civil service. The most significant step in the privatization process was the replacing of administrative law with civil law rights and procedures in the governance of employee relations within the public sector. In order to promote the creation of a more managerial culture, the legislation also sought to clarify the relationship between the policy-setting powers, politicians and the internal management function of senior managers. Too often in the past the roles became confused as politicians at every level of government exercised considerable interference in the internal management of departments. This was also the period in which the first steps were taken toward the creation of a French style *grand corps*. In future, top managers would be separate from the ministries or organization to which they were assigned and would be recruited through public competition and on renewable contracts of no more than seven years. It became possible at that time to appoint senior managers from outside the service on a merit basis. In the past, the few outside appointees had been political 'placemen' recruited according to the rules of a 'spoils system'.

In order to generate public confidence in the work of public officials, the 1990s also witnessed the creation of a vast number of public service charters in central and local government and in a wide variety of public organizations providing services directly to the public. By 1997 almost 7,000 government agencies had established public service charters in health, education, pensions and public utilities. The charters were accompanied by *codice di stile* for managers and *manuale di stile* for lower level employees to ensure that all documents were written in a language that was comprehensible to the ordinary citizen. This reform process took a quantum leap forward with the so-called Bassanini reforms of 1997–98. Named after the sponsoring minister, the legislation not only sought to further develop the process of 'privatizing' civil service employment relations but to transform the whole architecture of the political and administrative system and drive it in the direction of greater subsidiarity.

In terms of employment relations the Bassanini reforms built upon the work that was already in progress. What was radically new within the reforms was the attempt to redefine the mission of public institutions with the downsizing of central institutions, stripping them back to their core services. This process would be achieved through the launching of an ambitious process of institutional reform through the re-allocation of a wide range of powers and resources from the central state to the regions and municipalities, as will be discussed in more detail below. The reforms of the 1990s were impressive by any standards. An OECD report of 2001 stated that Italy had made impressive progress in just a few years in terms of the quality of regulation, bureaucratic simplification and administrative modernization (OECD 2001).

Given the ambitious nature of the Bassanini proposals it is perhaps not surprizing that the implementation process has been slow and, in certain instances, non-existent. The administrative culture that had developed under the system of administrative law proved extremely resilient. Much of the blame for the failure of many of the reforms to take root must be laid at the door of the central government. Despite the tinkering with the voting system to provide for more stable government, in the 20 year period of the reforms there have been no fewer than 11 different governments. Each government sought to place its own stamp on the reforms and, in so doing, slowed the process down by changing the focus of the reforms. The managerial controls in many governmental organizations were never implemented and so the expected benefits never materialized. The reforms did not change three areas of a malfunctioning public sector: 'high absenteeism, increasing expenditures and very low customer satisfaction and citizen trust' (OECD 2010).

In 2009 a further round of reforms was introduced to put the reform process back on track. These took the name of the sponsoring minister Renato Brunette. At the heart of the reforms was the introduction of the Charter of Duties of Public Administration (*Carta dei doveri della Pubblica Amministrazione*). The charter set out the role and responsibilities of public administrators in providing services to the ordinary citizen and the business community.

While large sections of the Italian press represented the new law as little more than a war against the *fannulloni* (shirkers), the real emphasis of the reform has been to address one of the major failings of Italian democracy – its inability to ensure that the state and its administrative organs is answerable to the ordinary citizen for what it does. In this sense the Brunette reforms seek to address the problem of open government by turning the administrative system into a giant goldfish bowl. Transparency and customer satisfaction form the central pillars of the reform, to which all the other provisions are designed to contribute. Under the so-called 'transparency operation' an enormous amount of information is made available to the public. Data that has to be made public includes information on proceedings, tenders, evaluations, absences, remuneration, companies in which the state has a share, assignments for consultants and external contractors. Information is available online concerning remunerated assignments to civil servants, salaries, curricula vitae, e-mail addresses and the contact details for managers and secretaries at municipal and provincial level. With all this information out in the open the policy-makers hope to make corruption in public office a thing of the past.

## The regional government

The 1948 Constitution divided Italy into 20 autonomous regional governments. Five were designated 'Special regions' and the remainder 'Ordinary regions'. The special regions were so designated to reflect their linguistic and cultural differences (Trentino-Alto Adige/Südtirol and Aosta Valley) or their geographical isolation (Sardinia and Siciliy). Their special status was conceded to these regions in order to lessen the very real demands that existed at the end of the war for secession from the rest of Italy. In the case of Trentino-Alto Adige/Südtirol the region does little more than co-ordinate the activities of the two autonomous provinces of Bolzano and Trento. There were many among the constitutional designers who firmly believed that the regional governments would transform the nature of the Italian political system. The regional governments were seen as a panacea for the ills that had afflicted the Italian state since the debate between centralists and autonomist had been settled in favour of the former in the 1860s. Defined as the most profound innovation introduced by the constitution with the potential to have a decisive importance for the history of the country, the regional governments were included in the constitution to be, in one way or another, a remedy to the over-centralized system of national decision-making, the inefficient and grossly overstaffed administration of the central government departments and to facilitate popular participation in the decision-making process. Nevertheless, over 20 years would elapse before the necessary secondary legislation was passed to make the ordinary regions a reality.

Despite the high hopes that accompanied the formation of the regional governments following the first regional elections in 1972, a large gap appeared between the intentions of the constitutional designers and the reality of regional governments. As we noted above, Putman and others have sought to explain the partial failure of the regional experiment as the consequence of the absence of 'civic republicanism' in certain regions. While this may partially explain the differences between some northern and central regions and those of the south, it does not explain why many became disillusioned with the whole regional experiment. The fact of the matter was that the 1948 Constitution did not provide a fully articulated blueprint for assigning functions to the different levels of government. This failure allowed short-term political consideration to over-ride the spirit if not the letter of the constitutional designers. The central government tended to view the regional governments as not much more than field offices of the national administration, executing orders and policies handed down from Rome. Despite legal provision being made in 1977 for the transfer of a large number of state functions to the regions in areas such as housing, health care, social welfare, public works and transport, they were bundled up with so many rules and regulations that little, if any, discretion in service delivery was left to the regional governments. Even if there had been any discretion, the demands of electoral coalition-building at the centre would have ensured that national party considerations would over-ride any attempts at policy experimentation in the regions.

The role of the regional governments was to change significantly in the early years of the 1990s. Political leaders of all persuasions now began to speak in terms of finding federal solutions to Italian ills. There was nothing new in this. As we have seen, federal solutions were discussed at the time of unification of the state over 150 years ago. However, a number of factors came together in the early 1990s to place federalism firmly on the political agenda.

One of the new actors rising to fill the political vacuum following the demise of the old political parties, was the Northern League (*Lega Nord*). The League developed out of the amalgamation of several protest movements in northern regions that were hostile to what they considered to be the iniquity of transferring northern taxes to support feckless and corrupt regions of the south. The entry of the League into the right of centre coalition government headed by Berlusconi in 1993 and again in 2001 and 2008 ensured that demands for greater regional autonomy could not be ignored. Once firmly established on the political agenda, federalism became a central theme in the manifestos of all the political parties, whatever their political persuasion. Federalism appeared to take on a life of its own and became the panacea for all Italian ills. For free-marketers it provided a solution to the inefficiencies and inequities of the welfare state. In the hands of the centre-left it provided an opportunity to democratize the welfare state by making it more responsive to local needs. For those wishing to modernize the whole system of public administration, greater subsidiarity became the staring point for the introduction of New Public Management techniques for managing personnel and ensuring value for money. European enthusiasts saw federalism as a way of adapting the Italian state to the European desire to support and strengthen the role of the regions within the EU.

The first significant step toward devolving power to the regions came with the so-called First Bassanini Law in 1997. Named after the sponsoring minister, the law and the subsequent enabling legislation devolved a series of spending and regulatory powers to all the three levels of local government. What the reform did not do was to grant the sub-national units of government any real taxation powers to cover the costs of their new responsibilities. The institutional set-up created by the reform required sizeable central transfers of resources, which were negotiated on a region-by-region basis and were based on historical expenditure patterns. This arrangement did little to enhance genuine regional autonomy and much to discourage inefficient regions from carrying out the necessary reform.

The process of devolution took a major step forward following a referendum held on 7 October 2001. The referendum asked the Italian voters if they approved of a vote passed in the Senate amending the constitution to give more powers to the regions on a wide range of issues including agriculture, education, health care and taxation. When the regional governments were established in the 1970s, the central ministries decided which functions they would transfer to the regions and, in so doing, severely restricted their room for manoeuvre. The change to the constitution turned this on its head. The core business of the central state would henceforth be restricted to: public order and security; defence and foreign policy; monetary policy; citizenship and immigration matters; the creation of electoral rules and systems; general norms and standards for education and health care; social security; and environmental and cultural heritage protection. Everything else would not be the responsibility of the sub-national organs of government.

The major achievements of the constitutional change were to clarify spending roles, firmly establish the principle of fiscal autonomy and address the issue of how the central transfers could be used to improve service delivery in the less efficient regions. However, defining the principles did not mean that the necessary legislation would be passed to operationalize these principles. The 2003 Berlusconi government set up a High Commission of Fiscal Federalism to address these issues but it did not survive the change of government that occurred in 2007. It would be another two years before necessary legislation would be passed. This occurred with the passage of Law no. 42 in 2009 on Fiscal Federalism, discussed under the heading below 'Financing the system'.

Given the different perspectives of the political actors it is perhaps not surprising that the reforms have not really produced a clear path toward a true federalist system of government. Instead, observers began to speak in terms of quasi-federalism, administrative federalism or moving things in a 'federalist direction'. What is not in doubt is the fact that the Italian system of government has changed radically as a result of the reforms.

In order to ensure that the regional governments had the necessary power and authority to carry out the new tasks allocated to them, a series of minor constitutional amendments had been passed before the transfer of powers took place. The 1948 Constitution placed the elected assembly at the heart of the regional power structure. Elected by popular vote, the assembly in turn nominated the members of the *Giunta* (or cabinet) composed of *assessori*, who are departmental heads, and the executive head (or regional president). Changes to the constitution in 1999 gave both Ordinary and Special regions the power to determine their own political structures and, more importantly, made it legally binding on the regions to directly elect the president through a popular vote. The changes brought the regions in line with the communes and provinces, which had had direct election of their respective chief executives since 1993. Presidents now had the power to choose their own executives and their electoral mandate was co-determinate with that of the assembly and the winning coalition was given a top-up of seats to guarantee a majority. At the heart of the change was the desire to inject a more managerial style into regional governance by endowing the presidents with greater legitimacy and lessening the control exercised by the political parties over the president once elected. These would in turn lead to more stable government in the regions and render the governments more responsive to issues and needs.

## Local government

Despite the massive transformation that has taken place in Italian society since the Second World War, the structure of Italian communal government has proved extremely resilient to change. In 1934 the fascist general law of local government was passed to make local government more efficient and responsive. Responsive in this context meant being responsive to the needs of the central state and not the citizen. The role of local government in fascist legislation was to act as a decentralized local office of the central bureaucracy in general and the Ministry of the Interior in particular. Municipal government only took on a third role as an expression of local autonomy when democratically elected representatives returned after the war. Despite this injection of democratic legitimacy the structure and functions of municipal government remained little changed. The key to the continuity was the roles performed by the prefect and the communal secretary. The prefect was the representative of the Ministry of the Interior based in the province. The provinces, unlike the communes, cannot lay claim to a glorious history, being as they were inventions of the post-unification period of Italian history. They have also been Janus-like figures in the system of local government. Facing one way they served as units of local governments with their own directly elected assemblies, provincial *giuntas* and administrative structures that mirrored the structures of the central ministries in Rome. Facing the other way they served as field agents of the Ministry of the Interior with the prefect playing the central role in providing central control and supervision by the centre. The communal secretary, who was a central government appointee and who acted as an overseer of communal activity further strengthened the controls exercised by central government. The reform of local government has eroded the power of the provinces. In the large metropolitan areas where they are overshadowed by the large municipalities, the most striking feature of Italian local government is its fragmentation. The fragmentation is represented not just by the number of communes but their geographical and sociological heterogeneity. The largest communes, Milan, Turin and Naples have populations of over one million. Rome, the political capital of the country has a population in excess of three million. At the opposite extremes, there are communes with populations measured in hundreds. Around 8 per cent of communes have under 500 inhabitants. The average geographical size of communes is about 37 square kilometres. Some are smaller than 0.1 square kilometres while the municipality of Rome extends to about 1,000 square kilometres.

Italy, along with France, continues to be outside the trend elsewhere in Europe with regard to the incorporation of units of local government into larger entities. A number of legislative measures have been passed in an attempt to create larger units of communal government, Law no. 142 in 1990 and again in 2000 (d.lgs 267), but neither have had a substantial effect. Recent legislation has provided the communes with two alternative ways of overcoming their size limitations in order to provide more efficient services. The first encouraged the communes to co-operate in the provision of specific services to the public or to share the administrative offices. The second provided the necessary legal structure for communes to amalgamate into larger municipal entities. While

*Table 6.1* Size of communes in Italy

| Population | Number of communes |
|---|---|
| Less than 3,000 | 4,630 |
| 3,001 to 10,000 | 2,359 |
| 10,001 to 100,000 | 820 |
| 100,001 to 250,000 | 29 |
| 250,001 to 500,000 | 7 |
| 500,001 to 1,000,000 | 3 |
| Over 1,000,000 | 3 |
| Total | 8,101 |
| Average population | 7,037 |

Source: Istat

there are literally thousands of examples of the former, there have only been five instances of the latter involving only 11 communes in Piedmont, Lombardy and Veneto. These have to be balanced against the creation of eight new communes as a result of movements in the opposite direction (Spalla 2006).

The internal structures of municipal government prior to the recent reforms mirrored the organization of the government apparatus at the centre. Citizens elected an assembly, which then elected a mayor and the heads of the local administrative departments who formed the local cabinet (*giunta*). In the elections that took place every five years, the political parties fought on issues of a national and international significance. As such, the elections were never judgments on issues as banal as the record of local councillors in providing clean streets or efficient public transport.

The direct election of mayors, which provided the model for regional presidents, was introduced in 1993 and was an attempt, among other things, to provide a remedy to precisely this problem. The intention of placing this power in the hands of an elected mayor was aimed at streamlining decision-making and increasing accountability. Mayors who failed to improve local services or fail to implement their campaign promises would have little chance of re-election. In this regard Italy was mirroring similar changes taking place elsewhere in western Europe where directly elected mayors were becoming commonplace. The streamlining of the decision-making process by placing executive power in the hands of the directly elected mayors has been achieved at the expense of the communal councils, which now serve only to scrutinize the activities of the mayor.

One of the immediate impacts of the mayoral reform was the introduction into local politics of a whole new cohort of political leaders with no obvious links to the old political parties. In the election held in 1993 over a quarter of all successful candidates fell into this category (Baccetti 2008). Though the opportunity for independent candidates has declined as the new political parties have re-regained a degree of control over the election process, the 'personalization' of the mayoral role had become well established. This personalization of the role is destined to become even more pronounced as the use of primary election for the choice of candidates becomes more widespread. The executive powers granted to the mayors ensured that those holding the reins of power would become personalities of importance at both local and national level. As such, the new mayors became an important constituency for concerted action aimed at the creation of a more robust system of local autonomy (Pasquino 2000; Triglia 2005).

This strengthening of the political leadership in the communes has been matched by a similar reform to the administrative structure. The Bassanini reforms changed the administrative leadership in the communes. Since their inception, the dominant administrative role in the communes was that of the general secretary who, like the prefect, ensured the conformity and legality of communal actions. In essence the secretary general performed a kind of command and control role on behalf of the central government. The reform removed the secretary general and replaced the role with that of the city manager. The city manager role was introduced in communes with populations in excess of 15,000 and was charged with generating greater managerial effectiveness and efficiency in policy implementation. The city manager was conceived of as both the co-ordinator of the departmental heads (*dirigenti*) and as a crucial conduit between them and the elected mayor.

Alongside the political administrative changes, there has been a minor revolution in the way in which services are delivered. In the past services to the community were delivered directly by the communes according to detailed rules and regulations dictated by the centre. The reforms of the 1990s gave the municipalities greater organizational flexibility in the way in which social and economic services are organized and delivered. Among the various reform initiatives has been the externalization of public services, such as corporatization, contracting out, public–private partnerships and privatization. The communes are now able to experiment with different kinds of 'quangos' and, in the wake of the privatization process, the introduction of local public enterprises. The Italian municipal landscape is now full of joint stock companies (*società per azione*) and limited companies (*società a responsibilità limitata*) providing services that were once delivered by locally publically owned municipal corporations. Many of the public–private partnerships in what are termed public utilities (water, electricity, gas, waste disposal, etc.) involve investments from foreign multinational companies (French water companies are particularly active in this area) and extend well beyond the historic boundaries of the communes. While the privatization of local service delivery has had many beneficial effects, there is a growing awareness that there are a number of negative consequences. There is growing concern that local politicians and managers are out of their depth in dealing with the management teams of the private companies. Also, the relationship between the mayor and the local corporation has become a little opaque and increasingly personalized with all that that entails.

Over the years, there have been a number of proposals regarding the future of the provinces. Attempts have been made to abolish some of the smaller provinces, but these have never got anywhere, due in no small measure to the damage such a change would cause to the local bases of the political parties. In fact, the number of provinces in Italy has actually increased from 94 in 1970 to 109 today.

The future of the provinces has been put in doubt as part of the technocratic government's debt-reducing measures within the spending review. The government is seeking to amalgamate provinces with populations less than 350,000 and/or geographic areas of less than 2,500 square kilometres with the whole process due to be completed by the start of 2014. The number of provinces that will disappear is unclear. Some have suggested that the figure could be around 60 and as high as 70 if the Special regions, which have a degree of autonomy in the matter, follow the national trend. The proposed legislation has once again sparked life into the debate concerning the establishment of metropolitan authorities based upon Italy's major cities. Despite numerous pieces of legislation beginning with Law no. 142 in 1990 and their inclusion in the constitution following a change introduced in 1998, the creation of metropolitan authorities has fallen foul of a lack of political will at the centre and a great deal of infighting among the sub-national tiers of government themselves. The regional authorities, for example, were fearful that large metropolitan authorities might pose a threat to their own situation. As a consequence, no metropolitan authorities have so far been created.

The reduction in the number of provinces would offer a real opportunity to incorporate the provinces around Italy's 10 largest cities into large metropolitan organs of local government. However, supporters of both provincial reform and metropolitan government should not hold their breath. Before the 2014 deadline for the reforms to be implemented, Italy is due a general election. There is every chance that these reforms will be one of the first casualties of the change in political leadership.

## Financing the system

The dual processes of decentralization and liberalization of public services have been at the heart of Italy's attempt to reduce the public debt and provide value for money in public services and bring them closer to the end user/taxpayer. For most of the post-war period the expansion in the functions of the regions and communes, as a consequence of the development of the welfare state, were not matched by increases in locally raised revenue. As a consequence, at least from the perspective of revenue raising, Italy was one of the most centralized political systems in Europe.

In terms of public expenditure, at the beginning of the 1990s sub-national organs of government were responsible for approximately 15 per cent of the total. By 2006 the figure had risen to 35 per cent. If the social security and the interest payments on the public debt are excluded, the figure rises to over 50 per cent of government expenditure (OECD 2007). The vast bulk of this expenditure was the product of devolving responsibility for health care management to the regional government, which could amount to over 80 per cent of regional expenditure.

This increase in the autonomy of sub-national organs of government in terms of expenditure, had until quite recently, only been partially matched on the revenue side. Nevertheless, even here the changes have been quite profound. The constitutional reforms, in accordance with the desire to promote greater fiscal federalism, were intended to lead to a situation in which the sub-national organs of government would have complete revenue autonomy for their normal activities, supplemented by the introduction of an equalization fund for the poorer regions with a lower tax base. Discretionary central government transfers were to become a thing of the past except in cases of extraordinary spending that might arise as a result of some natural disaster or other unforeseen event. The communes would be permitted to borrow to finance their investment according to the 'golden rule', which permits public authorities to run public-investment-oriented fiscal deficits.

The law on Fiscal Federalism (Law no. 42, 2009) developed the principle of fiscal autonomy and sought to operationalize them in a number of policy objectives. The law stipulated that the regions should have the power to raise taxes on productive activity within their jurisdiction and to share in the value-added and income tax raised in the region. For the sub-regional levels of government the main source of income would be a local property tax, some minor local taxes and charges for certain services. In recognition of the fact that there were vastly different tax bases both between and within regions, equalization measures were included. Here the distinction was made between delegated services such as health and education, for which full equalization would occur as standard, rather than historic, costs and an allocation for non-essential services with only partial equalization dependent upon the tax base.

The law on fiscal federalism laid down a number of principles that almost did the impossible by meeting the demands of a diverse political audience. The principles of 'fiscal autonomy', that spending and tax revenues should be in balance, and 'territoriality', that taxes should be spent in the regions in which they were collected, pleased the wealthy regions where the right dominated. The principle of 'tax autonomy' pleased the more efficient regions that stood to benefit from tax competition. Finally the 'equalization principle' gained support from the poorer regions and the left who were concerned with the question of unequal access to public services.

The net result of the changes on the revenue side has brought about a complete turnaround in local public finances. From being one of the most centralized countries in the 1970s, Italy in 2010 has the highest rate of locally raised revenue among non-federal states and is even on a par with some federal states.

## Accountability, secrecy and openness

'Public accountability is the hallmark of democratic governance. Democracy remains a paper procedure if those in power cannot be held accountable in public for their acts or omissions, for their decisions, their policies and their expenditures' (Bovens 2007: 182). When measured against such criteria, the Italian state has for most of its existence suffered from a massive democratic deficit.

Genuine political accountability in Italy has been almost totally absent. Political accountability can manifest itself in a number of forms but usually amounts to some form of control by elected representatives of political parties. In a parliamentary system this usually takes the form of responsibility being exercised through ministers or the equivalent department heads in the relevant regional or local governments. In the Italian case very little accountability of this kind ever took place. According to an Italian observer this was due to the fact that politicians were more concerned with exploiting the administrative system for their own advantage rather than ensuring administrative compliance. The concept of individual ministerial responsibility in which a minister resigns as a consequence of maladministration in his department, as has been the case in the UK, is not one an Italian politician would recognize. In the absence of political controls, the weight of overseeing bureaucratic activity fell to the administrative courts that were, at least in theory, independent from politicians and bureaucrats. The most important body in Italy was the Court of Accounts (*Corte die Conti*). The origins of the court can be found in the pre-unification period dating back to 1862 when it acted as a consultative, juridical and monitoring body within the government and administration of Piedmont. Its role was formalized in the post-war republic through Article 100 and was further enhanced with the creation of the regional governments in 1972 when it became the court of appeal for the Regional Administrative Courts (*Tribunale Amministrativi Regionali*). The court provides both ex-anti and ex-post control over government activity. Its ex-anti controls involve the court in the provision of preventative controls to ensure that proposed actions are in accordance with the law. No government contract or payment can be made without the prior approval of the court. To help the court perform its function it has officers permanently located in each of the spending ministries. The Court of Accounts exercises preventative control on the legitimacy of government measures, and also subsequent control on the management of the state budget. It participates, in those cases and in ways established by law, in control of the financial management of those bodies to which the state contributes in the ordinary way. It reports directly to the Houses on the results of audits performed. The law ensures the independence from the government of the two bodies. Its ex-post activities have focused primarily upon the production of annual reports to parliament and, in so doing, has often provided damning indictments of successive government failures to maintain adequate budget controls.

The system of controls focused upon the court has not been without its critics. The close working relationships between the court and the ministries has resulted in a situation of agency capture, in which the court has been criticized for helping the ministries to circumvent the regulations it was supposed to be enforcing. Another frequently voiced criticism of the court has been that it tended to define the public interest in terms of conformity with legal requirements with scant attention paid to whether the policies and actions involved the most efficient and effective use of public resources. Perhaps the most damning criticism was that, despite the court's controls, the public sector became embroiled in corruption on a massive scale.

One of the major driving forces behind the administrative reforms has been the desire to provide greater openness and accountability in the formation and implementation of policy. Whether the new public management paradigm is the only show in town is beyond the scope of this chapter. What is certain, however, is that many of the reforms undertaken in recent years have the potential to render the Italian state far more open and transparent than has been the case in the past. The whole *raison d'être* of the reforms has been to remove the kind of corrupt political practices that threatened the country's economic and political standing in the world and to restore public confidence in the state and the political system. Many of the measures alluded to above involve the devolution of decision-making and service delivery to the lower levels of the state apparatus in accordance with the principal of subsidiarity. The direct election of mayors at the communal level has been matched by a similar process at the regional level with direct elections of regional presidents. The introduction of personnel management techniques and accounting procedures has been part of the same design to increase the transparency of public decisions. The introduction of information and communication technology is destined to play a major role in the reform process both as a method of streamlining administrative procedures and giving the citizen the opportunity to participate in the policy process (Kudo 2008). A major barrier to the involvement of the ordinary citizen in the administrative process has been the highly complex and legalistic way in which the most mundane documents are expressed. One of the early measures to counter this was the creation of the *codice di stile*, or codes of style, designed to render the language of everyday administrative documents more accessible. All public managers now receive a *manual di stile* that contains guides on how to promote simplicity in communicating with the public. The introduction of Public Service Charters (*Carta dei servizi publici*) along the lines of those introduced in the United Kingdom and the creation of a local ombudsman (*defensore civico*) are attempts to provide the citizen with some defence against unfair and arbitrary decisions of local officials.

## Further developments and issues

From being a state characterized as anomalous, dysfunctional and incapable of democratic renewal, Italy has undergone a transformation unparalleled anywhere else in the developed world. In this respect, a recent book on Italian politics seeks to do what La Palombara did some 26 years earlier – to place Italy among the club of developed industrial democracies: 'I mean (too) that in terms of the quality of its democracy Italy is in most respects no worse than other countries in the category and in some respects much better' (Newell 2010). While recognizing that democracy Italian-style still has many idiosyncrasies, in which the phenomenon of Berlusconi is an obvious example, Newell is right to suggest that the reforms undertaken in recent years have changed the nature of democracy in Italy for the better. Whether Italian democracy is as normal as the subtitle of the book suggests is a matter for conjecture.

The changes made to the political and administrative system have been the product of careful thought and planning by forward-looking politicians and numerous research institutes and university departments. Given the close links between the academic and political world in Italy, they are often one and the same. The very size and ambition of the reform process has inevitably given rise to the law of unforeseen and unintended consequences. The gap between the intentions of the legislators and the effect of the changes on the ground is the subject of an increasing body of literature searching to understand the causes of what has become known as the 'implementation gap'. These studies are important because, 'when laws are not properly implemented, that undermines the credibility of government officials, fuels corruption, and presents serious challenges for business, which in turn hampers economic growth' (Global Integrity: Report on Italy 2010). The implementation gap is not an Italian phenomenon, it is common to all countries seeking to bring about changes on the scale of those introduced in Italy.

The factors contributing to the implementation gap in Italy have been discussed by a number of authors, Ongaro and Valotti (2008) and Turrini *et al.* (2010), who have identified certain key themes in the Italian experience. There is what they term the 'social capital theory stream'. This corresponds to the comments made above concerning the absence of a culture of civic republicanism as an explanation of the underperformance of many regional governments in the south of Italy. Here the implication is that the lack of the necessary social capital will hinder the full implementation of the reforms. Another factor embedded in the concept of social capital is the prevalence of clientelistic practices among local politicians and officials. Clientelism is seen as being so deeply embedded in administrative culture and practices that it will inevitably lead to a breakdown of administrative performance. Another factor common to many countries, not only Italy, is the dominance of the administrative law cultural paradigm in Italy. The problem is not caused by the existence of administrative law per se, but by the fact that administrative law becomes an all-embracing cultural paradigm shaping every aspect of bureaucratic behaviour.

One factor worth consideration is the extent to which decentralized/regionalized/federal systems prove more difficult to reform than highly centralized systems. If this is the case, the decentralizing measures in the reforms may actually make the task of the reformers more difficult. While political leaders in many regions in Italy have often proved to be ahead of their national counterparts in reform and management of public services, this has not been the rule everywhere.

Yet another factor, which has the potential to widen the implementation gap, as has been alluded to above, can be found in the different attitudes among the leading social forces as to what the precise meaning and implications are of many of the terms being used. The concept of federalism, like the proverb from the Indian sub-continent concerning seven blind men and an elephant, means different things to different people. For the supporters of the Northern League in Italy, a federal solution inspires images of a kind of micro-ethnocentric nationalism, and the related concept of 'fiscal federalism' is born of a desire for the rich north not to have to pay any tax to support the poor southern regions. If supporters of the Northern League had their way it would undoubtedly result in a more pronounced north–south divide, the creation of a good deal of political instability and rendering impossible a viable system based upon subsidiarity.

Finally, despite a good deal of tinkering with the electoral system in order to create more stable governments by reducing the number of parties and providing the electorate with a clear choice between alternative political programmes, Italy is still no nearer to achieving that goal than it was 20 years ago. There was a brief period in the late 1990s when it appeared as though a fragmented party system at the national level was about to coalesce around the two poles of Berlusconi's PDL on the centre right and the PDI on the centre left. The desire of many Italians for a British style bipolar party system with its clear winners and losers and governments capable of surviving for the full term of their mandate is further away than ever following the election results of February 2013. The lack of continuity and stability at the centre has the potential for widening the implementation gap even further.

# References

Baccetti, C. (2008) *La Nuova Political Locale*, Novara: UTET.

Banfield, E. (1958) *The Moral Basis of Backward Society*, Glencoe: Free Press.

Bovens, M. (2007) 'Public Accountability' in Ferlie, E. Lynn, L. Pollitt, C., *The Oxford Handbook of Public Administration 2007*, Oxford: Oxford University Press. pp. 182–208.

Cassese, S. (1983) *Il Sistema Amministrativo Italiano*, Bologna: Il Mulino.

Cavazza, F. L. and Cazzola, F. (1992) *L'italia del Pizzo*, Turin: Einaudi.

Chapman, B. (1959) *The Profession of Government: The Public Service in Europe*, London: Allen and Unwin.

Global Integrity: Report on Italy (2010) Online, available at: globalintegrity.org/global_year/2010

Graubard, S. R. (ed.) (1974) *Il Caso Italiano*, Milan: Garzanti.

Hofstede, G. (1991) *Cultures and Organisations*, London: McGraw-Hill.

Klickert, W. J. M. (ed.) (1997) *Public Management and Administrative Reform in Western Europe*, Cheltenham: Elgar.

Klein, N. (2007) *Shock Doctrine*, Harmondsworth: Penguin Books.

Kudo, H. (2008) 'Does E-Government Guarantee Accountability in the Public Sector? Experiences in Italy and Japan'. *Public Administration Quarterly*, 32, 1: 93–120.

La Palombara, J. (1987) *Democracy Italian Style*, New Haven: Yale University Press.

Ministry of Public Administration (n.d.) Online, available at: www.funzionepubblica.gov.it/cerca.aspx?search=assenteismo (last accessed 2 March 2014).

Negri, N. and Sciolla (ed.) (1996) *Il Paese dei Paradossi*, Rome: La Nuova Italia Scientifica.

Newell, J. L. (2010) *The Politics of Italy: Governance in a Normal Country*, Cambridge: Cambridge University Press.

OECD (2001) *Regulatory Reform in Italy*, Paris: OECD.

OECD (2007) *Economic Survey of Italy*, Paris: OECD.

OECD (2010) *Modernising Public Administration: A Study of Italy*, Paris: OECD.

Ongaro, E. and Valotti, G. (2008) 'Public Management Reform in Italy: Explaining the Implementation Gap'. *International Journal of Public Sector Management*, 21, 2: 174–204.

Owen, B. (2000) 'France' in Chandler, J. A. (ed.) *Comparative Public Administration*, 1st edn, London: Routledge, pp. 50–74.

Panozzo, F. (2000) 'Management by Decree: Paradoxes in the Reform of the Italian Public Sector'. *Scandinavian Journal of Management*, 357–73.

Pasquino, G. (2007) 'A Long Quest in Vain: Institutional Reforms in Italy, *Western European Politics*', 30, 4: 670–91.

Porta, della D. (1992) *Lo Scambio Occult*, Bologna: Il Mulino.

Putman, R. (1993) *Making Democracy Work*, Princeton: Princeton University Press.

Quaglia, L. and Radaelli, C. (2007) 'Italian Politics and the European Union: A Tale of Two Research Designs'. *West European Politics*, 30: 924–43.

Sartori, G. (1966) 'European Political Parties: The Case of Polarised Pluralism' in La Palombara, J. and Weiner, M. *Political Parties and Political Development*, Princeton: Princeton University Press.

Spalla, F. (2006) 'L'accorpamento dei Comuni in Europa e La Controtendenza Italiana'. *Amministrare*, 36, 1/2: 121–31.

Trigilia, C. (2005) *Sviluppo Locale: un Progetto per l'Italia*, Rome: Laterza.

Tulio-Altan, C. (1986) *La Nostra Italia. Arretratezza, Socio-culturale, Clientelismo, Trasformismo e Ribellismo Dell'Unita ad Oggi*, Milan: Feltrinelli.

Turrini, A., Cristofoli, C., Nasi, G. and Soscia, I. (2010) 'Lifting the Veil of Maya: Measuring the Implementation Gap of Public Management Reforms in Italy'. *International Journal of Public Sector Management*, 23, 1: 5–21.

# 7   The United States

*Howard Elcock*

## Political culture: the legacy of revolution

The United States of America was founded by a revolution that began with the Boston Tea Party in 1770, which was provoked by the autocratic imposition of a tax on imported tea by King George III's prime minister, Lord North, who Alistair Cooke described as 'a timid and apologetic bumbler' (1972: 100). In response to British autocracy and the growing threat from a reinforced British garrison, the 13 American colonies formed a Constitutional Congress in 1776 to formulate a Declaration of Independence leading to the vicious War of Independence against Britain with France supporting the American rebels. The colonies declared their independence in June 1776, opening their Declaration of Independence with the ringing words, 'We hold these truths to be self evident: that all men are created equal, that they are endowed by their Creator with certain inalienable rights, that among these are life, liberty and the pursuit of happiness.' The Declaration went on to declare that 'thus to secure these rights, Governments are instituted among men, deriving their just powers from the consent of the governed'. This proposition, derived from the political philosophies of the Enlightenment, notably those of John Locke and David Hume, constituted a 'stick of dynamite . . . the flame of a quite new revolutionary doctrine' (Cooke 1972: 122). To realise this revolutionary vision, the same Continental Congress prepared the first written constitution to govern the former colonies that had broken with British rule to form the United States of America, but the resultant Articles of Confederation and Perpetual Union soon proved to be inadequate, especially in the face of the sometimes desperate war against the former British colonists.

In consequence, in 1787 the States were asked to send delegates to a convention held in Philadelphia who determined that rather than amend the Articles of Confederation, they needed to draft a new constitution. The result was the shortest and oldest written constitution in the world, which is still in force to day, a knowledge of which is an essential prerequisite for anyone who wishes to understand the American system of government. Its content was largely shaped by the three authors of *The Federalist Papers*: John Jay, James Madison and Alexander Hamilton, who subsequently led

a campaign to persuade the 13 States to ratify it. This process was not concluded until 1790 and then only after the addition of the first 10 Amendments,
commonly known as the Bill of Rights. These include the prohibition of
any establishment of religion and defending free speech and a free press (the
First Amendment), the right not to be compelled to incriminate oneself
(the Fifth Amendment), and more regrettably, the citizen's right to bear arms
as a member of 'a well regulated Militia' (the Second Amendment). The
drafters' central purposes were to avoid the development of another centralised
tyranny by creating strong defences of the rights and powers of the states in
relation to the federal government.

## Principles of the constitution

For the student of public administration, two constitutional principles form
the essential basis for understanding the nature of the American administrative
system. The first is the separation of powers but it might be better defined as
the sharing of powers (Neustadt 1960). The second is the system of federalism.

### *Separate or shared powers*

The federal government consists of three institutions: the president, the
Congress and the Supreme Court, whose executive, legislative and judicial
functions are separate but overlap. The president is elected by the electorate
of the entire country once every four years, albeit that he is elected through
the medium of delegates elected from each state according to its population
to an electoral college, who then assemble to elect the president himself. This
explains the unusually long transition period when a new president is elected
– over two months from the election held on the first Tuesday in November
until the inauguration on 20 January the following year. Originally this was
the time needed for the electoral college delegates to ride to Washington to
assemble for the election. The president is constitutionally designated the
country's Chief Executive and Commander in Chief of the armed forces.

At the same time a vice president is elected but his only defined functions
are to take over the presidency if the president dies or is incapacitated and to
take the Chair of the Senate. The vice president is one heartbeat away from
the the presidency but many have been nonentities. However, the vice
president may be asked by the president to become a leader in specific areas
of policy or to act as a link between president and Congress. Lyndon Johnson
as vice president sought to smooth the passage of President Kennedy's
legislation through Congress, using political skills and experience that the
young president lacked. Al Gore was given major policy responsibilities by
President Clinton, including the development of the National Performance
Review, although another major policy initiative, the reform of the health care
system, he delegated to his wife Hillary.

The US president is often popularly described as the most powerful leader on earth but in reality his powers are far more restricted than those of, say, a British prime minister. Richard Neustadt (1960: 38) argued that

> the separateness of institutions and the sharing of authority prescribe the terms on which a President persuades. When one man shares authority with another but does not gain or lose his job on the other's whim, his willingness to act upon the urging of the other turns on whether he conceives the action right for him.

The essence of a president's persuasive task is to convince such men that what the White House wants of them is what they ought to do for their sake and on the president's authority.

Many of his powers are subject to approval or ratification by the Congress. This consists of two Houses. The House of Representatives now consists of 416 members elected every two years by simple plurality voting in electoral districts. These districts are supposed to be equal but as in other democracies, this ideal has proved to be impossible to achieve and has been the subject of many allegations of gerrymandering, some of which have ended up in the Supreme Court. The upper house, the Senate, is elected on a territorial basis; each state electing two senators regardless of its size. Hence the representation of mighty Texas and California is the same as that of miniscule Rhode Island. They are elected for six-year terms and a third of senators retire every two years. Lastly, the Supreme Court consists of nine justices appointed by the president to hold office 'during good behaviour' but their nominations must be approved by the Senate.

The real interest for the student of public administration lies in the relationships among these three institutions, because the way the powers of the state are divided among them by the Constitution mainly defines the environment in which public administrators must operate. First, legislation must be passed by both Houses of Congress in the same form, then be signed into law by the president. The powers of the two Houses are co-equal, so the passing of a Bill usually requires more or less extensive negotiations between their members in a Joint Conference Committee. The president can then refuse to sign the Bill, thus giving him a decision-making role in the theoretically separate legislative process, although his veto can in turn be over-ridden by two-thirds majorities in both Houses of Congress. Hence legislative power is shared rather than separated.

Another example of shared powers relates to issues of peace and war. The president is Commander in Chief of the armed services but the power to declare war is vested in Congress. Also, the president is entitled to negotiate treaties on behalf of the United States but any treaty he signs must then be ratified by a two-thirds majority of the Senate. The most famous refusal by the Senate to ratify a treaty occurred in 1919 when its members refused to ratify the Treaty of Versailles, thus denying the new League of Nations

American support and withdrawing the USA from influence in world affairs for the next 20 years, arguably with disastrous results (Elcock 1972). Yet another shared power is the president's right to make appointments to his Cabinet, which consists of the heads of the 10 major government departments. He also has the right to appoint the heads of the extensive network of executive agencies but most of these appointments must be confirmed with the 'advice and consent' of the Senate (see Drury 1959 for a gripping account of the nomination of a fictional Secretary of State).

Lastly, the Supreme Court has had the power, at least since the *Marbury v Madison* case in 1820, to strike down legislation duly passed by Congress and signed by the president, if the justices rule that it is unconstitutional. This means that the Court is drawn into political controversies in a way that could not happen in other developed democracies and therefore the political significance of judicial appointments is debated in a way largely unknown elsewhere, resulting in the development of a social science known as 'jurimetrics' under which the past decisions of individual Supreme Court Justices are analysed to determine whether their votes in the Court are predominantly 'liberal' or 'conservative' (Schubert 1963). Thus the Court has had a major impact on the development of the federal system through the judgements it has handed down, for example, the extent to which the federal power to regulate inter-state commerce permits it to ban socially undesirable practices like child labour – this was reserved to the states in 1919 but turned over to federal prohibition in 1941. The constitutional limit on the federal regulation of inter-state trade was notably used in the Court's initial refusal to approve president Franklin D. Roosevelt's 'New Deal' legislation in the early 1930s.

The justices have a long history of reversing their own decisions, usually because the Court's composition has changed or a single justice changes his or her vote, producing a 5 to 4 majority reversing the previous decision. Thus the New Deal legislation was saved by the single vote of Justice Owen Roberts after the 1936 presidential election produced a landslide victory for President Roosevelt. Such reversals have also had a major impact on such social issues as free speech. Here a judgement against the leaders of the American Communist Party in 1949 enabled the government to imprison them at the height of the Cold War on the basis that they constituted a 'clear and present danger' to the United States and the constitution. However, their second stringers were released after the Court declared two years later that the test had to be a 'clear and probable danger'; academic discussion of the revolutionary overthrow of the government was now allowed but not incitement to stage such a revolution.

Perhaps the most far-reaching decision the Court has ever made was that in *Brown v Topeka Board of Education* in 1952, when the Court reversed an earlier ruling in favour of the 'separate but equal' doctrine and ruled that educating black and white children separately was a denial of the black children's right to equality under the Fourteenth Amendment to the constitution, even if their separate education was of equal standard. This ruling gave rise to the subsequent fight for and eventual achievement of racial equality throughout the country. Another highly controversial decision was that in *Roe v Wade* in 1962, which confirmed the right of a woman to choose to have an abortion. Hence the Supreme Court's influence on the political, economic and social development of the United States has been far greater than would be expected of courts in other democratic states, where they are denied the right to overrule legislation duly passed by the country's parliament.

### Federalism

The second constitutional principle that must be recognised as crucial for public administration is federalism. The Tenth Amendment to the constitution declares that 'the powers not delegated to the United States by the Constitution nor prohibited by it to the states, are reserved to the states respectively, or to the people'. However, the history of the USA is littered with allegations that the federal government constantly seeks to usurp the powers of the states; indeed in modern times the process is sometimes referred to as 'coercive federalism'. Joseph Zimmerman (1992: 190) declared that 'If the drafters of the United States Constitution were resurrected and viewed in the 1980s the federal system they established in 1789, they would be amazed by the concentration of political power in the Congress'. He argues (1992: 202) that modern federalism consists chiefly of a mixture of co-operative relations between the federal and state governments and the coercion of the latter by the former: 'The current federal system should be viewed as a continuum in terms of national-state relations, ranging from nil to co-operative to coercive with the precise location of a given relationship on the continuum determined by the functional component concerned.' Disputes about the regulation of inter-state commerce and other issues have forced the Supreme Court repeatedly to redefine the doctrine of 'states' rights', which determines the limits on the federal government's powers and which the Court has often first left to the states but later agreed that it was appropriate for federal legislation.

The effect of federalism on public administration is that many government functions that in other countries would be carried out by the central government are in the United States carried out by state and local governments. The daily lives of Americans are thus affected far more by the decisions of their state governor and legislature and those of the local governments established under their state's constitution, than they are by the actions of the federal government. Examples of functions largely or wholly delegated to state and local governments are education, including higher education, welfare support, most policing, many highways and environmental protection. The federal government frequently tries to influence state and local policies and can adopt devices to persuade or coerce state and local governments to comply with federal policies but such interventions can be and are from time to time overruled by the Supreme Court.

The only governmental function that is unreservedly reserved to the federal government is foreign policy. That principle was determined by the Supreme Court only in 1936: Mr Justice Sutherland declared in the case of *United States v Curtis-Wright Export Company*: 'As a result of the separation from Great Britain by the colonies, acting as a unit, the powers of external sovereignty passed from the Crown not to the colonies severally but to the colonies in their collective and corporate capacity as the United States of America' (quoted in Potter 1955: 211). This has remained the position since and may explain why many presidents come to concentrate on foreign affairs, where their discretion is relatively unfettered rather than focussing on the endless wheeling and dealing that characterises domestic policy and law-making.

## The administrators: in-and-outers and others

The United States does not have a senior career civil service like those of other 'developed' states; there is no equivalent of the British Senior Civil Service (the 'Mandarins') or the French *Énarques*, because most of the posts that would be filled by such elites elsewhere are filled by presidential appointees subject to approval by the Senate. A modern president makes over 3,000 such appointments (Dillman 1998: 144); Peters (2002: 134) suggests that by 2002 this number exceeded 4,000. This means that sometimes appointments are made for reasons more or less divorced from the ability of the appointee, who may be given a cabinet post or an agency headship as a reward for making financial contributions to the president's campaign or having supported him in other ways. Thus, the head of the Disasters and Emergencies Relief Administration appointed as a crony by President George W. Bush, proved unable to deal with the catastrophe that hit the city of New Orleans following Hurricane Katrina in 2005. This also means that the political neutrality required of British civil servants is largely unknown in the American system.

Furthermore, Americans are traditionally suspicious of administrative power because of their belief in individual enterprise and the 'frontier spirit'. One consequence of this is that the USA has only slowly developed a unified civil service. Until the 1880s corruption and nepotism were widely practised in the appointment of public servants – the 'spoils system'. A unified civil service was created as late as 1883 by the Pendleton Act, after which the administrative culture 'evolved into a culture characterized by relative openness, professional specialization and commitment to particular policies and programmes' (Dillman 1998: 143). Since then, corrupt methods of appointment have been largely replaced by appointments by merit but this method is confined to administrative rather than policy-making posts, which are still filled by political appointees and therefore still subject to the vagaries of the 'spoils system' and the whims of individual presidents. The powers of the Civil Service Commission were strengthened under the leadership of John W. Macy during the Kennedy and Johnson presidencies (Dillman 1998); his 'lasting legacy is his quest for quality', which he established through both reform and example (ibid.: 152).

Public administration generally is a relatively low status, low-wage occupation at the operational level. Lawrence E. Lynn declared that 'the instruments of the state are held in lower esteem than in continental Europe' (2008: 254). Recruitment problems arise from the fact that 'the best and brightest' do not apply for civil service jobs (Peters 2002: 144). Also, because of the 'in and outer' system, the opportunities for career civil servants to achieve high office as it would be understood elsewhere are limited if not non-existent – presidents do fill some posts with civil servants rather than political appointees. Furthermore, many appointments at the local and state level have been and are still made through nepotism and other forms of corruption, rather than on the basis of merit.

## Departments and agencies

The core of the federal administration is the 10 departments with Cabinet status. These include the State Department, the Department of Defense, the Department of Homeland Security and the Department of Health, Education and Welfare. They are headed by political appointees who are of right cabinet members but the cabinet does not function as a collective entity in the way long-established in the United Kingdom: Theodore Sorensen recalled that President Kennedy consulted his cabinet 'occasionally'. These department heads are appointed by the president, subject to senatorial approval.

Outside the departments but subordinate to them there is now a plethora of executive agencies. Among the most famous (or infamous) are the Central Intelligence Agency, the Bureau of the Budget, the Federal Bureau of Investigation and the Internal Revenue Service. These are sometimes headed by political appointees, sometimes by senior professional figures – a decision that may be determined at least in part by the preferences of individual presidents. Hence posts filled at one time by a professional civil servant will at other times be filled by a presidential appointee. Other agencies, such as the Coast Guard, the Immigration and Naturalisation Service and the National Oceanographic and Aquatic Administration, are more exclusively professional. They have much greater budgetary and regulatory freedom than the Departments but they are all ultimately within the aegis of one or other of the 10 Departments.

## State and local government

Under the constitution the fifty states enjoy a degree of autonomy that would be the envy of their equivalents in most other democracies. Each state has its own constitution, which defines the powers and status of its governor and legislature. They are responsible for many public services such as welfare, state highways and higher education – public universities are state responsibilities, although they are governed by their own boards of governors but their members are appointed by the state governor and hence are subject to political scrutiny. In 1985 the states provided on average 51.3 per cent of non-education public services (Lynn 2008: 175). The states determine their own electoral processes, even for federal elections – a feature of the system that became notorious in the 2000 presidential election when George W. Bush eventually won against Al Gore on the basis of defects in the Floridian electoral system. Everyone involved in that election remembers the problems involved in counting 'hanging chads' – ballot papers where the punching machine had not completely removed the punched paper core from the hole, as needed to count the vote reliably. The result was finally decided by the Supreme Court.

The state constitutions also establish the 86,000 local governments that exist throughout the country and define the forms of government local governments may adopt. Most local governments are granted charters by the states, which guarantee them varying degrees of autonomy from the state and other local governments; 'home rule' charters grant the greatest local autonomy (Zimmerman 1992: 172). Local governments are empowered to levy their own taxes but most receive some state and federal support, which averages 30 per cent of local expenditure – a far lower proportion than the 70 per cent of central finance given to British local authorities (Zimmerman 1992: 173), which makes them heavily dependent on Whitehall.

Local governments determine their forms of government under the state constitution, often through referendums. There are a range of forms but two generally prevail, the elected mayor and council form and the council-manager form. In the older north-eastern states the elected mayor and council form is common, although other forms exist too. In New York State, for example, the majority of local governments, including New York City, are headed by elected mayors but some have adopted the council-manager form, where the administration is led by a professional manager appointed by the council and reporting to it. A formal distinction between 'weak' and 'strong' mayors is largely irrelevant because in modern conditions, all mayors need to be 'strong' to co-ordinate the government of their communities (Elcock 1995, 2001). In the south-western states, by contrast, the council-manager form is prevalent, although some larger councils have appointed or directly elected mayors to provide policy guidance to the manager (Svara 1990). The development of the council-manager form dates from the 1880s and was a response by the 'reform' movement to the corruption that was endemic in many mayoral systems, especially in the big cities. A famous example is the Chicago Democratic 'machine', which long maintained its control of the council by offering the voters in its impoverished downturn wards material or other inducements to vote for the Democratic candidates. For many years this 'machine' was headed by Mayor Richard J. Daley and his son, Mayor Richard M. Daley (Banfield 1961; Royko 1971). Another 'machine' was Tammany Hall, which dominated New York City's government for many years and was notorious for its corruption and gang violence. Edward Banfield and James

Q. Wilson (1963: 115–17) identified the source of the machine's power: 'control becomes possible when people place little or no value on their votes or, more precisely where they place a lower value on their votes than they do on the things which the Machine can offer them in exchange for them'. Most 'machines' have disappeared as educational standards have improved and affluence increased but traces of them still linger in some cities.

Local governments have extensive powers to provide public services, including water supplies, sewers and waste disposal, local policing, libraries and leisure facilities. However, American local governments are bound by 'Dillon's law', which like the British *ultra vires* rule, lays down that they can only take those actions they are legally empowered to take. School education is provided by separately elected local School Boards and other services may be hived off to single purpose bodies. However, unlike British local 'quangos', these single purpose bodies are usually headed by elected boards or councils, unless their function is highly technical or specialised, in which case their boards may be appointed but this is not the norm (Davis and Hall 1996).

## Finance and budgeting

Taxation is a vexatious issue in a nation that has a long-entrenched belief in small government, free-markets and low taxation. It has become more contentious still since the rise of the New Right in the 1980s. All levels of government have taxation powers. State and federal governments both collect income taxes, hence the amount of income tax citizens pay varies significantly from one state to another. Other taxes include sales taxes, gambling taxes and many others, which are levied in varied ways and amounts by state and local governments. Most of the latter levy a property tax because local government services such as highway maintenance and waste collection benefit property owners rather than the generality of citizens.

Budgetary processes tend to be both lengthy and controversial. At the federal level, the president prepares the budget, which is in reality prepared by an agency, the Bureau of the Budget, but it then has to be approved by both Houses of Congress, over which the president has no formal control. Members of Congress can delete, reduce or increase items in the president's budget and the process is not always completed before the financial year ends. Often expenditure items will be added or increased to promote the economic or other interests that are influential in the states or districts of individual senators or representatives. One Congressman's remark that 'if a legislator is sent here from a "bean" section, he will – and seemingly must – protect beans. His constituents demand it to be his first interest' (quoted in Potter 1955:169), indicates the sectional nature of much Congressional budgetary and other debates. Such amendments to benefit specific interests or individuals are referred to as the 'pork barrel'. Budgets may be delayed in Congress for all sorts of reasons. Theodore Sorenson (1963: 345) recalled how President Kennedy's 1962 budget was held up for three months by a wrangle between

two committee chairmen, both in their eighties, over 'who should call conference committee meetings, when and where'.

The president for his part can veto items included in the budget by members
of Congress. In 1995–6 President Clinton's budget had not been passed by
the Congress, which was then dominated by the Republicans since the mid-
term elections of 1994, before the financial year ended. In consequence, many
government facilities, including the Smithsonian Institution, had to be closed
and services had to be suspended until the impasse could be resolved. Even
under the acute pressures of the banking collapse of 2008–09 and the subsequent recession, Congress took several weeks and a good deal of persuasion
to pass President Obama's emergency financial rescue package, in contrast
with the British government's almost instantaneous decisions to partly nationalise several major banks and launch a major stimulus package. They were not
hindered from nationalising the failed banks or stimulating the economy by
parliamentary obstruction (see Cable 2009).

Major problems can arise for budgeters in the states and local governments
too. California passed by referendum a law restricting the amount of taxation
the governor and the legislature can levy, the most recent result of which has
been to drive that state into effective bankruptcy with governor Arnold
Schwarzenegger being forced to issue promissory notes instead of currency
to pay the state's wage and other bills. Similar tussles arise in local governments. Mayors propose budgets but councilmen can amend or defeat them.
The mayor can then in his turn veto the Council's proposals, thus giving rise
to a tug of war similar to that which arises between president and Congress
and the federal level. A former Mayor of the City of Buffalo recalled not only
having his budget rejected by the Common Council but also having his own
vetoes repeatedly over-ridden by the Council (Elcock 1995).

## Co-ordinating the system: inter-governmental relations

The American system of government is highly fragmented in several ways.
First, there are the relationships within the federal government and between
the federal government and the states. Earlier we discussed many examples
of the problems caused by the separation of powers at the federal level, which
result in a pronounced tendency for federal decision-making to stall at top
dead centre. Also, the federal government's constant attempts to secure the
adoption of its policies by the states can be mind-boggling in their variety
and cunningness. They include the giving of grants for state services together
with threats to withhold them if federal policies are not complied with, or the
imposition of unfunded mandates – imposing legal requirements to provide
services or develop projects but not offering the money to pay for them. Many
state services are supported by federal subsidies and the federal government
can reduce or remove these subsidies when state governments refuse to comply
with federal policies. For example, most states have been obliged to increase

the minimum age for consuming alcohol from 18 to 21 because the federal government refused to fund the building of federal highways, notably the Interstate Throughway network, in any state that failed to do so. Doing this has not solved problems of teenage drunkenness.

Similar issues arise between state and local governments. The latter are constrained by Dillon's Law but local authorities still have substantial areas of discretion. As with federal–state relations, the giving or withholding of grants and subsidies are the main methods used by the state governments to secure compliance with their policies but if local communities decide to provide a service from their own resources, the state government may be powerless to stop them. Also, local governments engage extensively in negotiations to win grants, subsidies or loans from the states; one mayor in Western New York described one of his major functions as being an 'ambassador' for his city but not just at state level: he had travelled to Canada and China in search of inward investment opportunities. A former city Mayor stressed the importance of his personal links with state and federal politicians, including two presidents, for getting money and other resources for his city (Elcock 1995). The overall picture is one of constant negotiation and 'log-rolling' to secure the maximum advantages for the states and the communities within them.

## Public management: a thousand flowers bloom

Improving the efficiency of governments and reducing their propensity to corruption has long been a preoccupation of American presidents and other political leaders. Lawrence E. Lynn (2008: 233) states that 'governments run with business-like efficiency has been a dream of American Presidents from Theodore Roosevelt through Franklin D Roosevelt, Ronald Reagan and George W Bush'. A major attempt at reform in the late nineteenth century was inspired by an essay written by T. Woodrow Wilson, then a professor at Harvard University, who condemned corruption and incompetence: he attacked 'the poisonous atmosphere of city government, the crooked secrets of state administration, the confusion, sinecurism and corruption ever and again discovered in the bureaux at Washington' (quoted in Lynn 2008: 235). One result was the introduction of the council-manager system, in the hope that installing professionalism in local government leadership would elim- inate the corruption that then surrounded many mayoral elections and local governments. Another innovation at this time was the replacement in some places of ward elections of councilmen by 'at-large' elections whereby the councilmen were elected *en bloc* by all the local government's electors; this reduces the possibility of bribing particular occupational or ethnic groups to secure the election of councilmen in wards with concentrations of those groups. Neither reform was by any means universally adopted, however, because of the inherently fragmented system of government and the different requirements of the state constitutions and local charters.

Although successive presidents have sought to reform and shrink the federal and local bureaucracies, such reform is not easy to achieve because of the decentralised nature of the country's administration. Peters (2002: 137) argues that 'each agency within a department has its own constituency and very often its own linkages to Congress and to powerful interests'. In consequence, a president's attempts to reduce an agency in size or abolish it altogether is liable to run foul of this 'iron triangle' system, which ensures 'multiple lines of accountability' (Peters 2002: 137). Hence, attempts at reform will be resisted in Congress and by powerful interest groups outside the government. In consequence more general reform programmes are likely to have a limited effect or be slow to have an impact. Vice president Gore's National Performance Review sought to reduce rigid rules and hierarchies in the interest of liberating enterprise among public managers, in line with the fashionable 'Reinventing government' prescription (Osborne and Gaebler 1993). Peters says that the public bureaucracy 'has been transformed substantially by the Gore Commission and its ideas' (2002: 141). One in six posts were abolished and the management style in government departments and agencies was changed 'substantially' by the relaxation of many rules. However, these changes took time to achieve, as did the introduction of performance measurement and assessment systems under the Government Performance and Results Act. From the beginning, it was acknowledged that this legislation would take at least five years to have 'any significant impact' (Peters 2002: 142).

One managerial device of which the United States is relatively free is structural reorganisation. Reorganisations of local government structures has become an obsession, even an addiction for British governments and the British Civil Service (Fenwick, Elcock and McMillan 2009). In the United States too, frequent and repeated attempts are made to consolidate local governments, merging them into larger units in the belief that these will be more efficient and lead to lower local taxes but these efforts usually fail because they have to be approved by referendums of the citizens of the existing local governments. Local citizens almost always vote to keep their own community governments intact, so dashing the hopes of the reformers. In some states, such as Pennsylvania, such consolidations are impossible under the State constitution (Peters 1997).

A more recent result of this fragmentation is that the impact of 'New Public Management' in the USA has been surprisingly limited, although most of its advocates are American citizens (Peters and Waterman 1987; Osborne and Gaebler 1993). The federal government was subjected to a National Performance Review, an attempted 'bonfire of bureaucracy' led by Vice President Al Gore after 1992. The impact of such federal government programmes on the state and local governments, which provide most public services, is limited because they are under no obligation to accede to the federal government's demands for reform, so the NPR's impact is limited.

Another issue that has been increasingly pursued in many countries has been the contracting out of the provision of public services by local governments to external providers, usually private companies or voluntary agencies. Such reforms have been evident in the United States but the extent to which public services are contracted out to private firms or voluntary agencies or directly provided by local and state governments varies widely. Even in a sample of small neighbouring local governments in Western New York State the balance between government, private and voluntary service provision varied widely from one local government to the next. Collaboration in providing specific services such as an emergency telephone call-out system is easier to achieve (Elcock 1995, 1998).

## Accountability, secrecy and openness

The First and Fourteenth Amendments to the constitution provides a clear and unambiguous protection for free speech and a free press. They also protect the right of free assembly, so any discussion of accountability and open government must be premised on the assumption that all government policies and activities can and will be vigorously investigated and debated. Also, there is a long-standing expectation that American governments are expected to be open to scrutiny and such scrutiny is vigorously exercised by Congressional committees but temptations to secure secrecy and the requirements of secret government agencies in the interest of national security or for more dubious reasons have long led to scandals involving the withholding of information or at worst, the concealment of governmental malpractice. The most infamous example was the Watergate affair in 1972, when agents acting on behalf of President Nixon burgled and bugged the Democratic Headquarters during the presidential election of that year. The eventual disclosure of widespread malpractice, including the taping of conversations in the White House, which themselves revealed both malpractice and foul language, forced Nixon's resignation in disgrace in the summer of 1973 (Woodward and Bernstein 1974, 1976).

The USA passed a Freedom of Information Act in 1966, which has since become a model for other countries (Thomas 1987). It was amended in 1974. For many years the absurd situation existed whereby because of the existence of the US Freedom of Information Act and the absence of equivalent legislation in Britain, documents to which access was denied under the British Official Secrets Acts could be obtained by travelling to Washington DC and making a request for them under the Freedom of Information Act at the Library of Congress. Despite problems associated with the maintenance of business and commercial privacy, as well as the need of the Federal Bureau of Investigation and the Central Intelligence Agency for secrecy, the Act provides a basic guarantee of public access to government documents and records for all American citizens, although its main users have been politicians, lawyers and business interest groups (Thomas 1987: 143). By 1975, 35 States had also passed Freedom of Information Acts (Thomas 1987: 145). Openness has been further assured through the Administrative Procedures Act of 1946, which requires that individuals and interest groups who are likely to be affected by departmental or agency policies or legislation must be consulted about them. This, plus rigorous Congressional scrutiny by committees and the General Accounting Office (a Congressional organisation), has resulted in a system that is 'distinctly open and participatory compared to Westminster systems' (Peters 2002: 137). However, the pressures that resulted from the destruction of New York's World Trade Centre on 11 September 2001 have resulted in renewed pressures for secrecy, as well as abuses of both American citizens' and foreigners' human rights.

## Democracy and the administrative system

In the main, American politicians and public servants are held effectively to account by a number of mechanisms. Short electoral terms guarantee that the interests of politicians' constituents are constantly in political office-holders' minds at all levels. Members of the House of Representatives are re-elected every two years and must therefore be constantly mindful of their constituents' views. State legislators and local councilmen are also subject to frequent re-election, usually having to face the voters every year or at least every other year. Hence, elections of some sort are held every first Tuesday in November and at other times too.

Scrutiny of executives is always vigorous. At the federal level, committees of Congress carry out painstaking investigations into all branches of government, sometimes with dramatic results and under the glaring scrutiny of the mass media. They also control legislation because almost all Bills are referred initially to committees and may be held up indefinitely by committee deliberations or delays by committee chairmen in scheduling debate on them. As a result, many Bills are lost in Congress's labyrinthine committee system. Either House may also set up a special investigatory committee to delve into government mistakes or misdeeds; the results can sometimes be spectacular.

At the state and local levels of government, scrutiny by both elected representatives and members of the public is frequent and demanding. For example local citizens can raise complaints or grievances at the 'public portion' of council meetings when they can question the Council and its executive, whether mayor or manager, on any matter over which they have competence and without having to give them prior warning. Such sessions can become both lively and confrontational: the author saw at least one threat of personal violence on such an occasion.

The impact of party politics on legislators' behaviour is far weaker than it is in Britain and many other western democracies because the Whips in the House and Senate have little power to maintain party discipline, hence legislators are to a greater or lesser extent beholden to one or more of the mass of lobbies that strive to secure support in Congress by offering inducements and threats to politicians. Local lobbies in their constituencies are also influential because they can influence voters at the next election, which is never far away. Theodore Sorenson (1963: 344) gives a vivid account of the difficulty President Kennedy faced in getting his Medicare Bill through the Senate in 1962. In the end the result hinged on the single vote of Senator Randolph of West Virginia: 'The President talked to Randolph. He arranged for West Virginian and national party leaders, labour leaders and other group leaders to talk to him. The pressure was unprecedented – and unsuccessful.' The Bill was only passed later under a more skilful legislative manipulator, Kennedy's successor Lyndon B. Johnson. Presidents can secure the passage of legislation only by 'log-rolling' – collecting the votes of legislators from whichever party by offering inducements to them such as government contracts for their constituents or concessions on other policies, until he has attracted sufficient votes to pass his Bill but the Bill's opponents offer inducements and threats too. It was in this context that Mr Speaker O'Neill famously declared that 'all politics is local', so for example 'a politician learns that if a constituent calls about a problem, even if it's a street light one, you don't tell them to call City Hall. You call City Hall' (O'Neill 1994: xvi). However, a long-term tendency for the Republican Party to become ideologically more right wing has accelerated with the advent of the 'Tea Party' movement within it, which is strongly committed to small government, low taxes and minimum regulation. This may now produce more coherent ideological voting by Republican politicians at all levels.

All this means two things. First, rapid action is impossible unless the president can find ways around the legislative delays that otherwise impede or baulk his need for action. For example, presidents have circumvented the right of Congress to declare war by provoking hostile states to declare war on the United States instead. President F.D. Roosevelt was powerless to enter the Second World War on Britain's side until Japan attacked the US Navy in Pearl Harbour in December 1941– an act of aggression arguably provoked by the president's imposition of an oil embargo on Japan earlier that year to try and halt her aggression in China (see Storry 1963). Alternatively, the president may choose to wage an undeclared war without getting Congressional approval for it.

## Further developments and future issues

There is a constant search for increased efficiency in government but the fragmentation of the system inhibits the coherent or systematic implementation of managerial prescriptions such as New Public Management. On the other hand it gives rise to a wide range of experiments and initiatives at all levels of government that provide examples of beneficial practices that others may learn from and follow: the practice of 'Reinventing Government' is therefore both constant and beneficial (Osborne and Gaebler 1993). Lawrence E. Lynn (2008: 240) suggests that the current trend of administrative reform places 'far less emphasis on the kinds of neo-liberal, market mimicking reforms that had already become popular in America', especially under President Reagan and the two Bushes. Hence the history of the NPR and other reform movements demonstrate that the future of administrative reform and reinvention is likely to continue to produce highly varied results and a wide range of innovations at all levels of government but much change originates away from presidential attempts to bring it about from their Washington DC perspective.

The greatest problem is the system's entrenched tendency to inertia, which often prevents badly needed reforms being implemented or results in their more or less extensive dilution. The American health care system has long been widely acknowledged to be a disaster, with 40 million Americans having no health insurance and public health provision being minimal, but public and Congressional opposition has either diluted or blocked successive attempts to reform it. President Kennedy's modest Medicare and Medicaid proposals to provide health cover for the poor and elderly were passed by Congress only after protracted and bitter opposition from doctors, insurance companies and others had been overcome. The Clinton Healthcare Plan of 1992 failed entirely after the initially strong public support for it was eroded by effective advertising against it by insurance companies and others during the summer of 1994. President Obama's reform scheme has been approved by Congress after a major struggle and was not fully implemented until 2013. He achieved reform because his party commanded majorities in both Houses of Congress but the Republicans gained control of the House in 2010, which seriously impeded passage of Obama's emergency legislation to address the banking crisis. Speedy action to correct economic imbalances is made difficult if not impossible by the slowness and sometimes reluctance of Congress to approve emergency measures, which would be taken immediately by government fiat in other countries. Hence there are real questions about whether the United States will be able to respond quickly or effectively enough to the growing pressures coming from outside in an increasingly globalised world economy. This is perhaps the most severe threat to her long-term power and prosperity.

# References

Banfield, E.C. and Wilson J.Q. (1963) *City Politics*, Cambridge, Mass: Harvard and MIT University Presses.

Banfield, E.C. (1961) *Political Influence*, New York: Free Press.

Cable, V. (2009) *The Storm: The World Economic Crisis and What It Means*, London: Atlantic.

Cooke, A. (1972) *Alistair Cooke's America*, London: British Broadcasting Corporation.

Davis, H. and Hall, D. (1996) *Matching Purpose and Task: The Advantages and Disadvantages of Single and Multi-purpose Bodies*, London: Joseph Rowntree Foundation.

Dillman, D.L. (1998) 'Leadership in the American civil service', in M. Hunt and B. O'Toole (eds), *Reform, Ethics and Leadership in Public Service: A Festschrift in Honour of Richard A Chapman*, Aldershot: Ashgate Press, pp. 142–58.

Drury, A. (1959) *Advise and Consent*, London: Collins.

Elcock, H. (1972) *Portrait of a Decision: The Council of Four and the Treaty of Versailles*, London: Eyre Methuen.

Elcock, H. (1995) 'Leading people: Some Issues of local government leadership in Britain and America', *Local Government Studies*, 21 (4): 546–67.

Elcock, H. (1998) 'German lessons in local government: The opportunities and pitfalls of managing change', *Local Government Studies*, 24 (1): 41–59.

Fenwick, J.H., Elcock, E. and McMillan, J. (2009) 'Local governance and the problem of English governance', *Local Government Studies*, 35 (1): 5–20.

Lynn, L.E. (2008) 'The study of public management in the United States. Management in the New World and a reflection on Europe', in W. Kickert (ed.), *The Study of Public Management in Europe and the US*, London: Routledge, pp. 233–62.

Neustadt, R. (1960) *Presidential Power*, New York: Wiley.

O'Neill, T. (1994) *All Politics is Local*, New York: Times Books.

Osborne, D. and Gaebler, T. (1993) *Reinventing Government: How the Entrepreneurial Spirit is Transforming the Public Sector*, New York: Penguin Books USA.

Peters, B.G. (1997) 'Regional economic development and political mechanisms: Western Pennsylvania in comparative perspective', in M. Keating and J. Loughlin (eds), *The Political Economy of Regions*, London: Frank Cass, pp. 262–74.

Peters, B.G. (2002) 'The Federal bureaucracy', in G. Peele, C.J. Bailey, B. Cain and B.G. Peters, *Developments in American Politics 4*, Basingstoke: Palgrave Macmillan, pp. 133–46.

Peters, T. and Waterman, R. (1987) *In Search of Excellence*, New York: Harper Row.

Potter, A.M. (1955) *American Government and Politics*, London: Faber & Faber.

Royko, M. (1971) *Boss: Mayor Richard J Daley of Chicago*, Boulder, Col: Paladin Books.

Schubert, G.A (1963) *Judicial Decision Making*, New York: Free Press.

Sorensen, T.C. (1963) *Kennedy*, New York: Columbia University Press.

Storry, R. (1963) *A History of Modern Japan*, London: Penguin Books.

Svara, J. (1990) *Official Leadership in the City*, New York: Oxford University Press.

Thomas, R. (1987) 'The experience of other countries', in R.A. Chapman and M. Hunt (eds), *Open Government*, London: Croom Helm, pp. 135–72.

Woodward, R. and Bernstein, C. (1974) *All the President's Men*, London: Quartet Books.

Woodward, E. and Bernstein, C. (1976) *The Final Days*, London: Coronet Books.

Zimmerman, J. (1992) *Contemporary American Federalism*, Leicester: University of Leicester Press.

# 8　Russia

*Marina Nistotskaya*

## Political culture

Modern Russia emerged as an independent state in 1991 from the remains of the USSR – once one of the most powerful states in the world, but whose capacity – ability to make and implement policies – was severely undermined in the course of Mikhail Gorbachev's reforms in the late 1980s. The dismantlement of the Communist Party's monopoly on power was followed by the proliferation of institutions with competing claims to authority. At the central level the USSR Congress of People's Deputies challenged the powers of the president; and at the subnational level, the leaders of the constituent members of the USSR, strengthened by their electoral mandates, called for the independence of the republics. The uncertainty about the future of the USSR led to colossal defection and asset-stripping by the party and state officials (Gregory 1990; Solnik 1998), which incapacitated the Soviet state even further.

New Russia experienced considerable difficulties in state building. Institutionally, fractures within the Russian state unfolded along both the vertical and horizontal axes. The early 1990s were marked by a showdown between the national legislature and the president. Not only did each of them claim to be the supreme governing body, but they were ideologically diametrically opposed. This hampered the ability of the state to formulate cohesive policies and to pass co-ordinated legislation. In the early 1990s much policy was carried out in the form of presidential decrees and government regulations. The dissolution of the national legislature and the adoption of the constitution in 1993, which considerably empowered the president, resolved the acute legislative-executive stalemate. However, significant ideological heterogeneity between the branches of authority continued to persist throughout the 1990s, providing for a low degree of co-operation between them and therefore impeding coherent law-making. In addition, as with the republican leaders of the USSR, the regional elites of new Russia sought greater political and fiscal autonomy and even independence, while the federal center tried to keep the federation intact through the policies of 'executive bilateralism' (Tafel 2010) and 'selective fiscal appeasement' (Treisman 1999).

Consequently a system emerged in which diverse constituent units enjoyed different rights and obligations and were governed by the centre in an ad hoc and opaque manner. Furthermore, relying on political influence rather than on competitiveness for their success, much of post-Soviet big business developed a cosy relationship with the state (Guriev and Rachinsky 2005; Slinko, Yakovlev and Zhuravskaya 2005) thereby undermining its autonomy. The early 1990s also witnessed a large-scale exodus of state officials to the private sector (Huskey and Obolonsky 2003). While the success of sweeping economic reforms critically depended on the ability of the state apparatus to implement them, by 2000 Russia's public bureaucracy remained largely unreformed, and also was older and less educated than its Soviet counterpart (Brym and Gimpelson 2004). Overall, through the 1990s the ability of the Russian state to structure a coherent policy-making process and the ability to implement policy decisions remained low.

Vladimir Putin made 're-building the state' a cornerstone of his presidential agenda in the 2000s. The political component of Putin's '*etatization* project' was concerned with the autonomy of the state in general and the president/federal government policy-making center in particular (Hashim 2005; Remington 2003, 2006; Sakwa 2008). The major initiatives in this sphere are:

- the indictment of several politically active business tycoons;
- weakening of the regional executives' sway over key policy-making centers through the reform of the upper house of parliament and suspension of gubernatorial elections;
- weakening the autonomy and the role of the parliament via the institutionalization of the 'party of power' – an electoral vehicle that brings 'to the national legislature politicians who are loyal to the federal executive' (Golosov 2004: 29).

The improvement of the administrative or implementation capacity of the state was another component of state-building. Public administration reform has been processed through three interconnected strands – civil service, budget and administrative reform. These developments have taken place against the background of the vastly improved macroeconomic situation and the waning of the political polarization in society that characterized the early transition period.

## The constitutional framework

According to the constitution of 1993 Russia is a democratic federal state. Therefore *de jure* the country's system of government reflects both the democratic principles of the separation of powers into executive, legislative and judicial branches, and the federative principle of a shared sovereignty between the federal authorities and the authorities of the constituent members (regions).[1] *De facto*, however, a clear separation of powers has never been achieved in post-Soviet Russia, and the intergovernmental relationships have evolved from the 1990's system of 'asymmetric federalism' with a weak central government and a considerable difference among regions in their rights and obligations, to the contemporary arrangement known as 'the power vertical', reflecting the supremacy of the federal authority in general and the institute of president in particular.

The Russian president, who since 2012 is elected by an absolute majority in a two-round national election for a term of six years, is the head of state. Within the constitution, this is distinct from all branches of power. At the same time, the president possesses considerable powers that belong to both legislative and non-legislative domains (see list below). This range of powers makes the Russian presidency 'more dominant than the French, and about as powerful as the American, but well short of the Mexican and several other Latin American presidencies' (White and Mcallister 2008, 605). The selected powers of the Russian president are:

- issue decrees with the force of law, draft federal laws, veto legislation passed by the parliament, and suspend acts passed by the regional executives;
- nominate and/or appoint and dismiss key officials from the prime-minister, federal ministers, key judges and supreme military personnel;
- directly oversee the ministries of the federal government with coercive powers: Defense, Interior, Security, Justice and Emergency;
- chair the meetings of the federal government;
- dissolve the State Duma (in certain circumstances) and dismiss the federal government as a whole without reference to the parliament;
- settle disputes between the federal and regional governments and between the regions;
- announce referenda and introduce a state of emergency;
- shape the directions of the domestic and foreign policies.

The system of institutional checks and balances is weighted heavily in the president's favour. He may veto legislation and dissolve the obstructionist assembly, but there is no practical way for the legislature to block or overrule the president's decrees. In his analysis of the Russian presidency in the 1990s, Stephen White concludes that 'In terms of the constitutional powers of president, prime minister, and parliament, the president was clearly the dominant figure' (1999, 222). During Putin's first two presidential terms this feature of Russia's constitutional framework has been further reinforced.

Since at least the parliamentary elections of 2003 the State Duma, the lower 450-member chamber of the Russian parliament, has been controlled by the pro-Kremlin majority party. This has been done through a series of changes in electoral law (Golosov 2011), and has ensured that not only the president's legislative initiatives and personnel decisions that require the approval of the parliament are passed smoothly but, more importantly, that the policy agenda of the president and government dominates the floor (Remington 2006; 2008). The most recent elections to the State Duma took place on December 4, 2011. Under party-list proportional representation system the pro-government party *United Russia* received 49 per cent of the vote, which translates to 53 per cent of the Duma's seats.

Most commentators agree that up until the year 2000 the Federation Council, the upper 178-member chamber, populated by the incumbent governors and the heads of regional legislatures, served as a constitutional venue for center-regions' bargaining, and was capable of defending the interests of Russia's regions, or at least their elites, by delaying or blocking legislation (Remington 2003; Tafel 2010, 267–270). However, since 2000 under the initiative of the president the composition of the Russian senate has been altered several times and its political clout has been diminished to the 'rubber stamp' of the Kremlin. Thus, in the spring of 2011 the Federation Council approved 264 laws and rejected one, in the autumn session of 2011 it approved 153 and rejected 2, and in the spring of 2012 it approved 101 drafts, rejecting none (Vedomosti 2012a). Soon after commencing his third term as president, Vladimir Putin initiated a new law altering the rules for the formation of the upper chamber once again. Under the new rules regional parliaments choose one of the senators from their own members through a vote. The procedure for the second representative is linked to the elections for governors, which were re-instituted in May 2012. Each gubernatorial candidate nominates three candidates for the Federation Council post, and the winner of the gubernatorial race appoints one of them at their own will. The law also sets forth a new residential qualification for senators. They must have lived in the region for at least the past five years before the nomination. At the same time the age qualification was relaxed from 30 to 21 years. In contrast to the previously existing rules, neither governor nor regional parliament can recall the region's representatives in the Federation Council.

While formally the president is not the head of the executive, the post-holder wields many executive powers, including some that are not clearly specified in the constitution but conferred by office. The president nominates the top state officials, including the prime minister, who must be approved by the State Duma. In turn ministers are formally nominated by the prime minister, but the power of appointment lies firmly in the hands of the president. Russian presidents have been more likely to draw ministers from their personal networks than from the national parliament or regional leaders. Furthermore the president directly oversees ministries and agencies with coercive powers such as Defence, Interior, Security, Justice and Emergency, and steers foreign policy (see the list of selected presidential powers above). The work of the president is supported by his executive office, one of the largest administrative bodies of the central state. It drafts federal laws and presidential decrees, oversees the implementation of presidential decisions and co-ordinates the work of the governments of all levels.

It should be noted that the real distribution of power in Russia goes beyond the constitutional prescriptions and 'a great deal depends on the individual office-holders' (White and Mcallister 2008, 606). Thus, although formally the current system is heavily 'stacked' in favour of the president, scholars of Russia agree that in his spell as prime minister between 2008 and 2012 Vladimir Putin had more influence over events than the actual president (Colton 2012; Orttung 2013). The recent return of the most influential figure of Russian politics to the most influential office of the Russian state leaves no doubt that in the next six to 12 years the locus of power and the decision-making center in Russia will be located in the Kremlin.

## The civil service

The early 1990s were the heyday of neo-liberalism, and post-communist reformers focused on privatization and price liberalization with the civil service featuring low on their reform agendas. Yet when Russia's Civil Service Act was passed in 1995, this was one of the first among the post-communist countries. The 1995 law introduced the rules and procedures for hiring, firing and promoting career bureaucrats and this had the potential to create a competent and impartial bureaucracy. However, it was never fully implemented (Huskey 2004; Huskey and Obolonsky 2003; Nistotskaya 2009) and was subsequently replaced with a new law.

A new civil service act, 79-FZ, effective from 2005, preserved large parts of the existing system, namely the key personnel policy provisions. 79-FZ provides a clear definition of the scope of the civil service vis-à-vis political posts and other forms of public sector employment. The term 'civil service' refers to professional activity pertaining to the fulfilment of the powers of the state, i.e. the execution of decisions made by elected officials and state organs. Civil service can be in the federal or regional levels (see Table 8.1). The former, which is sub-divided into the federal bureaucracy in Moscow and the federal bureaucracy in the regions, considerably outnumbers the regional bureaucracy (see Table 8.2). As local self-government is formally separated from the state, municipal officials do not form part of the civil service. Similarly individuals working in other sectors of public employment, such as teachers, doctors and about 4 million employees of the semi-autonomous organizations operating under the auspices of the central and regional governments (Vedomosti 2012b) are not part of the civil service.

The legislation also distinguishes between the senior civil service, known as managers, or advisors to managers and the rest of the public bureaucracy, labelled as specialists (see Table 8.1). According to the law, personnel decisions with regard to the former two categories are a matter of political judgment. That is, while officials such as ministers and governors can hire and fire managers at will, managers have a free hand in personnel decisions relating to the posts of advisors. At the same time, the law authorized vacancy contests as the main procedure for hiring specialists. Such elements of the hiring

*Table 8.1* Structure of Russia's Civil Service

| Classification grounds | Main groups of state service posts |
| --- | --- |
| Branches of authority | Legislative<br>Executive<br>Judicial |
| Levels of authority | Federal in Moscow<br>Federal in regions<br>Regional |
| Categories of posts | *Managers*: deputy heads of the state organs, heads of the structural units of the state organs<br>*Advisors*: organizational, information and analytical support to managers<br>*Specialists*: including support-specialists |
| Grades/ranks of specialists, including support-specialists | Level 8 = most senior level<br>Level 1 = most junior (entry) level |

*Table 8.2* Russia's Civil Service and municipal service (executive branch): 2001, 2011 (in thousands)

| | Federal civil service in Moscow | Federal civil service in regions | Regional civil service | Municipal service |
| --- | --- | --- | --- | --- |
| 2001 | 26 | 287.1 | 130.2 | 280.3 |
| 2011 | 29.9 | 454.6 | 182.6 | 358.3 |

Source: Rosstat 2009a

procedure as the compulsory advertisement of job vacancies in the mass media and the presence of independent experts in the commissions adjudicating the competition were sought to enable the emergence of a competent bureaucracy, free from undue political influence, cronyism and nepotism.

Promotion-wise, Russia adopted a position-based system, in which senior bureaucratic posts are open to both internal and external job seekers, and advancement in ranks is carried out through competitive contests. In reality, however, insiders are hugely favoured. Act 79-FZ also provides for a rather limited use of such personnel policy tools as demotions and discretionary dismissal of specialists. Overall, while Russia's Senior Civil Service is highly politicized by design and in practice, the lower ranks, which account for the overwhelming majority of the civil servants in the executive branch (see Table 8.3), are modelled more on a Weberian/Progressivist bureaucracy.

Unlike some post-communist countries such as Poland or Hungary who experienced reform backslide after gaining accession to the EU (Meyer-Sahling 2011), Russia has maintained its effort to reform public bureaucracy without

*Table 8.3* Civil service personnel (executive branch) by levels of authority and categories of posts, 2009 (in per cent)

|  | Managers | Advisors | Specialists | Support-specialists |
|---|---|---|---|---|
| Federal in Moscow | 10 | 1.1 | 74.4 | 14.2 |
| Federal in regions | 17.4 | 0.2 | 58.8 | 23.6 |
| Regional | 22 | 1.6 | 60.3 | 16.1 |

Source: Data on local self-governments as of January 1, 2011 (Rosstat, 2011a); on the number of Ministries, Agencies and Services as of June 1, 2012 (Government of the Russian Federation 2012c)

facing strong external pressure. However, the road to the full implementation of 79-FZ and related legislation (including that on standards of conduct and conflict of interests, and standard operating procedures that regulate bureaucratic behavior) has remained bumpy. For instance, although public notice of job vacancies in the state organs has become a permanent feature of the labour market, a considerable proportion of vacancies still remain unadvertized. According to the federal government, in 2011 about 40 per cent of all appointments in the regional civil service circumvented this provision and were made through the so-called 'cadres reserves', pools of pre-qualified candidates (Federal Portal of Managerial Cadres 2012). Other impediments include, but are not limited to, the absence of an independent merit-protection agency, coherent competence standards for bureaucratic positions, and a non-judicial system of appeal for unsuccessful job candidates and aggrieved civil servants, as well as the problems of the objectivity of the examination system and the selection commissions.

Although 79-FZ provided for salaries tied to the seniority of the position and service length as the main form of remuneration for bureaucrats, civil service reform was also concerned with strengthening performance incentives for individual officials. This element of the reform is part of an ongoing move to a performance-based management style within the public administration, which has been followed not only through civil service, but also administrative and budget reforms. It was expected that individual civil servants would be assigned performance targets that would influence their regular appraisal and the overall level of pay. While such indicators are being developed, the law provided for an interim measure in the form of monetary rewards for good performance distributed at managerial discretion. Consequently, the pay formulae are 'extremely complex and thus opaque' (Tompson 2007 19). Although some progress has been made since, especially in the central government (Gorodetski 2012; Verheijen and Dobrolubova 2007), today a fully functioning pay-for-performance system based on the formally assessed effectiveness of individual civil servants seems as far away as it was at the end of the 2000s.

In the executive branch of the civil service 85 per cent of personnel at all levels of government have university degrees (Rosstat 2009c, 2009d); however, only about 5 per cent hold a specialized degree in public administration (Vedomosti 2012c). Degrees in public administration are offered by institutions of higher education throughout the country, including specialized academies of state service. Service-related specialized training is available through educational establishments attached to the federal ministries and agencies. While in service officials may pursue graduate, postgraduate and other training with the financial support of the state. Despite this, the quality of Russia's Civil Service remains low as the bulk of university educated civil servants graduated in the Soviet times (Vedomosti 2012c) and the quality of Russia's higher education remains low (Guriev and Tsyvinski 2012).

## Central government agencies

The Russian government system is structured in three substantive tiers: federal, regional and local (see Table 8.1). The federal government is the chief executive organ of the state. The constitution has empowered it with considerable policy-making authority, especially with respect to macroeconomic and fiscal policies. The federal government initiates about half of all enacted laws (Bocharova and Gallay 2013). One of the key responsibilities of the government is the development of the annual budget.

The year 2004 witnessed a radical attempt to create an 'agency model' of central government, aimed at separating the core, rule-making, function of the government from its more operational routines. To this end a number of formerly ministerial functions, namely regulatory, monitoring and law enforcement, and public service provision, were devolved to services and agencies, which were supposed to operate at arm's length from their parent ministries. The initiative, however, was short-lived as most of the services and agencies were gradually brought back under direct control of their ministries. Thus, in a comparative perspective most of Russia's central government agencies and services are located on the right hand side of the 'quango continuum' (Greve, Flinders and van Thiel 1999, 142) as among the most restricted in terms of their independence. At the same time about 20 agencies and services, for example, the Federal Antimonopoly Service, the Federal Space Agency, the Federal Security Services, and the Federal Migration Service have remained as independent units of the central government.

The actual number of ministries and other units within the central government has evolved since 2004. As of June 2012, there were 20 ministries, 23 agencies and 34 services. At the end of 2011 almost 30,000 civil servants worked in the central apparatus in Moscow, with the Ministries of Foreign Affairs, Economic Development, Defense and Finance being the largest organizations employing 3,100, 1,800, 1,600 and 1,300 civil service staff respectively (Rosstat 2012). Most of the departmental units of the federal government have their own territorial structures to exercize their jurisdiction throughout the country. In 2011 there were almost 455,000 civil servants working in such field units of the government (see Table 8.2).

The different ways in which the structural units of the federal government are configured can be illustrated by the following examples. The Ministry of Finance is one of the largest and one of the most influential ministries of the central administration. It is subordinated to the prime minister. The Ministry has three services within its structure – the Tax Service, Financial and Budgetary Oversight, and the Treasury. It also has 11 quasi-autonomous organizations operating under its responsibility (as of June 2012). In turn the Tax Service, which is a subordinate unit of the Ministry, has offices in all territorial units of the Russian Federation, with 14 specialized field offices and 11 other sub-service organizations.

The Federal Civil Defense and Emergency Management Ministry is one of the oldest ministries, and one of those that is directly subordinated to the president. It is responsible for the protection of people and territories from natural and human-made disasters. Functionally its responsibilities include all phases of the policy process from rule-making to co-ordinating the response to the disaster. Although there are no agencies or services within its structure, the Ministry has territorial branches in all 83 regions of the Russian Federation and about 1,130 sub-ministry quasi-autonomous organizations that operate under its responsibility (Federal Civil Defence and Emergency Management Ministry 2010).

At the sub-ministry level one can observe a variety of organizations that do not make strategic decisions independent of their parent ministry, agency or service, but enjoy varying degrees of operational autonomy. They are the outcome of 'agencification from below' – the emergence of public organizations that charged user fees of various types or were engaged in direct commercial activities – that was typical of the first decade of transition in post-communist countries (Lehmbruch 2012). The legal forms of these organizations vary from joint stock companies with majority state ownership, state unitary enterprises that are under ministerial responsibility but 'work on the basis of commercial accounts and commercial legislations' (Kraan et al. 2008, 16) to a variety of so-called 'budgetary organizations'. These are non-profit organizations established by the central, regional or municipal authorities and financed by the state in whole or in a part. As of April 2009 there were about 25,000 such budgetary organizations at the central level and about 300,000 at the regional level, receiving financial resources from the state in exchange for the provision of public services (Government of the Russian Federation 2009).

Currently the amount of money that the state allocates to a budgetary organization depends on the amount of money it spent in the previous budget period (so-called cost budgeting) and not on performance evaluation (performance budgeting). Although financial reporting of the budgetary organizations has improved since the budget reform of the early 2000s, the overall efficiency and effectiveness of the quasi-autonomous organizations and their accountability remain low (Klyachko, Mau and Sinelnikov-Murylev 2010).

Since the middle of the 2000s the political leadership of the state has pushed for a complete overhaul of the system of the budgetary organizations in the spirit of performance-based management. This ambitious reform is currently still in progress with many questions being raised about the feasibility of its implementation (Diamond 2005; Timoshenko and Adhikari 2009). Indeed, while some elements of performance-based management have been successfully implemented at the level of ministries (Verheijen and Dobrolubova 2007), performance-related contracts are not an established feature of the relations between the ministries, services or agencies on the one hand and their quasi-autonomous organizations on the other.

# Regional and local government

## *Regional authorities*

The Russian transition of the 1990s entailed a change from a highly centralized state to the largest federative state in the world. Currently it is made up of 83 constituent members, known as subjects of the federation or regions each with a broad jurisdiction and its own legislative and executive authorities.

Since 1990 Russian regions have had several rounds of elections for regional parliaments. Two rounds of gubernatorial elections took place between 1996 and 2004, when they were substituted by a system of presidential appointees. In May 2012 the direct elections of governors were reinstated, however restrictions on who can run for governor raise doubts as to whether the elections will change the status quo (Golosov 2012; Orttung 2013, 469). Indeed in five regions that held such elections in 2012 the Kremlin managed to ensure victory for its preferred candidates. A similar trend was observed in the course of gubernatorial elections held in eight regions in September 2013.

In contrast to the benchmark principles of effective federalism (Weingast 1995), the formation of center–periphery relations in Russia in the 1990s was conducted 'without a map' and driven largely by transient political reasons (Shleifer and Treisman 2000). Consequently a system of 'federalism, Russian style' emerged with asymmetric powers enjoyed by formally equal constituent units, governed in a highly idiosyncratic and non-transparent manner by the centre. The regions' response to 'the delinquency, inconsistency and caprice of the central state' (Goode 2010) was chronic noncompliance with federal laws and the constitution. Regional confrontation with the federal centre was also fuelled by the interests of the local economic elites, on whose behalf regional administrations set up tariff and other barriers for inter-regional trade and allowed nonpayment of federal taxes (Sonin 2010) and preferential treatment of local firms (Slinko, Yakovlev and Zhuravskaya 2005). Overall, Moscow's legal and financial leverage over the territories was so weak that by the end of the 1990s the system of centrer–periphery relations was evaluated by most observers as a threat to the cohesion of Russia as a single political and economic space (Stoner-Weiss 2006, 4).

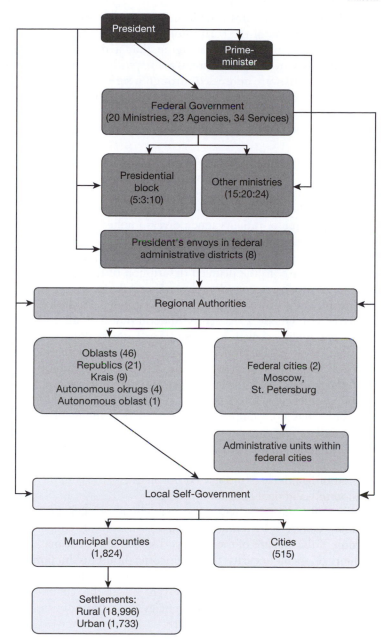

*Figure 8.1* Russia's structure of government, June 2012

Source: Data on local self-governments as of January 1, 2011 (Rossat 2011b); on the number of Ministries, Agencies and Services as of June 1, 2012 (Government of the Russian Federation 2012c)

Vladimir Putin addressed this issue in his election campaign in 2000, and made federal reform one of the cornerstones of his 'state building' political agenda. As of today, most observers agree that a new center–periphery balance, heavily tilted towards the centre, is achieved. The immediate problems of the federal relations were addressed through a series of political measures in the early 2000s. The most important of them were: reform of the system of presidential oversight in the regions (Goode 2010), reform of the Federation Council (Remington 2003) and eventual suspension of gubernatorial elections.

More fundamentally, the entire distribution of authority between the federal, regional and local governments was revisited. In June 2002 a special presidential commission, known as the Kozak commission, came up with a detailed list of public services and functions for regional authorities, which substituted a catalogue of rather vague powers implied by Articles 72–73 of the constitution. Most constitutional powers of the regions remained formally intact, but a shift from defining them broadly as, for example, 'co-ordination of issues of health care' to the detailed description of functions and services pertaining to health care, considerably reduced the scope of the regions' policy authority. Many powers that regions held jointly with the federal centre were simply gutted (Goode 2010). Also bilateral power-sharing treaties with 42 regions were abolished, with exceptions for Tatarstan and Chechnya. At the same time, some of the most demanding state responsibilities involving little or no policy authority, such as the bulk of social security obligations were assigned to the regions (see list below). Currently the distribution of authority between different levels of government is regulated by about 300 legal acts, and the process has not completely finished (Government of the Russian Federation 2012a). The main responsibilities of regional authorities can be summarized as follows:

- provision of health care (specialized hospitals);
- provision of vocational education;
- planning and financial provision for pre-school, primary and secondary education, delivered by municipalities;
- provision of the welfare of the elderly, disabled and orphans;
- provision of social security to low-income households, families with children, victims of political repressions, workers of the Second World War defense enterprises, and unemployed;
- environmental protection and emergencies prevention;
- regional roads and other infrastructure;
- intercity public transport;
- culture and sports events, regional libraries, and museums.

The redistribution of powers in favour of Moscow translated to an increase in the number of people working for the federal authorities in the regions. Between 2001 and 2011 the total number of civil service and auxiliary staff employed in the territorial offices of the federal government increased by a staggering 74 per cent, compared to the 31 per cent increase in the number employed in the central apparatus of the federal government in Moscow and the 29 per cent growth in the regional governments (Rosstat 2013). As far as the civil service per se is concerned, in 2011 the average ratio of federal to regional officials (the executive branch) in the regions was 2.5 to 1 (see Table 8.2).

The effort to delineate the scope of authority was coupled with the reform of intergovernmental fiscal relations. The reform had three major components. First of all, subnational governments were assigned new revenue sources. 'Own revenue' is made up of a few taxes, three for regional authorities and two for municipalities. The tax rates are set by the subnational governments and retained by them in full. In addition 'own revenue' is comprised of nontax revenues that include income from property and business operations, administrative fees and fines. Second, all subnational authorities retain a fixed and equal for all regions/municipalities proportion of some federal taxes raised in their jurisdictions. Hitherto the share of the federal taxes that went to subnational budgets was often set individually for each region/municipality in an ad hoc manner, and frequently renegotiated. Third, the system of redistribution of cash from richer to poorer regions via so-called equalization grants has been overhauled. In the 1990s the allocation of transfers was an important tool of Moscow's regional policy: cash transfers served to appease regions ill-disposed toward the centre (Treisman 1996, 1998a, 1998b) or to reward the loyal ones (Popov 2004). A new, formula-based, grant allocation system has been in place since 2001. The formula reflects the regions' capacity to raise sufficient resources to cover the costs of delivering public services in their jurisdiction (de Silva et al. 2009, 37) and covers the gap between the spending responsibilities and the region's fiscal strength.

Most commentators agree that these were important changes for the better. The current system is based on an adequate legal framework and ex-ante specified rules for tax sharing and transfer allocation. Therefore it is more stable and transparent, and ensures that the responsibilities of subnational authorities are sufficiently provided for (de Silva et al. 2009; Kraan et al. 2008; Zhuravskaya 2010). However, as a result of this reform lower governments also found themselves overall more dependent on the federal government than they had been before. Thus, while in 1998 the share of subnational revenue in the total state revenue was at its highest at 55 per cent, in 2010 it was only about 37 per cent (de Silva et al. 2009, 44; Strategy 2020, 776).

## *Local self-government*

The third substantive level of government in modern Russia is local self-government. Russia, compared to most European countries, has had a very short history of local self-government: introduced in late imperial Russia, it effectively did not exist during the Soviet period and was re-established in the

1990s. The 1993 Constitution legally separates local self-government from the state in a sense that it is seen more as a type of 'social organization' dealing with issues of 'local significance' through their own revenue sources rather than the lowest level of a vertically organized system of government. However, throughout the 1990s in sharp contrast to the proclaimed principles, both federal and regional authorities transferred numerous responsibilities onto local governments, including some of the state's social security obligations, pre-university education, some health care and recreation, and subsidies to loss-making enterprises. For the majority of the municipalities the spending obligations exceeded their fiscal capabilities. In the 1990s local taxes and other locally derived revenues made only up to 20 per cent of the budget of a typical Russian city with the rest coming from the taxes shared with higher governments and annually renegotiated transfers from regional budgets. What is more, regional governments used to reduce the transfers to those municipalities that increased their own revenue (Alekseev and Kurlyandskaya 2003). As research showed such fiscal arrangements provide local governments with no incentive to promote local growth and thus collect more tax and has a negative effect on the efficiency of public goods provision (Zhuravskaya 2000).

The reorganization of local self-government was part of a broader political and public administration reform of the 2000s. In accordance with the new law on local self-government, effective since 2006, the local government system is a two-tiered one. Currently there are about 23,000 municipalities: about 90 per cent of them are the lower tier rural and urban settlements, and the rest are the upper tier municipal counties (or *raions*) and cities (see Figure 8.1). As under the previous legislation, all new municipalities, except for those with a population of less than 100 people have popularly elected legislatures and elected heads, that is, the highest local official with executive powers.

Today local self-government can take on one of the three organizational forms depending on whether the local head is elected in popular elections or by the members of the local legislature. If the local head is popularly elected, they can be either the local chief executive or the chairperson of the local legislature. In the latter case, the administration is led by a non-elected manager (known as city manager, although this form of local self-government is practiced not only by cities but also by other municipalities). In those localities where the head of municipality is elected among and by the members of the local legislature, the role of local chief executive can be carried out only by a hired manager. The concrete form of the local government is stipulated by local charters and may be changed by the local population in a referendum-type event. According to the Ministry of Regional Development, in 2011 about 9,000 municipalities had a council-manager form of government (Reznikova 2011).

The concept of 'tier', not present in the previous legislation, was meant to help in allocating responsibilities and resources for municipalities in accordance with their size and other vital characteristics. The law specified the lists of 'issues of local significance' for settlements, cities and counties (see Table 8.4),

Table 8.4 Main responsibilities of local authorities (issues of local significance)

| Municipal counties and cities | Settlements |
| --- | --- |
| Delivery of pre-school, primary and secondary education and after-class activities using special-purpose funds from the regional budget | Delivery of utilities (electricity, gas, water, heating), street lighting and provision of waste collection |
| Provision of health care (general hospitals, organizations of preventive medicine, maternity care and ambulance) | Housing, including that for low-income households |
| Provision of utilities (electricity and gas) and waste disposal | Urban planning |
| Municipal police (as yet not fully implemented) | Parks, gardens and cemeteries |
| Recreation and culture, including libraries of local significance | Libraries of local significance |
| Roads of local significance (inter-municipal) | Public transport of local significance (intra-municipal) |
| Public transport of local significance (inter-municipal) | Basic fire protection |

and the number of items on those lists has more than doubled over time from about 20 to approximately 50 nowadays.

The law re-allocated several important responsibilities from the municipal to the regional level, at the same time permitting the delivery of the functions of a higher government by a lower government, on the condition that adequate financial resources are provided. Thus, for instance, today municipalities have no authority over the provision of pre-college schooling. The provision of this function, i.e. the overall organization, including specification of the service standards and funding, was moved to the competence of regional authorities. Yet, municipal counties and cities are charged with the delivery (as opposed to the provision) of pre-school, primary and secondary education using special-purpose funds from regional budgets. Local governments continue to bear full responsibility for housing and public utilities (communal services), an immense task considering the deplorable state of the public infrastructure in Russia and that these are highly monopolized and unreformed areas (Yegishyants 2012).

The expert community is agreed that the imposition of the lists of 'issues of local significance' from above has stretched the centre's steering of local governments to the extreme. Moreover, these lists are too large for most municipalities, and the two-tier structure of local self-government inadequately reflects the variety of localities in terms of their financial and other capabilities (Glazychev 2011). Furthermore, the problem of municipal revenue has persisted. The federal personal income tax has remained the main source of revenue for local authorities: in 2011 its proceeds were 1.5 times larger than locally levied taxes and nontax revenues (Government of the Russian Federation 2012a). In addition, unlike the federal government that managed to establish a reasonably transparent system of grant allocation to the regions, regional-to-municipal equalization policies are neither fair nor transparent (Kraan et al. 2008, 54). Regional governments have a major say in municipal finances not only by determining the parameters of the equalization policies, but also through executive decisions on investment programs and loans. As most local revenue still comes from higher governments that are prone to opportunism, nowadays local authorities face similar problems with incentives to foster economic growth and to effectively provide public goods as in the 1990s.

## Financing the system

For most of the 1990s public finance did not rest on a modern footing. Suffice to say that the Tax and Budget Codes, governing the revenue and expenditure sides of the public finance, were passed only in 1998. As far as taxation is concerned, in the 1990s tax policy was greatly affected by elite bargaining. As the revenue extracting strategy developed in Russia relied mostly on enterprises in the commodity export sector rather than households, business representatives sought and often succeeded in securing concessions on tax rates, tax exemptions or simply not paying taxes at all (Easter 2002). Powerful governors acted in a similar way, often in collusion with local large enterprises, consolidating their claim over local revenue sources. 'Across the government, tax policy was made and remade in an idiosyncratic and personalistic manner' (Easter 2006, 31), i.e. in negotiations between corporate and regional elites on the one hand and senior officials in Moscow on the other.

Since 2000, the focus has been on shifting fiscal authority in favor of the federal center, equidistant from powerful economic interests and regional leaders. Together with the measures aimed to tame 'oligarchs' and governors, major tax and budget reforms took place in the 2000s. The number of taxes was reduced, the rates were lowered and numerous tax breaks were abolished. Moreover today only federal authorities can levy a tax, regardless of whether it is federal, regional or local tax. Federal legislation establishes the tax base for all taxes and rates' ceilings. The exact parameters of subnational tax rates and tax exemptions are set by regional and local authorities. Revenues from most federal taxes, including corporate, excise on goods and some natural resource extraction, are shared between Moscow and subnational governments in fixed proportions. Revenues from one of the most productive taxes, personal income tax of 13 per cent, are split 70 to 30 per cent between regional and municipal authorities.

The revisited Budget Code sets out the process of preparation, adoption and execution of the consolidated budget of the state in great detail. The draft budget is prepared by the Ministry of Finance and must be agreed by key spending ministries before it is approved by the government and by both chambers of parliament and signed by the president after which it becomes a law. Budget laws are getting increasingly detailed. The 2012 budget law contained 4,289 pages compared to the 423-page-long 2002 and 8-page-long 1992 laws.

Although the Russian state does not have a uniform internal audit system, financial monitoring and reporting are quite well developed. Audit is carried out by the internal audit units within the ministries and by the Ministry of Finance, the Federal Treasury and the Federal Service of Financial and Budgetary Control. In addition, the Audit Chamber conducts an external audit of the entire central government and those regions that receive the majority of financing from the federal budget. External audit of subnational governments is also carried out by the regional audit chambers. The weakness of the system of external audit is the absence of strong procedures to follow up the findings of the auditors as the auditors themselves do not have the power to bring legal charges.

Detailed reports of federal budget execution, aggregated by the Ministry of Finance, are submitted to the government and parliament quarterly and annually. The lower chamber of parliament draws upon annual reports of the Ministry of Finance and the Audit Chamber to approve the budget execution. International organizations, such as OECD and World Bank regularly assessed the Russian budget process, and their recommendations have been largely incorporated by the Russian government (Kraan et al. 2008).

In the years since the 2008 economic crisis government expenditures have remained at the level of about 38 per cent of GDP, moreover this happened on occasion with a budget balance surplus rather than deficit (World Bank 2011, 3; 2012, 24). The federal budget increasingly relies on proceeds from oil and gas industries. If in 2009 oil and gas revenues made up 7.6 per cent of GDP, equal to two-fifths of the federal revenues, in 2011, they accounted for 10.4 per cent of GDP, equal to half of federal revenues (World Bank 2012, 25). The trend has remained the same in more recent years. Although high oil prices and the macroeconomic stabilization have been important to Russia's fiscal recovery, research also credits the contribution of the tax and budget reforms to financial stabilization (Appel 2008; de Silva et al. 2009; Easter 2006; Fritz 2007, 285–314; Jones Luong and Weinthal 2004; Kraan et al. 2008).

## Co-ordinating the system

Through the 2000s the dominant trend in relations between the organs of state power of all levels and branches was increasing centralization. At the top of the established 'power vertical' is the president, who not only has a major say on the content of public policies, but also ensures the co-ordinated functioning and interaction of all the organs of state power. The content of public policy is decided in policy communities around three decision-making centres: the president, legislature and the federal government. It is further developed as rules and regulations by the federal government and passed down the line to the departments of the federal ministries, their field offices and semi-autonomous organizations, and the regional and municipal governments. Since 2000 special presidential envoys have attuned the work of the regional authorities in line with the federal public policies and co-ordinated the work of the territorial branches of the federal ministries in several adjacent regions assigned to their jurisdiction (known as federal districts). The office of the president also plays an important role in co-ordinating and monitoring the performance of the regional authorities. In turn regional authorities have a major say in co-ordinating the work of municipal authorities within their jurisdictions. The expert community considers that political and financial centralization in Russia has reached the point where it becomes counter-productive as public managers at the subnational level face no incentives to innovate in the name of economic growth and adequate provision of public goods (Strategy 2020, 775).

The role of voluntary organizations in the system of governance has been largely marginal since the onset of post-communist Russia. One reason for that is that in a comparative perspective Russia stood out as a country with a particularly low level of civic participation (Howard 2002; Bartkowsky and Jasinska-Kania 2004). The most recent data from the World Values Survey Association (2009) shows that, excluding trade unions and consumer organizations, 96 per cent of Russians do not belong to any voluntary association. The number of voluntary groups is also relatively low, as of December 2011, there were about 224,000 registered civil society organizations. However, experts estimate that as many as 60 per cent of them are inactive (USAID 2012, 168). Furthermore, many of these non-government organizations (NGOs) such as consumer co-operatives, do not have goals of achieving political or social change and therefore do not actively seek participation in policy networks. Yet those civil society groups that engage in advocacy work and accept foreign financing were recently required to take on the stigmatizing label of 'foreign agent' (121-FZ of July 2012). This measure is widely seen as a tool of control that authorities wield selectively against targeted NGOs (Orttung 2013; Human Rights Watch 2013).

Second, the channels of intermediation between the state and voluntary organizations are poorly defined. Governmental control of the mass media considerably impedes the efforts of the NGOs for influencing the policy-making. The introduction of public chambers as a formal networking 'node' between interested voluntary groups and the executive agencies is seen, even by their own creators, as a veneer for genuine state–third sector co-operation (Putin 2012).

Unlike the situation in the 1990s when the key decision-making centres in Moscow and the regions were under the influence of business, particularly big companies (Fry 2002; Slinko, Yakovlev and Zhuravskaya 2005), today business's position in the governance networks is much less influential (Yakovlev 2006). The mode of business–state interaction also changed from direct, informal contacts and individual lobbying to co-ordinated actions via larger associations of business (Pyle 2011).

A new important line of interaction between business and the authorities is public–private partnerships (PPPs). Having been sprung into life by the deplorable state of the public infrastructure in Russia, the active development of public–private partnerships began in the middle of the 2000s. Although some successful projects have been carried out, such as the Western High-speed Diameter or the Orlovsky toll tunnel in St. Petersburg, observers note that the further development of PPPs in Russia is constrained, mainly by the absence of a general law on public–private partnerships (The Expert Institute 2010). Concessions remain the most popular form of PPP projects in Russia, enabled by the passage of the appropriate law in 2005. However, the law is vague with regards to the relationship between the state and the private party. It also lacks the provision to protect the rights of the concessionaire and allows the pledging of the concession's assets as security for bank loans only after the projects have been commissioned and with the explicit consent of the grantor. Interestingly, regional authorities seem to be ahead of the federal government on the issue: as of June 2012, 59 of them passed acts regulating PPPs in their jurisdictions. Practitioners find regional acts, like for instance the pioneering law of Saint-Petersburg, to be more flexible regarding the types of PPPs relationships, tender process and support from the authorities (Schwartz and Ivanov 2008).

## Managing the system

The overall template for managing the Russian administrative system represents a mix of the Weberian rational-legal model and New Public Management (NPM) initiatives. On the one hand, an array of measures has been introduced in the name of making the government more client-oriented and efficient. It puts much emphasis on performance-based management and budgeting. On the other hand there has been a move to regulate administrative behavior through clearly defined job descriptions, standards of conduct for public officials and administrative procedures. While budget reform was grounded more on performance principles, civil service reform was less reflective of the NPM ideas such as 'let the managers manage'. A distinct strand of the public administration reform called 'administrative reform' blends both approaches. The adoption of explicit standards and targets for the quality of government services (NPM) is supported by a rational-legal approach through the development of administrative regulations detailing how services are to be provided.

Russia is one of a few post-communist countries where the introduction of performance-based public management systems is at a, relatively, advanced stage (Verheijen and Dobrolubova 2007, World Bank 2011). However, it is still work in progress as neither a comprehensive system of performance indicators nor powerful incentive systems embracing individuals in all public administration organizations has been institutionalized. The performance of individual regional governments is assessed in its entirety on an annual basis. This is done against economic and social indicators, the number of which fluctuated from about 40 in 2007 to almost 300 in 2009 and to 11 in 2012 (Kulikov 2012; Vedomosti 2012d). A system of individual performance indicators is still under-developed, as 'evaluation tools are highly formal and disconnected from institutional performance management' (World Bank 2011, ix). An initiative to introduce key performance indicators for officials is currently under way, but only for the senior federal bureaucracy (Government of the Russian Federation 2012b; Vedomosti 2012e).

Contracting out, another NPM hallmark method, has been applied in Russia on a small scale so far, mostly in social services (Cook and Vinogradova 2006; USAID 2012, 172; Zobnin 2011) and also with respect to the noncore activities in other public services. For instance state education organizations tend to contract out such supporting services as catering, cleaning, security and accounting (Gadzhieva 2012). The limited use of contracting out (including its more radical vintage – customer choice method of service delivery or vouchers) could be due to the weak managerial autonomy experienced by Russian public administration organizations. Autonomy is expected to increase with the progress of budgeting reform.

Public procurement of goods and services for the needs of public administration is perhaps an area where the approach of introducing private sector practices in public administration is most evident. Since 2006 the law has required that most goods, services and works by the government and budgetary organizations be purchased through open competitive tendering and auctioning. The reality is, however, far from the legal ideal. According to the Audit Chamber, 70 per cent of large contracts have been concluded with a single supplier/provider without competition (Kotova 2012), and 17 to 20 per cent of all funds spent on public procurement is embezzled (Lutova 2013; Zakharov and Popov 2010).

## Accountability, secrecy and openness

The lack of transparency and accountability on the part of government organizations has been noted by many observers. Russia's rank on voice and accountability – one of the World Banks' Worldwide Governance Indicators measuring governments' preparedness to be externally accountable through citizen feedback, democratic institutions, and a competitive press has considerably deteriorated in the last 15 years (see Figure 8.2).

Until recently Russia lacked basic formal prerequisite for openness such as a freedom of information act (FOI). Having been in the legislative pipeline since 2002, Russia's first FOI Act was finally adopted in 2009. The law has two important elements. First of all, it regulates in detail what information government organizations should make publicly available by, for instance,

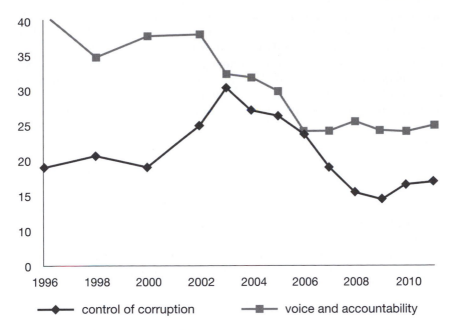

*Figure 8.2* Russia: Voice, accountability and control of corruption (as per centile rank, 0–100)

Source: Kauffman, Kraay and Mastruzzi 2010; The Worldwide Governance Indicators Project 2012

publishing it in the mass media, including the Internet, or allowing citizens to attend government meetings. Second, it regulates the practical aspects of the realization of the right to information about the activity of the state/ municipal organ. Although on paper the FOI Act (8-FZ of February 2009) marks a radical step toward greater public service transparency, the implementation of the law remains problematical. Recent monitoring showed that, on average, both federal and regional governments publish on their websites only about half of the information that is required by the FOI Act (Freedom of Information Foundation 2012a, 2012b). The effective implementation of the law has also been hampered by the lack of clarity on the notion of 'information about the activity of the state/municipal organ of power'. Often officials reject information requests and courts uphold such decisions on the grounds that the required information does not relate to the activities of a government body and is therefore not subject to the FOI law. The Constitutional Court consistently refuses to clarify the notion in question – one of the most recent instances was on June 19, 2012 (Constitutional Court 2012) – therefore permitting practices restricting the right of access to information.

The development of administrative law allowing citizens to seek redress against the state has proceeded at a slow pace. Although the Russian constitution lists the right to address the state by filing a request, complaint or suggestion, among the fundamental rights of Russian citizens (Article 33), the first legislation regulating complaints procedure was passed only in 2006 (59-FZ). The law covers mostly complaints over illegal treatment of citizens by the state. It does not provide for an independent institution that may review and adjudicate decisions made by public organizations, with exceptions for Human Rights and the Children's Ombudsmen. These two attributes make 59-FZ a rather weak legal instrument for improving the accountability of public officials.

A mechanism allowing citizens to seek redress against the state regarding poor provision of public services was adopted by the federal government in August 2012. As all governmental services are now codified in terms of basic quality standards and procedures regulating their delivery (such as deadlines, costs and documents required), this provides a solid foundation for the effective challenge of the authorities by citizens and hence improved bureaucratic accountability.

Hope for improved transparency and accountability also comes from the success of e-government in Russia. Having advanced 32 positions in the United Nations e-government world ranking from 2010 to 2012, Russia is currently the Eastern European leader and is above such western European countries as Italy or Ireland (UN 2012, 30). One of the most notable projects of e-government is the Internet portal of public services (www.gosuslugi.ru), which provides a single point of access to all references on government services and allows citizens and organizations to receive services and to file complaints electronically. The proliferation of this type of interaction between citizens and officials may help to overcome the pervasiveness of informal rules and personal contacts that for many years was the modus operandi of Russia's public bureaucracy (Jakobson 2001; Barabashev and Straussman 2007).

## Democracy and the administrative system

A clear consensus among observers is that over the past decade democracy in Russia has deteriorated. It has been classified as 'not free' (since 2005) and as a consolidated authoritarian regime (since 2009) by Freedom House (Orttung 2013). The fundamental feature of authoritarianism is the limited number of political players. Indeed Vladimir Putin managed to wrest authority away from oligarchs, regional leaders and parliament, and to emasculate the mass media and civil society. These measures resulted in a monopoly of power in the hands of the president that may have both advantages and disadvantages for state capacity and the quality of government. It is argued that systems with a limited number of veto players are capable of making quick policy changes compared to systems with many veto players who tend to limit the set of feasible policy changes, rendering governments less decisive (Tsebelis 2002). They can also implement their decisions effectively due to the advantages of their hierarchical monitoring system (Back and Hadenius 2008, Ertman 1997). Indeed, Russia's considerable improvement in tax administration, budget process, land property rights, judiciary and center–periphery relations and some improvement in the state's fiscal and other infrastructural capacities since 2000 cannot be gainsaid (Appel 2008; Aslund 2004; Colton and Holmes 2006; Taylor 2011).

On the other hand, the comparative advantages of autocracies are said to be unsustainable. This happens for a number of reasons, fundamental to which are the following. First, a wider account of the relationship between democracy and high quality of government holds that the absence of political competition breaks the link between the preferences of citizens and the policy output of the government. Therefore authoritarian 'steering from above' mechanisms as in Russia are 'standing on a perilously narrow base, out of touch with society and hence in danger of making bad decisions' (Shevtsova 2004, 74). Second, and more important, when power is concentrated in one pair of hands, there is a danger that the rules of the game are manipulated to the advantage of the ruler and her associates (North 1990). Thus assessing the current governance system created in Russia, Ekaterina Zhuravskaya notes that its sustainability rests upon 'the utopian assumption of honesty and self-limitation of federal authorities' (2010, 77).

It is interesting to note evidence suggesting that Russia's ruling elite understands some of these limitations of the government system it has built. In his 2012 election manifesto Vladimir Putin outlined a number of initiatives aiming to bridge the preferences of citizens and government policies. One such initiative, which is similar to the United Kingdom's e-petitions, presupposes a mechanism by which the government and parliament are obliged to consider a citizens' initiative that collects 100,000 or more signatures (Putin 2012). Another initiative is concerned with the re-launch of public chambers as a platform for intermediation between the state, business and the third sector. In addition to these measures, that are all located outside the realm of competitive politics, the authorities also undertook steps that were meant to improve the competitiveness of Russian politics. First, the law on political parties (28-FZ of April 2012) made it considerably easier for Russian citizens to set up political parties. As the law reduced the minimal number of members from 40,000 to 500 the number of officially registered political parties increased from 7 in April 2012 to 72 in August 2013 (The Ministry of Justice 2013). However, with the next parliamentary and presidential elections not due until December 2016 and March 2018, the practical effect of this change will likely be minimal. Second, the popular elections of regional governors were restored, and today 12 subjects of the federation, including Moscow city, have popularly elected heads with about a further 40 elections to be held in 2014–2015. However, as it was predicted by experts, the so-called 'municipal filter' – a feature of the law that stipulates that any candidate wishing to run for governor has to first ensure the endorsement of 5 to 10 per cent of the region's municipal lawmakers (each region establishes its own threshold), who are dependent on both the ruling United Russia party and the sitting governors – effectively allowed the incumbent authorities to manipulate the contest.

The nature of the political regime also affects the quality of Russia's bureaucracy. The authoritarianism built by Putin and Medvedev is an 'electoral authoritarianism' that presupposes the considerable involvement of public bureaucracy in elections to ensure the 'right' election outcome (Golosov 2011; Remington 2008). Consequently, within the public administration 'there are employees whose career prospects depend directly on the results of the elections' (Golosov 2011, 637). This is clearly in contradiction to the key structural prerequisite for a welfare-enhancing bureaucracy to place bureaucrats 'above politics' by creating a set of incentives that are different to those of politicians (Knott and Miller 2008; Miller 2000). Instead of separating the incentives of politicians and bureaucrats electoral authoritarianism aligns them, therefore inhibiting positive qualities of public bureaucracy, such as for instance impartiality in the implementation of the law (Rothstein and Teorell 2008).

Another important feature of the recent political regime that may have had a negative impact on the quality of bureaucracy is 'a Russian roulette' pattern of gubernatorial appointments (Petrov 2010). The environment of high uncertainty it had created was clearly conducive to the shortening of the time-horizons of individual governors, which is found to have a negative impact on the success of the institutionalization of politically neutral bureaucracies (Lapuente and Nistotskaya 2009).

## Further developments and issues with the system

Examination of the developments in Russia's public administration since 2000 has clearly shown that there has been a concerted drive to reform it. What is less clear is the extent to which the reform undertaken is likely to succeed. Both research and practitioners' accounts demonstrate that there is real progress in some important areas. For example, in terms of the budgetary process, intergovernmental transfers and public procurement, making the processes more rule-based and public has certainly made them less susceptible to abuse. Considerable developments have also taken place in the area of access to public documents and administrative redress.

While reform initiatives in public administration have led to some modest improvement in the infrastructural state capacity – the ability of the state 'to implement logistically political decisions throughout the realm' (Mann 1986, 113) – there is little evidence to suggest that there has been improvement in the quality of government and the provision of public goods. Russia today is no safer than in the past, the threat from terrorism and organized crime remains unabated (Taylor 2011, 82–94) and the military is 'poorly trained, ill-equipped and undisciplined' (Rummer and Wallander 2003, 63). There is a lack of improvement in public health and property rights protection (McFaul and Stoner-Weiss 2008; Taylor 2011, 102–107), nor does there appear to have been improvement in the level of corruption (Figure 8.2).

The state of the public infrastructure remains poor as corroborated by the recent admission by the Russian authorities that only half of Russia's roads satisfy government standards (Prosecutor General's Office 2012). Of course, one can point to the substantial economic growth of the recent past as an encompassing measure of the improved well-being of Russians and therefore the improved quality of government. However research shows that economic growth is unlikely to be a consequence of the Kremlin's steering (McFaul and Stoner-Weiss 2008; Robinson 2011).

There are competing explanations as to why the output of government has not improved despite a reform agenda that appears to have targeted the key areas for change. It may be argued that the full impact of the individual reforms has not yet had sufficient time to make itself apparent. In effect the reform has not yet 'kicked in'. Alternatively the lack of real progress may be due to an incorrect sequencing of New Public Management and the rational-legal approaches to public administration reform as it has long been argued that the NPM tools work only in countries where basic attributes of a Weberian bureaucracy are irreversibly institutionalized (Manin and Parison 2004, 54; Pierre and Rothstein 2011; Schick 1998).

In the most extensive study to date, Brian Taylor (2011) attributes Russia's low state capacity/low quality of government trap to the interplay between structural (Leninist legacy and hydrocarbon dependence) and organizational factors (patrimonial bureaucracy, the lack of strong monitoring of the state by citizens and the lack of organizational mission that encourages public-interested behavior on the part of the state officials).

Perhaps even more profound is the suggestion that the ultimate problem relates to the character of the current political regime, and a contradiction between the regime-strengthening and state capacity-building elements of Russia's *etatization* project (Hashim 2005; Taylor 2011). As part of a perennial debate about regime type and human well-being, the answer to this question remains largely open. However, current scholarly debate on Russia seems to link the hope for an improvement in the quality of Russia's government with the evolution of its political regime into a fully-fledged democracy rather than a developmental dictatorship (Taylor 2011; Shevtsova 2004; Zhuravskaya 2010).

## Note

1   In addition to this, there are also local self-governments that are formally separated from the state but in reality act within the scope of power prescribed to them by the higher levels of authority.

## References

Alekseev, M. and Kurlyandskaya, G. (2003) 'Fiscal Federalism and Incentives in a Russian Region', *Journal of Comparative Economics*, 31: 20–33.

Appel, H. (2008) 'Is It Putin or Is It Oil? Explaining Russia's Fiscal Recovery', *Post-Soviet Affairs*, 24: 301–323.

Aslund, A. (2004) 'Russia's Economic Transformation under Putin', *Eurasian Geography and Economics*, 45: 397–420.

Back, H. and Hadenius, A. (2008) 'Democracy and State Capacity: Exploring a J-Shaped Relationship', *Governance*, 21: 1–24.

Barabashev, A. and Straussman, J. D. (2007) 'Public Service Reform in Russia 1991–2006', *Public Administration Review*, 67: 373–382.

Bartkowsky, J. and Jasinska-Kania, A. (2004) 'Voluntary Organizations and the Development of Civil Society', in Arts, W. and Halman L. (Eds.) *European Values at the Turn of the Millennium*, Leiden: Brill, pp. 109–137.

Bocharova, S. and Gallay, A. (2013) 'What is Behind the Increased Legislative Activity of the State Duma?', *Vedomosti*, August 28 (in Russian). Online, available at: www.vedomosti.ru/politics/news/15668711/gosduma-vozvraschaetsya-k-perelomnoj-rabote?full#cut (accessed September 17, 2013).

Brym, R. and Gimpelson, V. (2004) 'The Size, Composition and Dynamics of the Russian State Bureaucracy in the 1990s', *Slavic Review*, 63: 90–112.

Colton T. J. and Holmes S. (Eds.) (2006) *The State After Communism: Governance in the New Russia*, Lanham: Rowman and Littlefield.

Colton, T. J. (2012) 'Medvedev – Former President Who Was Never Really President', Interview. Online, available at: http://valdaiclub.com/politics/42260.html (accessed September 17, 2012).

Constitutional Court of the Russian Federation (2012) Notion N 1245-O-P of June 19 (in Russian). Online, available at: http://base.garant.ru/70203746 (accessed August 30, 2012).

Cook, L. J. and Vinogradova, E. (2006) 'NGOs and Social Policy-Making in Russia's Regions', in *Problems of Postcommunism*, 53: 59–77.

De Silva, M. O., Kurlyandskaya, G., Andreeva E. and Golovanova, N. (2009) *Intergovernmental Reforms in the Russian Federation: One Step Forward, Two Steps Back?* Washington DC: The International Bank for Reconstruction and Development and The World Bank.

Diamond, J. (2005) 'Reforming the Russian Budget System: A Move to More Devolved Budget Management?' *International Monetary Fund Working Paper No. 05/104*. Online, available at: www.imf.org/external/pubs/ft/wp/2005/wp05104.pdf (accessed September 17, 2012).

Easter, G. (2002) 'Politics of Revenue Extraction in Post-Communist States: Poland and Russia Compared', *Politics and Society*, 30: 599–627.

Easter, G. (2006) 'Building Fiscal Capacity' in Colton, T. J. and Holmes, S. (Eds.) *The State After Communism: Governance in the New Russia*. Lanham: Rowman and Littlefield, pp. 21–52.

Ertman, T. (1997) *Birth of Leviathan: Building States and Regimes in Medieval and Early Modern Europe*, Cambridge: Cambridge University Press.

The Expert Institute (2010) 'Barriers for the Development of Public-Private Partnerships in Russia' (in Russian), Moscow: NPF the Expert Institute. Online, available at: http://pppinrussia.ru/userfiles/upload/files/Analitika/ppp-Results_24_11_2010_Fin_1.pdf (accessed August 23, 2012).

Federal Civil Defense and Emergency Management Ministry of the Russian Federation (2010) Order No. 488, 'The List of the Federal State Agencies under the Ministry of the Russian Federation for Civil Defense and Emergency Management' (in

Russian). Online, available at: www.mchs.gov.ru/ministry/?SECTION_ID=5791 (accessed July 15, 2012).

Federal Portal of Managerial Cadres (2012) 'The Analysis of the Use of Cadres Reserves in the Regions of the Russian Federation' (in Russian). Online, available at: www.rezerv.gov.ru/GovService.aspx?id=626&t=34 (accessed September 17, 2012).

Freedom of Information Foundation (2012a) 'Monitoring 2012: Informational Openness Rating for Federal Executive Government Bodies'. Online, available at: www.svobodainfo.org/en/print/1639 (accessed August 26, 2013).

Freedom of Information Foundation (2012b) 'The Results of the Monitoring of the Official Websites of Russia's Regional Authorities, Executive Branch' (in Russian). Online, available at: www.svobodainfo.org/en/print/1928 (accessed August 26, 2013).

Fritz, V. (2007) *State-Building: A Comparative Study of Ukraine, Lithuania, Belarus and Russia*, Budapest: Central European University Press.

Fry, T. (2002) 'Capture or Exchange? Business Lobbying in Russia', *Europa-Asia Studies*, 54: 1017–1036.

Gadzhieva, L. (2012) 'Transferring Non-Core Functions to External Contractors by the Educational Institutions of Perm as a Means of Their Performance Improvement' (in Russian), *Public Administration Issues*, 2: 174–182.

Glazycev, V. (2011) *Local Self-Governance: The Scene in the Middle of 2011* (in Russian). Online, available at: http://2020strategy.ru/g12/documents/32581823.html (accessed September 17, 2012).

Golosov, G. (2004) *Political Parties in the Regions of Russia: Democracy Unclaimed*, Boulder, CO: Lynne Reinner.

Golosov, G. (2011) 'The Regional Roots of Electoral Authoritarianism in Russia', *Europe-Asia Studies*, 63: 623–639.

Golosov, G. (2012) 'Dilemmas of an Authoritarian Political Reform'. Online, available at: www.polit.ru/article/2012/05/18/elect (accessed June 11, 2012).

Goode, P. (2010) 'The Fall and Rise of Regionalism?' *Journal of Communist Studies and Transition Politics*, 26: 233–256.

Gorodetsky, D. (2012) 'Key Indicator of the Country's Health' (in Russian), *Vedomosti*, July 31. Online, available at: www.vedomosti.ru/career/news/2334860/klyuchevoj_pokazatel_zdorovya_strany (accessed July 31, 2012).

Government of the Russian Federation (2009) 'Explanatory Note to the Draft of the federal law 83-fz' (in russian). online, available at: http://asozd2.duma.gov.ru/MAIN.NSF/(VIEWDOC)?OPENAGENT&WORK/DZ.NSF/BYID&EB91E2ECCDE54840C325769C00505AE5 (accessed September 17, 2012).

Government of the Russian Federation (2012a) 'Verbatim Report of the Meeting the Federal Government on the Realization of the Targets Set by Vladimir Putin in His Election Articles as a Candidate for the Post of Russian President' (in Russian), March 22. Online, available at: http://government.ru/docs/18490/ (accessed August 31, 2012).

Government of the Russian Federation (2012b) 'Verbatim Report of the Meeting of the Advisory Board of the Agency of the Strategic Initiative Chaired by the Prime-Minister Vladimir Putin' (in Russian), February 3. Online, available at: http://government.ru/docs/17986/ (accessed July 3, 2012).

Government of the Russian Federation (2012c), 'The Structure of the Government' (in Russian). Online, available at: http://government.ru/ministries (accessed June 12, 2012).

Gregory, P. (1990) *Restructuring the Soviet Economic Bureaucracy*, Cambridge: Cambridge University Press.

Greve, C., Flinders, M., and van Thiel, S. (1999) 'Quangos – What's in a Name? Defining Quangos from a Comparative Perspective', *Governance*, 12: 129–146.

Guriev, S. and Rachinsky, A. (2005) 'The Role of Oligarchs in Russian Capitalism', *The Journal of Economic Perspectives*, 19: 131–150.

Guriev, S. and Tsyvinski, A. (2012) 'A High-Yield Personal Investment' (in Russian), *Vedomosti*, April 10. Online, available at: www.vedomosti.ru/opinion/news/1620707/cena_vysshego_obrazovaniya (accessed July 31, 2012).

Hashim, M. S. (2005) 'Putin's Etatization Project and Limits to Democratic Reforms in Russia', *Communist and Post-Communist Studies*, 38: 25–48.

Howard, M. (2002) 'Postcommunist Civil Society in Comparative Perspective', *Demokratizatsiya*, 10: 285–305

Human Rights Watch (2013) World Report 2013: Russia. Online, available at: www.hrw.org/world-report/2013/country-chapters/russia (accessed August 23, 2013).

Huskey, E. and Obolonsky, A. (2003) 'The Struggle to Reform Russia's Bureaucracy', *Problems of Post-Communism*, 50: 22–33.

Huskey, E. (2004) 'Nomenklatura Lite? The Cadres Reserve in Russian Public Administration', *Problems of Post-Communism*, 51: 30–39.

Jakobson, L. (2001) 'Public Management in Russia: Changes and Inertia', *International Public Management Journal*, 4: 27–48.

Jones Luong, P. and Weinthal, E. (2004) 'Contra Coercion: Russian Tax Reform, Exogenous Shocks, and Negotiated Institutional Change', *American Political Science Review*, 98: 139–152.

Kauffman, D., Kraay, A. and Mastruzzi, M. (2010) 'The Worldwide Governance Indicators: Methodology and Analytical Issues', *The World Bank Policy Research Working Paper 5430*. Online, available at: http://papers.ssrn.com/sol3/papers.cfm?abstract_id=1682130 (accessed July 3, 2012).

Klyachko, T., Mau, V. and Sinelnikov-Murylev, S. (2010) 'On the Budgetary Organizations Reform', in Gaidar, E., Glavatskaya, N., Rogov, K., Sinelnikov-Murylev, S., Starodubrovsky, V. and L. Freinkman (Eds.) *Economy in Transition. Collection of Published Works, 2003–2009*, Moscow: Delo, pp. 157–174.

Knott, J. K. and Miller, G. J. (2008) 'When Ambition Checks Ambition Bureaucratic Trustees and the Separation of Powers', *The American Review of Public Administration*, 38: 387–411.

Kotova, J. (2012) 'Stepashin: 1 Trillion Roubles a Year Embezzled from State Procurement' (in Russian), *Vedomosti*, 14 November. Online, available at: www.vedomosti.ru/politics/news/6076361/stepashin (accessed August 23, 2013).

Kraan, D. J., Bergvall, D., Hawkesworth, I., Kostyleva, V. and Witt, M. (2008) 'Budgeting in Russia', *OECD Journal of Budgeting*, 8: 1–58.

Kulikov, S. (2012) 'The Efficiency Scale Is Cut Down' (in Russian), *Nezavisimaja Gazeta*, July 11. Online, available at: www.ng.ru/economics/2012–07–11/1_scale.html (accessed August 28, 2012).

Lapuente, V. and Nistotskaya, M. (2009) 'To The Short-Sighted Victor Belong The Spoils: Politics and Merit Adoption in Comparative Perspective', *Governance*, 22: 431–458.

Lehmbruch, B. (2012) 'It Takes Two to Quango: Post-Soviet Fiscal Relations, Political Entrepreneurship and Agencification from Below', *International Institute for Social*

*Studies, Working paper 538*. Online, available at: http://repub.eur.nl/res/pub/32156/wp538.pdf (accessed July 15, 2012).

Lutova, M. (2013) 'The Audit Chamber: 70% of All Large State Procurement Contracts Executed in Contravention to the Law' (in Russian), *Vedomosti*, 16 August. Online, available at: www.vedomosti.ru/finance/news/15277091/zakupki-v-seroj-zone (accessed September 17, 2013).

McFaul, M. and Stoner-Weiss, K. (2008) 'The Myth of Authoritarian Model: How Putin's Crackdown Holds Russia Back', *Foreign Affairs*, 87: 68–84.

Manin, N. and Parison, N. (2004) *International Public Administration Reform: Implications for the Russian Federation*, Washington, DC: The World Bank.

Mann, M. (1986) 'The Autonomous Power of the State: Its Origins, Mechanisms, and Results', in Hall, J. A. (Ed.) *States in History*, Oxford: Basil Blackwell, pp. 109–136.

Meyer-Sahling, J.-H. (2011) 'The Durability of EU Civil Service Policy in Central and Eastern Europe After Accession', *Governance*, 24: 231–260.

Miller, G. (2000) 'Above Politics: Credible Commitment and Efficiency in the Design of Public Agencies', *Journal of Public Administration Research and Theory*, 10: 289–327.

The Ministry of Justice of the Russian Federation (2013) 'The List of Registered Political Parties (as of August 23, 2013)'. Online, available at: http://minjust.ru/nko/gosreg/partii/spisok (accessed August 23, 2013).

Nistotskaya, M. (2009) 'Organizational Design of Welfare-Enhancing Public Bureaucracy: A Comparative Analysis of Russia's Regions', Ph.D. Dissertation, Budapest: Central European University. Online, available at: http://web.ceu.hu/polsci/dissertations/Marina_Nistotskaya.pdf (accessed September 17, 2012).

North, D. C. (1990) *Institutions, Institutional Change and Performance*, Cambridge: Cambridge University Press.

Orttung, R. (2013) *Nations in Transit: Russia*, Freedom House. Online, available at: www.freedomhouse.org/sites/default/files/NIT13_Russia_1stProof.pdf (accessed September 17, 2013).

Petrov, N. (2010) 'Gubernatorial Roulette', *The Moscow Times*. Online, available at: www.themoscowtimes.com/opinion/article/gubernatorial-roulette/397332.html (accessed September 5, 2011).

Pierre, J. and Rothstein, B. (2011) 'Reinventing Weber: The Role of Institutions in Creating Social Trust', in Christensen T. and Laegreid, P. (Eds.) *The Ashgate Research Companion to New Public Management*, Burlington: Ashgate Publishing Limited, pp. 405–416.

Popov, V. (2004) 'Fiscal Federalism in Russia: Rules Versus Electoral Politics', *Comparative Economic Studies*, 44: 515–541.

Prosecutor General's Office (2012) 'The Prosecutor General's Office Has Taken Steps to Ensure the Rule of Law in the Field of Road Construction' (in Russian). Online, available at: http://genproc.gov.ru/news/news-77590/ (accessed September 13, 2012).

Putin, V. (2012) 'Democracy and the Quality of the State' (in Russian), *Kommersant*, 20/_ (4805), February 6. Online, available at: www.kommersant.ru/doc/1866753 (accessed September 17, 2010).

Pyle, W. (2011) 'Organized Business, Political Competition, and Property Rights: Evidence from the Russian Federation', *The Journal of Law, Economics and Organization*, 27: 2–31.

Remington, T. F. (2003) 'Majorities without Mandates: The Russian Federation Council Since 2000', *Europa-Asia Studies*, 55: 667–691.

Remington, T. F. (2006) 'Presidential Support in the Russian State Duma', *Legislative Studies Quarterly*, 31: 5–32.

Remington, T. F. (2008) 'Patronage and the Party of Power: President-Parliament Relations Under Vladimir Putin', *Europa-Asia Studies*, 60: 959–987.

Reznikova, A. (2011) 'The Proliferation of City Managers Has Come to an End' (in Russian), *RBK Daily*, July 25. Online, available at: www.rbcdaily.ru/2011/07/25/focus/562949980767169 (accessed July 26, 2012).

Robinson, N. (2011) 'Political Barriers to Economic Development in Russia: Obstacles to Modernization under Yeltsin and Putin', *International Journal of Development Issues*, 10: 5–9.

Rosstat, Russian Federation Federal State Statistics Service (2009a) 'Civil Service Personnel of the Federal Level of Authority by Gender, Categories and Ranks of Posts, and Branches of Authority as of October 1, 2009' (in Russian). Online, available at: www.gks.ru/free_doc/2009/gos-kadr/f3.xls (accessed August 23, 2013).

Rosstat, Russian Federation Federal State Statistics Service (2009b) 'Civil Service Personnel of the Regional Level of Authority by Gender, Categories and Rank of Post, and Branches of Authority as of October 1, 2009' (in Russian). Online, available at: www.gks.ru/free_doc/2009/gos-kadr/f4.xls (accessed September 17, 2012).

Rosstat, Russian Federation Federal State Statistics Service (2009c) 'Civil Service Personnel of the Federal Level of Authority by Level of Education, Categories and Rank of the Post and Branches of Authority as of October 1, 2009' (in Russian), Moscow: Rosstat.

Rosstat, Russian Federation Federal State Statistics Service (2009d) 'Civil Service Personnel of the Regional Level of Authority by Level of Education, Categories and Rank of the Post and Branches of Authority as of October 1, 2009' (in Russian), Moscow: Rosstat.

Rosstat, Russian Federation Federal State Statistics Service (2011a) 'The Number of Civil Servants and Municipal Servants by Gender, Branches and Levels of Authority' (in Russian). Online, available at: www.gks.ru/free_doc/2011/gos-kadr/tab1.htm (accessed August 23, 2013).

Rosstat, Russian Federation Federal State Statistics Service (2011b) 'The Number and Types of Municipalities in the Subjects of the Russian Federation' (in Russian). Online, available at: www.gks.ru/free_doc/new_site/bd_munst/1-adm_2011.xls (accessed August 23, 2013).

Rosstat, Russian Federation Federal State Statistics Service (2012) 'On the Number of the Civil Service Personnel of the Federal Government (the Central Offices of the Ministries, Agencies and Services) in 2011' (in Russian). Online, available at: www.gks.ru/bgd/free/b04_03/IssWWW.exe/Stg/d03/rab_god2011.htm (accessed July 15, 2012).

Rosstat, Russian Federation Federal State Statistics Service (2013) 'The Total Number of Employed in the Organizations of Federal, Regional and Local Governments, Updated 13.04.2013' (in Russian). Online, available at: www.gks.ru/free_doc/new_site/gosudar/chisl_vetv.xls (accessed August 23, 2013).

Rothstein, B. and Teorel, J. (2008) 'What Is Quality of Government? A Theory of Impartial Government Institutions', *Governance*, 21: 165–190.

Rummer, E. and Wallander, C. (2003) 'Russia: Power in Weakness?' *The Washington Quarterly*, 27: 57–73.

Sakwa, R. (2008) *Russian Politics and Society*, London: Routledge.

Schick, A. (1998) 'Why Most Developing Countries Should Not Try New Zealand's Reforms', *World Bank Research Observer*, 13: 23–31.

Schwartz, M. and Ivanov, I. (2008) 'Russian Federation: Public Private Partnerships in Russia: An Overview'. Online, available at: www.mondaq.com/article.asp?articleid=70344 (accessed August 23, 2012).

Shevtsova, L. (2004) 'The Limits of Bureaucratic Authoritarianism', *Journal of Democracy*, 15: 67–77.

Shleifer, A. and Treisman, D. (2000) *Without a Map: Political Tactics and Economic Reform in Russia*, Cambridge: Cambridge University Press.

Slinko, I., Yakovlev E. and Zhuravskaya, E. (2005) 'Laws for Sale: Evidence from Russia', *American Law and Economics Review*, 7: 284–318.

Solnik, S. (1998) *Stealing the State: Control and Collapse in Soviet Institutions*, Cambridge Mass.: Harvard University Press.

Sonin, K. (2010) 'Provincial Protectionism', *Journal of Comparative Economics*, 38: 111–122.

Stoner-Weiss, K. (2006) *Resisting the State: Reform and Retrenchment in Post-Soviet Russia*, Cambridge: Cambridge University Press.

Strategy (2020) 'New Growth Model – New Social Policy, Final Report by the Expert Group on the Problems of the Socio-Economic Development of Russia through 2020' (in Russian). Online, available at: http://2020strategy.ru/data/2012/03/14/1214585998/1itog.pdf (accessed June 11, 2012).

Tafel, H. L. (2010) 'Regime Change and the Federal Gamble: Negotiating Federal Institutions in Brazil, Russia, South Africa, and Spain', *Publius: The Journal of Federalism*, 41: 257–285.

Taylor, B. D. (2011) *State Building in Putin's Russia: Policing and Coercion after Communism*, Cambridge: Cambridge University Press.

Timoshenko, K. and Adhikari, P. (2009) 'Exploring Russian Central Government Accounting in Its Context', *Journal of Accounting and Organizational Changes*, 5: 490–513.

Tompson, W. (2007) 'From 'Clientelism' to a 'Client-centered Orientation'? The Challenge of Public Administration Reform in Russia', *OECD Working Paper No. 536 ECO/WKP(2006)64*. Online, available at: http://eprints.bbk.ac.uk/505/1/ECO-WKP%282006%2964.pdf (accessed July 12, 2012).

Treisman, D. (1996) 'The Politics of Intergovernmental Transfers in Post-Soviet Russia', *British Journal of Political Science*, 26: 299–335.

Treisman, D. (1998a) 'Fiscal Redistribution in a Fragile Federation: Moscow and the Regions in 1994', *British Journal of Political Science*, 28: 185–222.

Treisman, D. (1998b) 'Deciphering Russia's Federal Finance: Fiscal Appeasement in 1995 and 1996,' *Europe–Asia Studies*, 50: 893–906.

Treisman, D. (1999) *After the Deluge: Regional Crisis and Political Consolidation in Russia*, Ann Arbor: University of Michigan Press.

Tsebelis, G. (2002) *Veto Players: How Political Institutions Work*, New York: Russell Sage.

United Nations (2012) 'United Nations E-Government Survey 2012: E-government for the People'. Online, available at: http://unpan1.un.org/intradoc/groups/public/documents/un-dpadm/unpan048580.pdf (accessed August 30, 2012).

USAID, US Agency for International Development (2012) 'The 2011 CSO Sustainability Index for Central and Eastern Europe and Eurasia', 15th Anniversary Edition.Online, available at: http://transition.usaid.gov/locations/europe_eurasia/dem_gov/ngoindex/reports/2011/2011CSOSI_Index_complete.pdf (accessed September 17, 2012).

Vedomosti (2012a) 'Editorial: How Will the Federation Council Change' (in Russian), June 26. Online, available at: www.vedomosti.ru/opinion/news/2214623/omolozhenie_starejshin (accessed June 26, 2012).

Vedomosti (2012b) 'Editorial: Bureaucrats are Many; They are Expensive and Useless' (in Russian), July 31. Online, available at: www.vedomosti.ru/opinion/news/2334831/ne_pashut_ne_seyut_ne_stroyat (accessed July 31, 2012).

Vedomosti (2012c) 'Editorial: Illiterates in the Civil Service' (in Russian), August 1. Online, available at: www.vedomosti.ru/newsline/news/2378531/neuchi_na_gossluzhbe (accessed August 1, 2012).

Vedomosti (2012d) 'Editorial: New Marks for Governors' (in Russian), August 28. Online, available at: www.vedomosti.ru/newsline/news/3218441/11_punktov_putina (accessed August 24, 2012).

Vedomosti (2012e) 'Video interview with Sergey Beliakov, Deputy Minister of the Ministry of Economic Development' (in Russian), August 29. Online, available at: www.vedomosti.ru/politics/video/21_1321 (accessed August 29, 2012).

Verheijen, T. and Dobrolubova, Y. (2007) 'Performance Management in the Baltic States and Russia: Success Against the Odds?', *International Review of Administrative Sciences*, 73: 205–215.

Weingast, B. (1995) 'The Economic Role of Political Institutions: Market-Preserving Federalism and Economic Development', *Journal of Law, Economics and Organizations*, 11: 1–31.

White, S. and Mcallister, I. (2008) 'The Putin Phenomenon', *Journal of Communist Studies and Transition Politics*, 24: 604–628.

White, S. (1999) 'Russia', in Elgie R. (Ed.) *Semi-Presidentialism in Europe*, Oxford: Oxford University Press, pp. 216–231.

World Bank (2011) 'Russia: Public Expenditure Review. Report No. 58836-RU'. Online, available at: www-wds.worldbank.org/external/default/WDSContentServer/WDSP/IB/2011/08/01/000356161_20110801010543/Rendered/PDF/588360ESW0Gray00702701100BOX361521B.pdf (accessed September 17, 2013).

World Bank (2012) 'Russian Economic Report: Moderating Risks, Bolstering Growth', Russian Economic Report No 27. Online, available at: www.worldbank.org/content/dam/Worldbank/document/rer-27-march2012-eng.pdf (accessed September 17, 2013).

World Values Survey Association (2009) *World Values Survey 1981–2008, Official Aggregate v20090901*. Online, available at: www.wvsevsdb.com/wvs/wvsdata.jsp (accessed January 20, 2013).

The Worldwide Governance Indicators Project (2012) 'Aggregate Indicators of Governance 1996–2011. 2012 Update'. Online, available at: www.govindicators.org (accessed January 20, 2013).

Yakovlev, A. (2006) 'The Evolution of Business-State Interaction in Russia: From State Capture to Business Capture?' *Europa-Asia Studies*, 58: 1033–1056.

Yegishyants, S. (2012) 'Russia: Oil, Budget and Life' (in Russian), ITinvest Online Broker. Online, available at: www.itinvest.ru/analytics/reviews/strategic-analysis/6792/ (accessed September 17, 2012).

Zakharov, M. and Popov, P. (2010) 'Kickbacks as a Mode of Production' (in Russian). Online, available at: www.polit.ru/article/2010/10/29/roz (accessed August 28, 2012).

Zhuravskaya, E. (2000) 'Incentives to Provide Local Public Goods: Fiscal Federalism, Russian Style', *Journal of Public Economics*, 76: 337–368.

Zhuravskaya, E. (2010) 'Federalism in Russia', in Åslund, A., Guriev, S. and Kuchins, A. (Eds.) *Russia after the Global Economic Crisis*, Washington DC: Peterson Institute for International Economics, pp. 59–77.

Zobnin, A. (2011) 'Social Outsourcing in Furmanskiy Municipal District of the Ivanovo Region' (in Russian), *Public Administration Issues*, 1: 167–178.

# 9 The People's Republic of China

*Thomas Johnson and Guohui Wang*

## Political culture

The People's Republic of China (PRC) is a one-party authoritarian state that was established in 1949 after Mao Zedong's communist forces triumphed in a protracted civil war against the nationalists led by Chiang Kai-Shek. The country's initial political and administrative system borrowed significantly from the Soviet Union. At its heart was a centrally planned economy, a highly centralised and hierarchical political structure dominated by the Chinese Communist Party (CCP), and the atomisation of society in order to maintain party control (Saich 2004: 28). The year 1978 marked a significant watershed in the history of the PRC when Deng Xiaoping, emerging victorious from a power struggle within the CCP following Mao's death in 1976, instigated market reforms that began to gradually dismantle the centrally planned economy while also relaxing to an extent party control over society. The resulting upsurge in economic growth, reflected in an average annual GDP increase of 9.6 per cent from 1979–2004 (Xinhua News Agency 2006), has lifted tens of millions of Chinese out of poverty and helped transform China into a major economic and political force on the world stage. Yet although party–state control has undoubtedly relaxed in the economic and social realms compared with the Maoist era, political reform has proceeded far more cautiously. Hence more than 60 years on from the founding of the PRC, the CCP still dominates politically and there is little sign that its ruling elites are likely to move the country towards anything approaching western liberal democracy.

After its victory over the nationalists, the CCP faced the daunting challenge of rebuilding a country torn apart by foreign occupation, civil war and warlords. In 1949 China was still economically backwards, with approximately 80 per cent of its population living in rural areas. Against this backdrop, the CCP embarked on a modernisation programme that largely drew from the Soviet experience. At the heart of this was the policy of heavy industrialisation characterised by socialised production, to be financed by increases in agricultural output. Rural reforms resulted in the communisation of agriculture by the mid-1950s, while private enterprises were virtually eliminated. At the same time, CCP leaders, and Mao in particular, imposed their own ideology on the population. As Kenneth Lieberthal (2004) has pointed out, a smoothly run administration was incompatible with the type of revolutionary change favoured by Mao. He frequently circumvented the cumbersome bureaucracy and mobilised the populace through regular mass campaigns including the Great Leap Forward (1958–60), which resulted in mass famine, and the tumultuous Cultural Revolution (1966–9). During the latter the party–state bureaucracy was decimated and plunged into chaos before Mao sent in the People's Liberation Army (PLA) to restore order. Throughout the Maoist era class background was favoured above expertise, resulting in many important positions in the bureaucracy and beyond being held by poorly educated peasants.

The 1978 reforms marked a significant shift away from a reliance on Maoist socialist ideology towards a new approach based on pragmatism and increasingly market-oriented economics. Rural communes were abolished in the early 1980s, and the subsequent dismantling of many state-owned enterprises (SOEs) has led to rising urban unemployment and the end of comprehensive social welfare provision previously guaranteed for urban workers by the 'iron rice bowl'. Yet despite the policy of economic liberalisation, the party's monopoly over political control remains non-negotiable. This was articulated at the start of the reform period in 1979 by Deng's 'Four Basic Principles', which were to be defended at any cost, namely adherence to the socialist road, maintenance of the dictatorship of the proletariat and CCP leadership, and finally the upholding of Marxism-Leninism-Mao Zedong thought. Politics in the PRC remains highly individualistic, with patron–client ties based on personal connections (*guanxi*) dominating over formal institutions and rules. Yet at the same time there have been efforts to institutionalise political power in the reform era. Greater institutionalisation within the party was evident in the 2003 transfer of leadership from the 'third generation' of leaders headed by Jiang Zemin to the current 'fourth generation' led by Hu Jintao, a transition widely praised for its smoothness. The principle of 'rule of law' was written into the state constitution in 1999, yet the party remains firmly above the law, which is merely viewed as another tool for exerting CCP control (Saich 2004).

The communist revolution succeeded in unifying the country once again after sustained foreign invasion. Several disputes with neighbouring countries over border demarcations aside, the only territorial issues left outstanding were the enduring colonial status of Hong Kong and Macau, and the occupation of Taiwan by fleeing nationalist forces. Hong Kong and Macau were handed over to China in 1997 and 1999, respectively, under the 'one country two systems' formula that enables the two territories to keep their existing political and economic systems for 50 years. Taiwan is viewed as a renegade province in the eyes of Beijing, which in 2005 passed the Anti-secession Law authorising the use of military force to reclaim any part of the country (including Taiwan) that secedes.

## The constitutional arrangement

Recent dislocations and upheavals in PRC politics are reflected in its constitutional arrangement. The PRC has altogether adopted four state constitutions, in 1954, 1975, 1978, and the current version adopted in 1982. Although the document in many ways resembles a constitution in a liberal western democracy, it does not enjoy the supremacy of constitutions in other countries. In reality, the CCP oversees the adoption of the state constitution and attempts to harmonise it with the party's own constitution (Zou 2006). Moreover, the party does not rule in a manner consistent with the state constitution and refuses to subject itself to constitutional checks and balances (Peerenboom 2002). Hence citizens' constitutional rights including equality before the law and freedom of speech, press, and religion, are not protected in practice, and state organs do not operate independently of party control. This does not mean that the PRC constitution is irrelevant, however. Constitutional changes frequently follow major realignments in party policy and can therefore function as a barometer of the current political climate. In this vein, the current constitution followed closely on the heels of the reform and the opening up of policy and strongly reflects Deng Xiaoping's reform agenda (Chen 2004). It has been regularly amended (in 1988, 1993, 1999, and 2004) in order to reflect changes in the CCP's outlook as it continues to shape its own brand of 'socialism'. A recent example concerns Jiang Zemin's theory of the 'Three Represents', which provides an ideological justification for allowing entrepreneurs to join the party, and which was written into the state constitution in 2004 after being enshrined in the CCP Constitution during the sixteenth National Party Congress in 2002.

The 1982 Constitution appeared to signify a desire on behalf of the PRC's leaders to move the country towards a more predictable and rules-based system that entailed greater separation between party and state, with the latter responsible for implementing CCP policies (Saich 2004). However, the party has continued to exercise considerable control over the state, and boundaries between the two are frequently blurred and overlapping. CCP units operate in parallel with state units at every level of administration, with real power held by the former. Hence decision-making power at the central level is concentrated in the CCP Politburo, and in particular its seven-person Standing Committee headed by Party Secretary and President, Xi Jinping. Overlap between party and state positions means that State Premier Li Keqiang and Chairman of the National People's Congress Standing Committee Zhang Dejiang also sit on the Politburo Standing Committee, while government ministers and provincial governors are nominated via the party's nomenklatura system. With few exceptions individuals from the latter two groups also hold, or previously held, positions in important party organs such as the CCP Politburo, Central Party Committee, and Central Committee for Discipline Inspection.

According to the constitution, the PRC is a unitary multinational state. The country is formally administered at five levels: central, provincial, prefectural, county and township. The National People's Congress (NPC) is the legislature and the highest organ of state power, and is replicated by Local People's Congresses down to and including the township level. The NPC is composed of approximately 3,000 deputies (the precise number of which varies between sessions) who are elected by provincial-level People's Congresses and the PLA. Due to its size, the NPC only convenes once a year. When not in session the NPC's duties are taken up by its Standing Committee of approximately 150 members who meet bimonthly. NPC sessions are numbered consecutively and last for five years, with the current twelfth NPC running from 2013 to 2018. In theory, the NPC has wide-ranging powers, including the authority to amend the constitution, elect and remove from office senior officials including the state president, and oversee national economic and social development plans. However, despite increasing numbers of abstentions and 'no' votes in recent years, the national legislature remains little more than a rubber stamp that merely confirms the CCP's policies.

The State Council is the executive organ of the NPC, and is presided over by an executive board made up of the state premier (currently Li Keqiang), several vice premiers, state councillors and a secretary general. The Chinese central government has undergone six rounds of administrative reform since 1982, with the most recent reform conducted in 2008. The main thrust of these reforms has been to reduce the number of central government departments, which numbered over 100 before 1982 and which currently stands at just 27 ministries and commissions. In 2003 the State Development and Planning Commission and State Economic and Trading Commission were replaced by a single entity, the National Development and Reform Commission (NDRC). The NDRC has responsibility for co-ordinating national economic and social development, as well as overseeing economic reform. In order to improve efficiency and reduce overlap, the 2008 reforms created five 'super ministries', in the areas of Industry and Information, Human Resources and Social Security, Environmental Protection, Housing and Urban–Rural Construction, and Transport. The State Council also incorporates various administrations, committees, bureaus, offices, and ad hoc organisations. Along with the ministries and commissions, these bodies' work includes the adoption of administrative measures, submission of proposals to the NPC, and the drawing up of the country's national economic and social development plans in addition to the state budget. State Council sessions coincide with those of the NPC, and the premier, vice premiers and state councillors are limited to serving two terms. Similar to Local People's Congresses, the central government apparatus is replicated by Local People's Governments at the local level.

The president and head of state is formally elected by the NPC, and concurrently serves as CCP party secretary and head of the Central Military Commission of the PRC. The length of office for presidents is limited to two terms. Until recently, party elders exercised considerable influence behind the scenes long after having 'retired' from their official posts. This was certainly the case with regards Deng Xiaoping, who had final say on all major decisions even after he relinquished his official positions. Although former party elites still exert influence from behind the scenes, previous leaders such as Jiang lack the charisma and personal authority that enabled Deng (and Mao before him) to remain powerful. The Central Military Commission of the PRC derives its authority from the constitution and is the state body responsible for supervising the PLA. Yet this organisation simultaneously convenes as the Central Military Commission of the CCP, and it is this party body that exerts real influence over the armed forces. When Jiang Zemin's presidency ended in 2002, he did not relinquish his formal position as head of the Central Military Commission until 2004 when this role was passed onto a new president Hu Jintao.

## The civil service

China's economic reforms have necessitated the establishment of a modern and effective civil service with enhanced capacity to govern the country and manage the economy. Since the early 1980s China has been reforming its civil service in a bid to improve governance capacity and efficiency. In the process Chinese reformers have adopted aspects of personnel management strategies typically found in western democracies, including competitive recruitment and pay, a merit-based approach and sanctions for poor performance. At the same time, the PRC's Civil Service displays various 'Chinese characteristics' that ensure considerable divergence with civil service systems elsewhere. For example, the idea that the civil service should be politically neutral along Weberian lines has been explicitly rejected. Chinese civil servants are bound by law to carry out CCP policy and accept party control. The CCP retains control over leading civil service appointments through its nomenklatura system, and civil servants operating in sensitive areas such as personnel departments are required to be party members.

After much deliberation and internal wrangling, the PRC formally established a modern civil service in 1993 with the promulgation of the Provisional Regulations on State Civil Servants (hereinafter referred to as the '1993 Regulations'). The 1993 Regulations created a new system for supervising government workers who had previously been managed under the Soviet-styled cadre management system, which had been in effect since the 1950s. The cadre management system employed a unified structure for managing all cadres, which was a blanket term referring to all party, government and army officials engaged in 'mental' (as opposed to 'manual') labour (Burns 2001). This system was highly autocratic, with recruitment secretive and based overwhelmingly on political loyalty and class credentials (Tong et al. 1999). After the onset of market reforms the cadre management system was widely criticised for being inefficient, ineffective, rigid, and prone to corruption, all of which threatened to hinder economic development (Liou 1997: 506). The 1993 Regulations defined civil servants as '"cadres" or administrators, managers and professionals who work for government agencies'

(Burns 2001: 80). The main thrust of the reforms embodied by the 1993 Regulations was to overcome problems associated with the cadre management system by creating a more meritocratic and effective civil service with the capacity to address complex challenges stemming from the economic reforms. The Chinese Civil Service system was to be institutionalised, standardised, codified and professionalised (Tsao and Worthley 2009: 89). This is partly manifested in the numerous pieces of legislation that followed the 1993 Regulations and which addressed specific areas such as civil servant training, discipline and working practices. Yet at the same time these reforms have been undermined by pervasive corruption and nepotism, as well as recruitment strategies that are frequently based on local level political considerations.

In the PRC politicians and civil servants are not treated as separate entities (Burns 2001). Therefore, the scope of the Chinese Civil Service is broader than those found in western democracies in that it incorporates the whole state bureaucracy, including many political positions such as the premier and provincial governors that would not be part of civil services elsewhere (Burns 2001). Yet it is also narrower than other countries by virtue of excluding those cadres working in public service units (in areas such as education and public health) and state-owned enterprises as well as all blue-collar state workers (Burns 2001). China's Civil Service is hierarchically organised, consisting of 12 positions distributed across 15 grades, ranging from the premier who occupies the top grade down to the position of clerk, which can fall in any of the bottom five grades. In 2005 the PRC promulgated its first Civil Service Law. According to Chan and Li (2007), this law expanded political control over the civil service by expanding the definition of civil service contained in the 1993 Regulations to include party organisations. The number of civil servants swelled from approximately 4.9 million in 2003 to 6.3 million after the law took effect (Chan and Li 2007: 389). The Civil Service Law had the effect of blurring the distinction between civil servants (as defined by the 1993 Regulations) and cadres while also providing a legal basis for party control of the civil service, reflecting the reality that had been ongoing since the founding of the PRC (Chan and Li 2007). Regarding the degree of politicisation in China's Civil Service, Chan and Li (2007) argue that political considerations are prioritised above competence when it comes to recruitment. However, Tsao and Worthley (2009) suggest that although political obedience remains a minimum requirement in recruitment and promotion decisions, expertise and professional qualifications have become more significant determinants of personnel decisions.

Reforms have helped to create a civil service that is better educated, better paid, and younger than was the case previously (Burns 2007). The civil service has also become more inclusive. Previously, applicants for entry-level positions at the central level had to be residents of Beijing. However, this policy changed in 1998 and examinations are now held in cities across the country, while Jiang Zemin's 'Three Represents' theory has facilitated the inclusion of businesspeople in the civil service. Yet at the same time, attempts to modernise

China's Civil Service have faced setbacks and results have varied significantly across different regions. Central level positions have successfully attracted society's 'best and brightest', and are characterised by a highly competitive and rigorous application process. In 2009, 775,000 applicants competed for just 13,500 central level civil service positions (Reuters 2009). Beyond the centre, however, the quality of China's Civil Service is highly variable. In wealthy provinces civil servants tend to be well educated and subjected to a highly competitive recruitment process (Tsao and Worthley 2009). In contrast, in poorer regions civil service capacity is considerably lower, nepotism and the corrupt buying and selling of positions remain serious problems, and the government is often considered an 'employer of last resort' (Burns 2007). Regional variations are further exacerbated by unequal access to training opportunities between richer provinces and poorer ones that view such activities as an unnecessary luxury (Burns 2007). Although the centre has aimed to optimise economic rationality through civil service reforms, local governments have frequently been more concerned with resolving conflict arising from the economic reforms, and many have merely implemented these reforms in line with their own interests (Chou 2004). Political factors still interfere with recruitment decisions in many cases. For example, government policy dictates that large numbers of demobilised soldiers are to be recruited into the civil service in a non-competitive manner (Chou 2004). Furthermore, government downsizing efforts in the reform era have often been undermined by the desire of local officials to prevent the social instability that could accompany rising unemployment. Attempts to stimulate better performance through appraisals have also faced difficulties. Following the promulgation of the 1993 Regulations, civil servants' performance was either rated excellent, satisfactory, or unsatisfactory, based on work performance and political integrity (Chou 2004). Yet research suggests that under this system over 99 per cent of civil servants were placed in the upper two categories (Chou 2005). Although the Civil Service Law altered the performance appraisal system to include a fourth category, reluctance to punish poor performers due in part to reciprocity and face-saving continues to undermine efforts to increase accountability (Chou 2008). In short, raising the capacity of the civil service while simultaneously maintaining party control is a difficult and on-going task for Chinese reformers.

## Central government agencies

At the Chinese central government level, apart from the formal civil service system, namely, central government departments and commissions, a number of semi-administrative public institutions are also established and function to formulate and implement policies as well as to provide public services. Although the legal status of these public institutions is not categorised as part of the civil service system, they are actually highly administrative and subordinated to the central government. According to their functions, these agencies can be classified into three different categories. The first category is supervision and regulatory agencies responsible for supervising or regulating certain trade or public service areas. Typical agencies of this category include the state-owned Assets Supervision and Administration Commission of the State Council (SASAC), China Banking Regulatory Commission (CBRC) and State Electricity Regulatory Commission (SERC). The SASAC, established in 2003 by the State Council, performs investor's responsibilities by supervising and managing the state-owned assets of the enterprises under the supervision of the central government (excluding financial enterprises). The SASAC is authorised by the central government to appoint and remove the top executives of the supervised enterprises and evaluate their performances. It is also responsible for the fundamental management of the state-owned assets of enterprises, drafting laws and regulations on the management of the state-owned assets, establishing related rules and regulations, and directing and supervising the management work for local state-owned assets. The CBRC and the SERC were also created in 2003. The CBRC's main functions include formulating supervisory rules and regulations governing the banking institutions, authorising the establishment, changes, termination and business scope of the banking institutions, conducting examination and surveillance of the banking institutions, and taking enforcement actions against rule-breaking behaviours. Similarly, the SERC is empowered by the State Council to perform administrative and regulatory duties with regard to the national electric power sector. It is responsible for the overall regulation of the national power sector, while also formulating regulatory rules for the sector as well as establishing rules for, and monitoring, electricity market operations.

The second category is policy research and consulting agencies that function as leading think tanks under the central government. The Development Research Centre of the State Council (DRC) and the Chinese Academy of Social Sciences are typical examples. Both of these agencies conduct intensive research into national economic and social issues and shoulder the responsibility for providing advice and proposals for central government policy-making.

The last category comprises institutions responsible for certain public service provision. For example, the National Council for Social Security Fund was created in 2000 and is responsible for the management and operation of the National Social Security Fund. The National Natural Science Foundation of China is a public institution directly under the State Council, and is in charge of managing the National Natural Science Fund. Its main function is to formulate and implement funding plans to support natural science research and to manage funded projects, and promote the effective allocation of research resources. It also co-operates with the state administrative departments in charge of science and technology in formulating state principles, policies and plans for developing basic research, and provides advice on major national issues concerning the development of science and technology.

The China Meteorological Administration (CMA) and the China Earthquake Administration (CEA) are public service agencies responsible for organisational and operational management of the national meteorological services and earthquake monitoring and disaster relief services respectively.

## Federal and local government

According to its constitutional arrangements, China is a multinational unitary state. Provincial and sub-provincial level governments are officially administrative units below the State Council and are obliged to implement its administrative measures, regulations and decisions. Yet the reality is rather more complex, as provincial governments have in practice enjoyed a growing degree of autonomy during the reform period due to the decentralisation of power away from Beijing. Following the highly centralised system of the Maoist years, decentralisation was carried out after 1978 in order to provide the stimulus for sub-central governments to grow their economies. It also occurred partly by default as responsibility for expenditure increasingly fell to local governments (Wong 2009). The latter now have significant autonomy, particularly in the realm of economic policy, and have been granted much greater flexibility in implementing central government directives (Zheng 2007). Concerns that further decentralisation would lead to the disintegration of the PRC prompted a recentralisation programme in the early 1990s including centralising reforms to the tax and banking systems. Yet the overall shift of authority away from the centre since 1978 has prompted some scholars to characterise central–local relations as a form of de facto federalism (Zheng 2007). Under this arrangement, both central and provincial governments have their own exclusive areas of influence. These include national defence and foreign policy in relation to the former, and, in the case of the latter, local security, school and road construction, and responsibility for the majority of economic matters. There is also a significant degree of overlap between the two, with local governments playing a crucial role in implementing central policies. As well as coercion, the centre relies heavily on bargaining and reciprocity in order to ensure that its policies are implemented at the local level (Zheng 2007).

Local government in the PRC occurs at four levels, namely provincial, prefecture, county, and township (see Figure 9.1).

Cities appear at each of these levels (excluding township) according to their size and importance. In addition, autonomous administrative units have been established at each of the four levels in regions with high concentrations of non-Han minority groups, which accounted for approximately 9 per cent of the population in 2008 (Cabestan 2009). Beneath the township level but not constituting a level of government in their own right are villages (in rural areas) and street committees and communities (in urban areas).

The highest level of local administration is the provincial level, consisting of 33 administrative units (excluding Taiwan). At the time of its founding, the

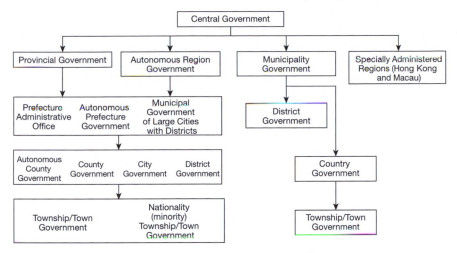

*Figure 9. 1* Governmental administrative structure of the PRC

Source: Zhong (2003: 48)

PRC included 21 provinces. In 1988 this became 22 provinces when the island of Hainan, which had previously been administered as part of Guangdong Province, was given provincial status. The provincial level also includes four municipalities administered directly under the central government, namely Beijing, Shanghai, Tianjin and Chongqing, with the latter administratively separated from Sichuan Province in 1997. In addition there are five special autonomous regions in areas with significant non-Han populations. Inner Mongolia had already been established as such two years before the PRC's founding, and was followed by Xinjiang Uygur in 1955, Guangxi Zhuang and Ningxia Hui in 1958, and finally Tibet in 1965. Despite their titles however, these regions enjoy little autonomy. For example, although the government head must belong to the ethnic minority in whose name autonomy is granted, this does not apply to party organs. The principle of limited autonomy for minorities is repeated at lower levels, where there are 30 autonomous prefectures, approximately 120 autonomous counties and banners, and over 1,000 autonomous townships. Finally, since 1997 and 1999, respectively, Hong Kong and Macau have been governed separately as Special Administrative Regions, with the guarantee that they keep their existing political and economic systems for 50 years. According to Kenneth Lieberthal (2004: 182), most provincial-level governments have a staffing allocation of between 5,300 and 7,500, although the sparsely populated provinces in China's western region employ fewer people.

Hierarchically arranged beneath the province are the prefecture, county, and township levels. Prefectures derive from Circuits, which were established during the Qing Dynasty as an administrative unit between the counties and provinces. Circuits were abolished in 1928, but restored soon after because provincial governments found it difficult to manage numerous counties directly. Prefectures replaced Circuits, and are decentralised administrative organs of provincial governments. Since the onset of the reform period, many prefectures have been converted to prefecture-level municipalities. In 2008 there were 333 prefecture-level units, including 17 prefectures (compared with 86 in 1996), 30 autonomous prefectures, and 283 municipalities (compared with 210 in 1996) (Ministry of Civil Affairs 2008). The third level of local administration is the county level. Provinces and autonomous regions are subdivided into counties, autonomous counties, and county-level cities, while municipalities directly under the central government are divided into counties and districts. As of 2008, China had 2,859 administrative units at the county level, including 1,463 counties, 856 municipal districts, 117 autonomous counties and 368 county-level cities (Ministry of Civil Affairs 2008). Townships form the lowest level of local administration, and are divided into rural townships (*xiang*) and urban towns (*zhen*) based upon their urban populations and importance of the locale. Since the mid-1980s a large number of rural townships have been re-designated as urban towns due to rapid urbanisation and industrialisation (Zhong 2003). In 2008 their numbers totalled 19,249 and 13,928, respectively (Ministry of Civil Affairs 2008). During the Great Leap Forward, townships were subsumed into the people's communes, and only regained their position as separate administrative units in 1982 with the abolition of people's communes. Although the structure of township governments is simpler than higher levels, the core party and government organs are all present (Lieberthal 2004).

Each level of local government basically replicates the administrative structure of the centre, with party and government organisations operating in parallel with each other. The only exception is the prefecture level, which is not a level of political power and which therefore does not establish Local People's Governments or Congresses (Saich 2004). Authority is concentrated in party committees (and their party secretaries) that can be found at every administrative level. Constitutionally, the highest organs of state power at the local level are Local People's Congresses (LPCs) which, like the NPC only convene once a year and also have their own standing committees. County and township LPCs are elected by the popular vote, although elections are tightly controlled. County-level LPCs elect delegates at provincial LPCs who in turn are responsible for electing delegates to the NPC. Deputies are elected for five years at the provincial level and in those cities divided into districts, and three years at lower levels. Local People's Governments (LPGs) are elected by LPCs and carry out executive duties at the local level. LPG officials' term of office corresponds to that of LPC deputies at the same level. At and above the county level, LPCs supervise the LPGs through examining and approving economic and social development plans, budgets of their respective administrative areas, and reports on their implementation. Studies suggest that since the 1990s LPCs have become more assertive in holding LPGs accountable, although they rely on cultivating party support in order to do so and still favour co-operation over confrontation (Cho 2002). Provincial and county-level LPCs are authorised by the constitution to promulgate their own regulations, on the condition that they do not contravene national laws.

Below the township level are administrative villages, which are considered grass-roots semi-administrative units. By 2009, there were around 680,000 administrative villages throughout China. The body responsible for running each administrative village is the villagers' committee, the status of which is defined in the constitution (Article 111) as 'mass organisations of self-management at the grass-roots level'. Villagers' committee leaders are directly elected by villagers and are responsible for village governance and management of public affairs within the village. Although villagers' committees are autonomous organisations by law and their leaders are not state officials, in reality they are largely treated as administrative organs by the township/town government and village leaders are highly responsive to the leadership of the township government.

## Financing the system

The management of financial resources in the PRC has undergone huge change with the transition towards a market economy, yet the reform of China's public finances has lagged behind other economic reforms and is still very much considered a 'work in progress' (Wong and Bird 2008). This is partly manifested in sharply rising regional inequality in the reform era as well as the under-provision of public goods and basic services in many localities (Hussain and Stern 2008).

Under the planned economy, revenues collected at the local level were remitted to central government coffers, before being redistributed to local governments based on their spending needs, which were determined centrally. This 'revenue sharing system' was highly redistributive between rich and poor provinces. For example, before 1978 approximately 80–90 per cent of Shanghai's revenue was kept by the centre, whereas over two-thirds of expenditure in Guizhou Province was financed by central government subsidies (Wong 2000: 5). Before 1978 by far the most important source of government revenue was state-owned enterprise (SOE) profits. However, the transfer of many SOEs from central to local government control in the early 1980s combined with the introduction of market competition severely reduced the government's tax base (Wong 2000). In the 1980s Beijing introduced a 'fiscal responsibility system' whereby provincial governments paid a lump sum to central coffers annually while keeping the rest to finance their own expenditure. This placed local governments on a self-financing basis for the first time in the PRC and encouraged them to maximise revenue generation through growing their economies (Wong and Bird 2008). However, the fiscal responsibility system did not arrest the decline in fiscal revenue compared with GDP, which plummeted from 31.2 per cent of GDP in 1978 to 10.7 per cent of GDP in 1995 (Hussain and Stern 2008: 15). In 1994, in order to reverse this trend while also seeking to increase the centre's share of government revenues, Beijing conducted a major overhaul of the country's fiscal system. First, the 1994 reform simplified the tax structure by creating three categories of tax, namely central, local and shared. The biggest tax, VAT, was designated a shared tax, with the centre claiming a share of 75 per cent of revenues. This move helped the centre increase its share of total fiscal revenues from 22 per cent in 1993 to 55.7 per cent in 1994 (Wong 2000: 9). Second, the central government established its own agencies at the provincial level for collecting central and shared taxes, while local government agencies only collected local taxes. This arrangement was designed to prevent local governments from siphoning off extra revenue (Wong and Bird 2008). In 1996, fiscal revenue as a percentage of GDP started to recover, reaching 19.3 per cent in 2004 (Hussain and Stern 2008: 15).

During the pre-reform era, the fact that resources were allocated from the centre meant that the state budget was merely a mechanism for implementing the plan (Ma 2009). The declining importance of the plan after 1978 necessitated the establishment of an effective budgeting system, yet reform in this area was slow in coming. Between 1978 and 1999 the PRC state financing system was highly fragmented across numerous ministries, departments and bureaus, and was also far from comprehensive, all of which hindered the exertion of expenditure control (OECD 2005). In 1999 steps were taken to overhaul this arrangement. Government departments are now required to submit departmental budgets, which, as well as having been opened up to slightly more scrutiny by the legislature than was previously the case, are also far more detailed than before. Furthermore, the 1999 reforms centralised the treasury management system into a single account and reformed government procurement (Ma 2009). Yet budgetary reform has been slow and many problems remain. Much government spending still takes place outside of the formal budget, and there remains a lack of effective oversight and transparency.

The PRC annual state budget is drafted by the government and formally approved by the NPC. The NPC Standing Committee reviews and approves budgetary adjustments that are necessary during the budgetary cycle, which runs from 1 January to 31 December. Local governments also draft budgets, which are approved by Local People's Congresses at the same level. However, the formal budget only partially explains the fiscal situation in China. Since the 1980s there has been a sharp growth in extra-budgetary funds, which are officially sanctioned by the centre and include revenue from sources such as leasing land and enterprises run by administrative units. These funds are reported to higher levels but under less stringent conditions than formally budgeted funds, and local authorities carry out their own control and oversight. Extra-budgetary funds have softened local government budget constraints and in some cases helped maintain a bloated public sector workforce and fund new infrastructure such as airports and shopping centres (Wong and Bird 2008). Despite attempts to increase the proportion of government expenditure covered by the formal budget, a large amount of government spending remains off budget and unreported. Particularly in rural areas, a significant quantity of expenditure is financed by illegal ad hoc fees, which still prevail despite attempts by the central government to convert these fees into taxes. When off-budget spending is included, estimates place China's public expenditure at around 32 per cent of GDP, which roughly equates with other emerging economies (OECD 2005: 255). The National Audit Office (NAO), set up in 1983, is responsible for auditing government departments and SOEs. The NAO was established as a department under the State Council and is therefore not independent of the government. Although some Chinese researchers have advocated that the NAO be subsumed under the NPC in order to improve its supervisory capabilities, this would represent a significant restructuring of the State Council, and political support for such a move appears lacking (Yang et al. 2008). Local audit bureaus tend to be understaffed and lacking in capacity, and are similarly compromised by their subservient relationship to the local government they are responsible for scrutinising (Wong and Bird 2008).

Local governments are almost entirely responsible for financing provision of basic services such as public health, education and social security. According to the OECD (2005), Chinese local governments account for around 75 per cent of government spending. Because local governments are largely self-financed, there is huge variation in fiscal revenue and therefore service provision across jurisdictions, which has only partially been overcome through a revenue transfer system. Local governments are not authorised to set tax rates or introduce new taxes. As a result, discrepancies between local government responsibilities and resources have resulted in growing reliance on extra-budgetary and off-budgetary funds (which for many rural governments have accounted for half of more of their expenditures including the funding of basic services), and illicit borrowing. In some cases this has created perverse incentives whereby, for example, environmental protection bureaus actually rely on pollution because it generates fines with which their activities can be funded. Public Service Units, which provide the vast majority of public services in China, from schools and cultural centres to hospitals, on average only obtain half of their funding from the budget, and must raise the remainder via fees and other sources (Wong 2009: 940). Some public service units have also been compromised by the need to raise funds, with the over-prescription of drugs by doctors being just one example (Wong and Bird 2008). A lack of revenue at many county and township levels is seen as a major impediment to the implementation of national policy in these areas, with poorer localities in particular forced to scale down basic service provision.

## Co-ordinating the system

China's bureaucracy is co-ordinated both vertically from the centre to the local level, and horizontally within a certain jurisdiction (Lieberthal 2004). This means that, for example, a provincial-level education bureau falls under the influence of the Ministry of Education as well as the provincial government in which it is situated. Ultimately, one of these bodies will have greater influence and enjoys what is termed a 'leadership relationship' (Lieberthal 2004). Decentralisation during the reform era has on the whole increased the influence of the horizontal over the vertical as local governments have been given greater discretion for managing their affairs. In addition, local governments must answer to the party committee at the same level as well as the government body directly above them in the hierarchy (Lieberthal 2004). In China's highly hierarchical bureaucracy, every unit is given a rank. Units of the same rank cannot issue binding orders to each other, which can sometimes create co-ordination problems especially when units refuse to co-operate.

Co-ordination of the central government apparatus in China is basically achieved by three forms: the State Council meetings; co-ordinating agencies/organisations; and major leaders taking the lead. Meetings of the State Council are divided into plenary meetings and executive meetings. The plenary meetings of the State Council are composed of all members of the State Council, whereas executive meetings are limited to the premier, the vice premiers, the state councillors and the secretary general. The premier convenes and presides over the plenary and executive meetings of the State Council. Important issues that require co-operation among different ministries and agencies are discussed and co-ordinated by an executive or plenary meeting of the State Council.

In order to organise and co-ordinate important tasks across ministries and agencies of the State Council, advisory and co-ordinating organs and provisional organs are set up under the State Council. Examples include the Committee of Aids Prevention and Cure and the Work Safety Committee. These organs are subject to constant change and adjustment according to prevailing circumstances. For example, the National Headquarters of SARS Prevention and Cure was set up in 2003 for tackling the SARS (Severe Acute Respiratory Syndrome) crisis and was formally abolished in 2008. By 2009, there were a total of 32 such advisory and co-ordinating organs and provisional organs under the State Council. In order to add authority and facilitate co-ordination, most of these organs are chaired by the premier, the vice premiers or the state councillors.

The third but less institutionalised way of administrative co-ordination is when a major leader takes the lead in important issues. This method largely relies upon the bureaucratic authority of a major State Council leader (usually the premier, vice premier or state councillor) to realise administrative co-ordination across ministries and departments. This can enhance administrative efficiency and make decision-making or policy-implementation easier. However, this is not an institutionalised way of co-ordination and is often used in urgent issues.

In order to improve public service delivery and provide infrastructure necessitated by the country's rapid development, the Chinese government has promoted public–private partnerships (PPPs). These PPPs can be divided into three categories: outsourcing, concession (typically based on 20–30 year contracts) and divestiture (Adams et al. 2006). Despite considerable growth in PPPs during the reform era, several issues remain unresolved. Poor access to investment capital is a significant barrier to small enterprises, and most PPP projects involve large consortiums of companies, some of which include foreign enterprises. This has limited the extent to which PPPs have been established in areas such as health and education. Another constraint on PPPs is related to the relatively high risks for private companies due to uncertainties regarding property rights (Adams et al. 2006). Nevertheless, PPPs have been used for many infrastructure projects, including a recent extension of the Beijing subway system, and look certain to play a bigger role in the future.

## Managing the system

After the CCP came to power it relied heavily on party discipline, ideology and the planned economy to control local officials (Zhong 2003). Since the start of the reform era, however, the latter two have been greatly weakened as the CCP has turned to pragmatism over ideology and set about dismantling the planned economy. Party discipline has remained important however, and the CCP retains control over key personnel decisions via the nomenklatura system. However, some local party officials have been able to abuse their power and establish what are referred to as 'dukedoms', ignoring or circumventing central government directives.

Some scholars have identified trends towards corporatisation and the (partial) privatisation of SOEs as evidence that China is embracing the principles of New Public Management (Lee and Lo 2001). At the same time, these scholars acknowledge that the Chinese experience diverges sharply from that of western countries. Any understanding of public management reform in the PRC must take into account the unique ideological, institutional and political context in which such reforms are embedded (Lee and Lo 2001). For example, attempts at downsizing the state bureaucracy have been seriously undermined because they conflict with the political imperatives of maintaining CCP patronage and promoting social stability through limiting unemployment (Burns 2003). Similarly, calls by the government to cultivate a system of 'small government, big society' have been tempered by a reluctance to grant autonomy to NGOs for fear that they might mobilise to challenge the party's monopoly on political power. These 'grass-roots' organisations struggle to raise revenue and operate under difficult political constraints. Indeed, the vast majority of Chinese 'NGOs' are in fact better described as government-organised NGOs (GONGOs), many of which grew out of government departments in order to seek international funds and absorb government workers who were being laid off due to downsizing. Some of these, such as the China Disabled Person's Federation, are engaged in service delivery and many have become more autonomous from the government, while also maintaining strong links with government departments.

The CCP faces a struggle to maintain political loyalty among cadres while also promoting greater efficiency. Managing the system is based upon party control of the government and party management of cadres. The CCP exercises management of cadres through the Cadre Responsibility System (CRS). The principles behind the CRS, including decentralisation of authority, a focus on outcomes rather than processes, and the use of contracts, quantitative goals and economic incentives, are consistent with those under-pinning the wider global trend towards New Public Management (Heimer 2006). The CRS is an outcome-based tool for evaluating the performance of leading local officials in meeting pre-arranged targets. Under this system, performance contracts stipulating clear targets for a certain jurisdiction are signed between that government and the level directly above it in the hierarchy. The CCP exerts control by dividing these targets into three categories in order of importance: soft targets, hard targets and priority targets with veto power. Soft targets might include items such as basic infrastructure provision, whereas hard targets typically relate to the economy. Priority targets include those that the party considers of fundamental importance and which must be met at all costs, such as maintaining social stability and adhering to family plan-ning policy. If a priority target is not met, then this negates ('vetoes') any achievements in other areas, and has a negative impact on officials' career prospects. Although the CRS is limited in the sense that it cannot deal with too many priority targets at any one time, it allows the party to be 'selectively effective' by prioritising goals (Edin 2003). In addition, the party possesses the power to move local leaders to different jurisdictions through cadre rotation and promotion. In order to strengthen CCP control over lower levels, cadres can be given a higher party ranking while remaining in the same post (Edin 2003). In 1984, the nomenklatura system was reformed. Whereas previously it extended two levels down the hierarchy, since 1984 it only extends down one level (Zheng 2007). Although this gave local governments greater control over personnel decisions it also enabled the centre to pay more attention to provincial level appointments.

## Accountability, secrecy and openness

Despite efforts to improve government accountability and transparency during the reform period, the PRC still suffers from serious 'governance deficits' in these areas (Howell 2004). Official accountability in China is overwhelmingly top-down, with officials answering to their superiors in the party–state hierarchy rather than the general public. Formal supervisory bodies such as the Bureau of Supervision, LPCs, the judiciary and the media have been given greater licence to hold officials to account, but on the whole are still not accorded enough authority to effectively monitor officials (Zhong 2003). This is not to say that officials are never held to account by citizens. In some cases citizen protests and complaints may lead to changes in policy or intervention from higher-ups who can then punish official wrongdoing.

The central government has implemented some reforms designed to increase accountability and openness. For example, government agencies such as industry and commerce, taxation, personnel management, labour, health care and residence administration, that provide services to the general public have based their field offices within communities so that people can have convenient access to government agencies, make fewer trips to and spend less time going to government offices. Since 1999 when the government launched 'Government Internet Program', there has been steady progress in e-government. For instance, the Ministry of Personnel started to provide services such as civil service exams, personnel mobility, issuing residence permits and employing Chinese nationals that return from overseas studies via the Internet. Governments at each level have constructed Internet platforms where people can have access to all information in the public domain, and wherever possible the government intends to deliver public services via the Internet.

Despite improvements in government transparency in recent years there still exists considerable tension between the trend towards greater information disclosure and fears that improved transparency might lead to social instability and jeopardise the party's political control. In many ways the SARS pandemic that emerged in late 2002 and early 2003 underscored the problem of a lack of transparency in the PRC. SARS is a severe form of pneumonia, and the pandemic killed almost 800 people. The Chinese media was initially instructed not to report on the disease, which originated in the southern province of Guangdong. After SARS spread to other regions, international pressure prompted the Chinese government to publicly acknowledge the disease, yet it downplayed the extent to which SARS had spread. It was only after a doctor in Beijing questioned publicly released statistics of SARS victims that the government became more open, with President Hu Jintao demanding accurate and honest reporting of the crisis and the removal from office of several senior officials involved in the cover-up (Tai and Sun 2007). The immediate response to the 2008 Sichuan earthquake was one of unparalleled openness with regard to media reporting, suggesting that lessons had been learnt from the SARS crisis. However, the media was subsequently banned from reporting stories related to claims that shoddy construction of schools linked to official corruption had contributed to the tragedy. In 2010 an activist named Tan Zuoren was reportedly poised to release his own report into the issue of substandard school construction in the earthquake zone, but was jailed for five years for a separate charge of state subversion that his supporters claim was merely an excuse to silence him (Reuters 2010). More recently the Chinese government has taken steps to improve transparency in order to limit corruption, improve public trust in government, and facilitate economic development (Horsley 2007). In 2007 the State Council promulgated the Ordinance on Openness of Government Information, which provided a legal basis for government information disclosure, including for public requests for information, for the first time in the PRC. In addition, many local governments have published their own government information regulations. Evidence suggests that members of the public are increasingly using information disclosure regulations to request disclosure and, in some cases, taking governments to court for failing to uphold these regulations (Horsley 2007). Yet loopholes in the regulations that, for example, exempt broadly defined 'state secrets' from disclosure, as well as poor enforcement mean that many citizens are still denied access to basic government information.

The beginning of the reform era heralded increased opportunities and higher stakes for official corruption. Problems have included the buying and selling of official posts, creation of slush funds, and siphoning-off of money from infrastructure projects including the Three Gorges Dam and, more recently, construction projects in preparation for the 2008 Beijing Olympics. Since the late 1990s the CCP has started to take the issue of vice more seriously due to its undermining of party legitimacy, to the extent that over 200,000 corruption cases were investigated between 1998 and 2003 (Saich 2004: 331). Improved accountability mechanisms such as the spread of government audits since the 1990s have helped identify a large number of corruption cases (Yang 2004), while others have been exposed through citizen complaints and the media. However, many more cases have gone unpunished and the party is loathe to implement structural solutions necessary to curb official vice including establishing an independent corruption monitoring body, while corrupt senior officials tend only to be targeted in cases where political gain can be achieved (Saich 2004).

## Democracy and the administrative system

The Chinese system of public administration is based not on democratic principles but on authoritarian ones, and substantial progress has not been made toward democratisation. Through public administration reforms, the PRC has attempted to restructure its organisations, improve public administrative efficiency, perfect management practices and improve the relations between the government and the public so as to acquire a high prestige and political legitimacy. All these factors are claimed to have pushed China toward the direction of 'socialist democratic politics'.

One of the most eye-catching political reforms in China, known as 'grassroots democracy' or 'village democracy', is village elections and self-government, launched in rural China in the 1980s. The 1982 constitution provides for villagers' committees, directly elected by village residents, to handle public affairs and carry out public administration within the villages. As demonstrated previously, the formal administrative system extends from the centre down to the township level, which is one organisational level above the village. In 1987 the National People's Congress (NPC) adopted a provisional law that was made permanent as the Organic Law of Villagers' Committees (VC) in November 1998. The VC Law incorporates important democratic elements designed to ensure that the villagers truly have a choice in selecting their leaders. These include:

- open, direct nominations by individuals rather than groups;
- multiple candidates;
- secret ballots;
- the mandatory use of secret voting booths to ensure the integrity of the individual vote;
- a public count of the votes;
- immediate announcement of election results;
- recall procedures.

The VC Law also strengthens measures on transparency and accountability to ensure 'democratic' self-government. It introduces the so-called 'four democracies': democratic election, democratic decision-making, democratic management and democratic supervision. The VC must not only abide by majority rule in making decisions and obtaining approval from the villager assembly for action on specified matters but must also adhere to the principle of 'open management' of village public affairs.

Some observers have optimistically argued that the implementation of village democracy has significantly improved public administration and governance in many Chinese villages and may make a significant contribution to China's democratisation from the bottom up (e.g. Brandtstadter and Schubert 2005). However, a great deal of evidence also indicates that the impact of village democracy functioning in an authoritarian environment is actually quite limited and even the democratically elected VCs are generally more responsive to the higher-level government than the villagers (Alpermann 2001). In addition, hopes that village elections might be extended to the township level have not been realised.

## Further developments and issues with the system

The PRC's system of public administration has undergone considerable changes in the past 30 years that have been necessitated by its market reforms. Reformers have been given the task of changing the role of government to one that can facilitate economic development. Much progress has been made in a comparatively short time frame. Yet these changes are ongoing, and China's public administration system is still very much a work in progress. As well as internal demand for a government apparatus more closely aligned with its move towards market economics, external pressures such as WTO membership will also continue to shape public administration. China has proven willing to learn from the experience of other countries, and its public administration reforms have sometimes consciously imitated western nations. However, the PRC has its own unique political context that also exerts significant influence. At times, the need to uphold CCP power can be seen as an impediment to public administration reforms. What is clear is that, some borrowing from the West notwithstanding, these reforms have displayed, and will continue to display, their own 'Chinese characteristics'.

There are several key issues that China needs to address in the coming years. One such issue is the need to improve the extractive capacity of the state in order that basic public services can be provided to all. Another key issue is the extent to which accountability and transparency can be improved within China's one-party state. The country's leaders have spoken about the importance of openness and accountability on many occasions, but appear unwilling to make the structural changes necessary, such as giving independence to the courts. Once again, the CCP will need to balance its goals in terms of establishing a modern and effective administration with the more important one of maintaining its grip on power.

# References

Adams, J., Young, A. and Wu, Z. (2006) 'Public Private Partnerships in China: System, Constraints and Future Prospects', *International Journal of Public Sector Management*, 19, 4: 384–96.

Alpermann, B. (2001) 'The Post-election Administration of Chinese Villages', *The China Journal*, 46: 45–67.

Brandtstadter, S. and Schubert, G. (2005) 'Democratic Thought and Practice in Rural China', *Democratization*, 12, 5: 801–91.

Burns, J. (2001) 'The Civil Service System of China: The Impact of the Environment', in Burns, J. and Bowornwathana, B. (eds), *Civil Service Systems in Asia*, Cheltenham: Edward Elgar, pp. 79–116.

Burns, J. (2003) '"Downsizing" the Chinese State: Government Retrenchment in the 1990s', *The China Quarterly*, 138: 458–91.

Burns, J. (2007) 'Civil Service Reform in China', *OECD Journal on Budgeting*, 7 (1): 1–25.

Cabestan, J.P. (2009) 'Provincial and Sub-Provincial Structure Since 1949: Overview', in Pong, D. (ed.) *Encyclopedia of Modern China*, Detroit: Charles Scribner's Sons, pp. 204–16.

Chan, H. and Li, E. (2007) 'Civil Service Law in the People's Republic of China: A Return to Cadre Personnel Management', *Public Administration Review*, 67, 3: 383–98.

Chen, J. (2004) 'The Revision of the Constitution in the PRC: A Great Leap Forward or a Symbolic Gesture?', *China Perspectives*, May–June, 15–32.

Cho, Y. (2002) 'From "Rubber Stamps" to "Iron Stamps": The Emergence of Chinese Local People's Congresses as Supervisory Powerhouses', *The China Quarterly*, 171: 724–40.

Chou, B. (2004) 'Civil Service Reform in China, 1993–2001: A Case of Implementation Failure', *China: An International Journal*, 2, 2: 210–34.

Chou, B. (2005) 'Implementing the Reform of Performance Appraisal in China's Civil Service', *China Information*, 19, 1: 39–65.

Chou, B. (2008) 'Does "Good Governance" Matter? Civil Service Reform in China', *International Journal of Public Administration*, 31, 1: 54–75.

Edin, M. (2003) 'State Capacity and Local Agent Control in China: CCP Cadre Management from a Township Perspective', *The China Quarterly*, 173: 35–52.

Heimer, M. (2006) 'The Cadre Responsibility System and the Changing Needs of the Party', in Brodsgaard, K. and Zheng, Y. (eds), *The Chinese Communist Party in Reform*, Abingdon: Routledge, pp. 122–38.

Horsley, J. (2007) 'China Adopts First Nationwide Open Government Information Regulations'. Online, available at: www.freedominfo.org/features/20070509.htm (accessed 20 September 2012).

Howell, J. (2004) 'Governance Matters: Key Challenges and Emerging Tendencies', in Howell, J. (ed.) *Governance in China*, Lanham: Rowman and Littlefield, pp. 1–18.

Hussain, A. and Stern, N. (2008) 'Public Finances, the Role of the State, and Economic Transformation, 1978–2020', in Lou, J. and Wang, S. (eds), *Public finance in China: Reform and Growth for a Harmonious Society*, Washington DC: The World Bank, pp. 13–38.

Lee, P. and Lo, C. (2001) 'Remaking China's Public Management: Problem Areas and Analytical Perspectives', in Lee, P. and Lo, C. (eds), *Remaking China's Public Management*, Westport: Quorum Books, pp. 1–18.

Lieberthal, K. (2004) *Governing China: From Revolution Through Reform* (2nd edn), New York: W.W. Norton.

Liou, K. (1997) 'Issues and Lessons of Chinese Civil Service Reform', *Public Personnel Management*, 26, 4: 505–14.

Ma, J. (2009) 'The Dilemma of Developing Financial Accountability Without Election – A Study of China's Recent Budget Reforms', *The Australian Journal of Public Administration*, 68, 1: 62–72.

Ministry of Civil Affairs (2008) *Zhonghua Renmin Gong He Guo Xingzheng Quhua Jiance (2008) (People's Republic of China Administrative Divisions Handbook (2008))*, Beijing: China Society Press.

OECD (2005) *Governance in China*, Paris: Organisation for Economic Co-operation and Development.

Peerenboom, R. (2002) *China's Long March Toward Rule of Law*, Cambridge: Cambridge University Press.

Reuters (2009) 'China's Civil Service Exam Cheaters Go High-Tech', 18 January. Online, available at: www.reuters.com/article/idUSTRE50I03020090119 (accessed 17 September 2013).

Reuters (2010) 'Chinese Advocate of Quake Victims Sentenced Over E-Mails', 8 February. Online, available at: www.nytimes.com/2010/02/09/world/asia/09 china.html (accessed at 17 September 2013).

Saich, T. (2004) *Governance and Politics of China* (2nd edn), Basingstoke: Palgrave Macmillan.

Tai, Z. and Sun, T. (2007) 'Media Dependencies in a Changing Media Environment: The Case of the 2003 SARS Epidemic in China', *New Media and Society*, 9, 6: 987–1009.

Tong, C., Straussman, J. and Broadnax, W. (1999) 'Civil Service Reform in the People's Republic of China: Case Studies of Early Implementation', *Public Administration and Development*, 19: 193–206.

Tsao, K. and Worthley, A. (2009) 'Civil Service Development in China and America: A Comparative Perspective, *Public Administration Review*, December, 88–94.

Wong, C. (2000) 'Central-local Relations Revisited: The 1994 Tax Sharing Reform and Public Expenditure Management in China', Paper for the International Conference on 'Central-Periphery Relations in China: Integration, Disintegration or Reshaping of an Empire?', Chinese University of Hong Kong, March 24–25.

Online, available at: www.cuhk.edu.hk/gpa/wang_files/C%20Wong%202000.pdf (accessed 17 September 2013).

Wong, C. (2009) 'Central–Local Relations in an Era of Fiscal Decline: The Paradox of Fiscal Decentralisation in Post-Mao China', *The China Quarterly*, 128: 691–715.

Wong, C. and Bird, R. (2008) 'China's Fiscal System: A Work in Progress', in Brandt, L. and Rawski, T. (eds), *China's Great Transformation: Origins, Mechanism, and Consequences of the Post-Reform Economic Boom*, New York: Cambridge University Press, pp. 429–66.

Xinhua News Agency (2006) 'China Revises 2004 GDP Growth to 10.1%', 9 January. Online, available at: http://news.xinhuanet.com/english/2006–01/09/content_ 4032734.htm (accessed 17 September 2013).

Yang, D. (2004) *Remaking the Chinese Leviathan: Market Transition and the Politics of Governance in China*, Stanford: Stanford University Press.

Yang, S., Xiao, J. and Pendlebury, M. (2008) 'Government Auditing in China: Problems and Reform', *Advances in Accounting*, 24, 1: 119–27.

Zheng, Y. (2007) *De Facto Federalism in China: Reforms and Dynamics of Central-Local Relations*, Singapore: World Scientific Publishing Ltd.

Zhong, Y. (2003) *Local Government and Politics in China: Challenges from Below*, New York: M.E. Sharpe.

Zou, K. (2006) *China's Legal Reform towards the Rule of Law*, Boston: Martinus Nijhoff Publishers.

# 10 The Federal Republic of India

*David Pell*

## Political culture

> [A] few million urbanites, white collar workers, trade union leaders, large farmers, blackmarketeers, politicians, police officers, journalists, scholars, stockbrokers, bureaucrats, exporters and tourists can now drink Coke, watch Sony television, operate Hewlett Packard personal computers, drive Suzukis and use Parisian perfumes, while the rest of the people live in anguish. (Tharoor 1997: 175)

The failure of the Indian democracy to make greater progress in combating widespread and extreme poverty among its people in spite of having huge natural and human resources at its disposal is dramatic. Such failures are commonly attributed to Indian 'bureaucracy', using the word in the pejorative sense and give credence to the claim by Harvard economist, Lant Pritchett, that India's public sector is 'one of the world's top ten biggest problems – of the order of AIDS and climate change' (*The Economist* 2008). A much less serious but more globally public example of this malaise presented to the world through the apparently poor organisation of the 2010 Commonwealth Games in Delhi. This contrasts with the, clearly, very competent organisation of the Beijing Olympic Games by the authoritarian regime in China in 2008 and that by the United Kingdom in 2012. The failure of India's public sector also contrasts with the considerable successes of its private sector. This has, for example, made good use of India's large educated, English speaking, workforce, commanding 44 per cent of the global market for IT business processes offshore according to Deutsche Bank Research (2005) and is seen as the 'world's back office'. The success of the private sector is also further evidenced in the eyes of the world, by its development of the very commercial 20/20 brand of cricket.

The huge scale of the failure of the Indian public sector and its administration makes its investigation an important task for the political scientist. It is also an interesting one because, as Soni (2008: 1161) argues: 'Given its large size, diversity, and vibrant social and political system, India is an exceptionally good case for examining themes of general significance in comparative public administration.'

The Indian system of government and public administration is, on the face of it, very similar to the British system. This is not surprising, of course, because it was modelled on the British system when India gained independence from Britain in 1947. Nevertheless, any such comfortable familiarity is misleading because the Indian context makes the operation of the system hugely different. A brief history is needed to begin to explain this context.

The Federal Republic of India (also known as Bharat) was established on 15 August 1947 as a parliamentary democracy when it ceased to be a part of the British Empire and became the Union of India, an independent dominion of the British Commonwealth from which, on 26 January 1950, the modern Republic of India was created. It is the world's biggest democracy having about 716 million electors in 2009 (Election Commission of India 2009) and, according to the CIA (2010), has about one-sixth of the world's population, at 1.173 billion. The United Nations (2006) draws attention to the very wide ethnic and religious diversity of this population and its many widely differing beliefs about the proper role of nationalism, suggesting that the country is more of a world civilisation than a simple nation state. It is a new, sovereign, socialist, democratic, republican nation based on an ancient civilisation and its traditional past has greatly influenced the nature of its political culture and democratic processes. Mohandas Karamchand Gandhi (Mahatma Ghandi) was the political and spiritual leader of the Indian Independence movement relying on civil disobedience and non-violence. Ghandi is recognised as the father (*Bapu*) of the Indian nation, commemorated there on 2 October each year (his birth date) by a national holiday and, worldwide, in the form of an International Day of Non-Violence. He was assassinated on 30 January 1948, only five months after his nation achieved independence.

The territory was a part of that known previously as British India under the tenancy of the English East India Company or the sovereignty of the British crown from 1612. British India included 17 provinces and 562 princely states. After the Second World War, an interim government in India was established, led by Jawaharlal Nehru. The Muslim League refused to take part in the Constituent Assembly and campaigned for a separate state for Pakistan. Lord Louis Mountbatten, the last Viceroy of India (and who subsequently became the First Governor General of the Indepenent Union of India, 1947–8), produced a plan for the division of India into India and Pakistan. Jawaharlal Nehru became the first prime minster and remained in post until his death in 1964.

The partitioning of the territory resulted in the Muslim majority in the east and north-west of British India becoming the Dominion of Pakistan in the Commonwealth of Nations. The partition of the Punjab in particular was accompanied by horrific casualties from conflict, including 1 million deaths, which accompanied the movement of about 16 million people, with Hindus moving one way and Muslims moving the other. Kashmir, in the sub-continent's far north, soon became a source of controversy that erupted into the first Indo-Pakistan war lasting from 1947 to 1949. The United Nations ultimately oversaw a ceasefire that left India with two-thirds of the contested region. Pakistan became a republic in 1956. The constitution of India became operative in Kashmir on 26 January 1957 and included special clauses for this state. East and west Pakistan were geographically remote from each other and, in 1971, following a civil war, the former became Bangladesh.

On partition, the princes could choose to remain independent or to join one or other of the two nations. India's leaders thus had a fragmented nation of medieval kingdoms and provinces previously ruled by sovereign powers. Vallabhbhai Patel (generally known as *Sardar* meaning 'chief' in many of the Indian languages) was a leading supporter of Ghandi in the struggle for independence and he went on to lead its integration as an independent and united nation as Home Minister. At the request of Ghandi he had stepped down in the 1946 Congress presidency election in favour of Jawaharlal Nehru. Patel is credited with having brought together all parts of India into a federation with the exception of Jammu and Kashmir. While, as India's first Prime Minister, Nehru was extremely popular with the people, it was Patel who had the loyalty and trust of congressmen as well as India's Civil Services.

The new nation faced massive challenges such as rapid population growth, large-scale poverty and inequality closely linked with a rigid caste system and widespread and endemic corruption. It has been argued that democracy was ill-suited to meeting these challenges. Moore (1966), for example, noted that it may seem odd to find a political democracy in an Asian setting without an industrial revolution. He argued that while, economically, India belonged to the pre-industrial age, politically, it belonged to the modern world. Moore explained this as the state's legacy as a colony arguing that democracy had been at the root of the nation's struggles to lift its population out of poverty when coercion was needed. He concluded that: 'Only the future will tell whether it is possible to modernize Indian society and retain or extend democratic freedoms' (Moore 1966: 315). In a similar vein and more recently, Jain (2001) observed that India's achievements as a democracy should not be underestimated because the Indian state was an experiment in establishing a sovereign republic with a 'parliamentary democracy' and not many commentators had thought that India would survive in this form. These included John Stuart Mill who claimed that 'democracy is next to impossible in multi-ethnic societies and completely impossible in linguistically divided countries' (Jain 2001: 1300) and Robert Dahl, who believed 'that widespread poverty and illiteracy are anathema to stable democracy' (Jain 2001: 1300).

India has defied these negative predictions because democracy has survived albeit heavily blighted by corruption. Moreover, considerable economic growth has been achieved, especially since trade liberalisation in the early 1990s. India's GDP real growth rate in 2011–12 is estimated as 6.8 per cent against estimates for 2010–11 and 2009–10 of 10.1 per cent and 5.9 per cent respectively. While this put India thirty-fifth in the world for 2011–12 it was the second highest after China among the major economies at 9.2 per cent and ninth (CIA Factbook 2012). In March 2010, Manmohan Singh, the

Prime Minister, announced a growth rate target of 10 per cent during the period of the Twelfth Plan (2012–17) (Business Standard 2010). Unfortunately, recent history has also shown that, in spite of this economic success, Indian society remains hugely unequal and most of its population remains exceedingly poor. According to UNEP (2010), for example, 27.5 per cent of Indians live below the national income poverty line.

The Eleventh Five-Year Plan, which covers the period 2007–12 (Eleventh Five-Year Plan para 1.4) points out that there has been some progress, however, because: 'The percentage of the population below the official poverty line has come down from 36 per cent in 1993–94.' It also concedes, however, that 'the rate of decline in poverty has not accelerated along with the growth in GDP, and the incidence of poverty among certain marginalized groups, for example the Scheduled Tribes, has hardly declined at all' (para 1.4). The UN Food and Agriculture Organisation (2008) estimated that India was home to more than 230 million undernourished people; 21 per cent of the national population. In addition to poverty and inequality, language, illiteracy, religion, caste and, especially, widespread corruption are also very significant to the political culture of India.

Hindi is widely spoken as the first language of 41 per cent of the people according to the 2001 Census (CIA Factbook 2012) and is spoken in most of the cities but there are 21 other languages recognised by the constitution including Bengali, Gujarati, Kashmiri, Punjabi, Sanskrit, Tamil and Urdu. There are hundreds of dialects in use. While English has only associate status it is the most used language for political and business purposes. India also has the largest number of adults who are illiterate in the world at 300 million (Planning Commission of India 2002).

While the constitution permits any religion as a secular state, those that predominate are Hinduism, Christianity, Sikhism, Buddhism and Jainism. Religion and caste are closely related and, in spite of the preamble to the constitution, which prohibits public discrimination on the basis of class, and continuing efforts to remove the caste system as a main cause of inequality in Indian society, it remains a major feature (Heitzman and Worden 1995: 2010). Social inequalities deriving from caste are also closely entangled with economic inequality. While in 2011–12 there was an estimated overall rate of unemployment of 9.8 per cent (CIA Factbook 2012), it is much higher for the lower castes. Thus, the social, political and economic fabric of the Indian state is much influenced by the impact of the caste system especially at the local level where caste-based politics is most apparent. Bidwai (2002), a former senior editor of *The Times of India*, for example, points out that:

> Oppression of 160 million Dalits is an enduring reality of India's countryside. To be a Dalit means having to live a sub-human, degraded, insecure existence. Every hour, two Dalits are assaulted. Every day, three Dalit women are raped; two Dalits are killed. This violence has a precise function: perpetuate social hierarchy, defend servitude, and preserve

conditions for the ruthless exploitation of the poorest people. Corrective measures are needed-urgently.

Against these, and other problems such as corruption, which is discussed later, India has enormous opportunities. While it is given as only the tenth largest economy in the world by nominal GDP (IMF 2012), Pricewaterhouse-Coopers (*The Times of India* 2010) argued that India could replace Japan as the third largest economy behind the US and China by 2012, when measured by purchasing power parity. Indeed, on this basis, India was very close behind Japan by 2011 (IMF 2012). PricewaterhouseCoopers further argued that India is likely to grow faster than China after 2020. These factors are likely to help to provide India with the economic means, at least, to make progress against its many problems and to achieve better lifestyles for all of her people. Jain (2008) similarly points out that the process of economic liberalisation and the rolling back of the state, which began in the early 1990s, has been aided by The Disinvestment Commission of India, which was set up in 1996 with some notable success. It has brought in foreign and private capital to ease the government's investment levels in some basic industries such as power, road and air transport, albeit against considerable opposition from trade unions and leftist political parties and also from the reality that in this huge developing country the private sector cannot be expected to meet the huge needs.

As Soni (2008) argues, however, while liberalisation of Indian markets in the early 1990s and globalisation have resulted in modernisation, greater wealth and a larger middle class they have also created a huge and urgent need for the reform of Indian public administrative administration, the development of infrastructure and the narrowing of the gap between rich and poor.

Since independence, the federal government has been dominated mostly by the Indian National Congress (INC) and that of the states by several national parties including the INC, the Bharatiya Janata Party (BJP) and the Communist Party of India (Marxist) (CPI(M)) and a variety of regional parties. The INC is seen as centre left in the Indian political spectrum and was established in 1885 and became the leader of the Independence movement and, after independence and until quite recently, has frequently been led by members of the Nehru-Gandhi family. India's second largest political party, the BJP, was created in 1980 and advocates conservative, right of centre, social policies and free-market capitalism as well as strong national defence. In alliance with others, it was in government from 1998 to 2004. This P. V. Narasimha Rao-, BJP-led government had a huge influence on the direction of the nation, which was on the brink of bankruptcy. It oversaw the dismantling of the 'Licence Raj' and major economic reform in favour of the free market as well as the introduction of a system of local self-governance for the rural population. This apparent dominance by a few major parties should not be allowed to obscure the fact that India has many political parties and that coalitions are usual at both union and state level. Very significantly, the political and governmental scene has become increasingly characterised by raucous debate, politicking and corruption rather than effective government (see 'Managing the system', below).

In May 2009, the Indian National Congress-led left of centre/centrist coalition (forming the United Progressive Alliance) was elected by a 'landslide', to serve a second term and Manmohan Singh (born 1933), an economic reformer, began a second term as Prime Minister. The opposition BJP conceded defeat. Smt. Pratibha Devisingh Patil became the twelfth, and first female, President of India on 25 July 2007. She was born in 1934, a trained lawyer, and was nominated by the Indian National Congress Party. In July 2012 on demitting the office and, having been accused of corruption in relation to her retirement home and 'gifts' to her home village, she pointed out that the scourge of corruption is the enemy of good governance. Her successor, Pranab Mukherjee, from India's governing Congress Party was sworn in as India's thirteenth President at 76 years of age and vowed to fight corruption (NDTV 2012).

## The constitutional arrangement

The Republic of India's written constitution was agreed by the Constituent Assembly on 26 November 1949 and it came into force on 26 January 1950. It is the longest of any country in the world having 117,369 words in 395 articles, 22 parts and 12 schedules. It has 94 amendments. There is an English version with an official Hindi translation (full text: India Gov 2010). It is India's supreme law, not only setting out the framework of political principles but also the governmental structure, powers and procedures. It declares that the Union of India is a sovereign and democratic republic and guarantees basic rights for its citizens including justice, equality, liberty. It also sets out to promote fraternity and the words 'socialist', 'secular' and 'integrity' were added in 1976 by constitutional amendment. The main principles of the constitution, which cannot be changed, include, supremacy of the constitution, the rule of law, the separation of powers, fundamental rights, judicial review, free and fair elections and the independence of the judiciary. The constitution now provides for a multi-level system of governance from the national level to the state, to the district and the village or municipality.

The state's central government is divided into three branches as in the British system: the legislative, the executive and the judicial. Also as in the British system, the leadership of the executive is derived from the legislative body. A separation of powers is almost achieved. Article 50 requires the separation of the judiciary and the executive but, in fact, the executive is in control of judicial appointments. A significant feature of the Indian polity has been a struggle between those wanting to use legislative power to change the constitution and those who have supported the efforts of the judiciary to retain its basic structure (National Portal of India 2010). The system has been durable. Elections have never been cancelled and all 400,000 plus votes are counted within just one day and governments get changed as a result of elections.

The constitution (Article 79) provides that the supreme legislative body is the Council of the Parliament of the Union consisting of the president and the two Houses known as the Council of States (*Rajya Sabha*), the upper house, and the House of the People (*Lok Sabha*), the lower house. In reality, though, much of the executive power of the Union effectively rests with the Council of Ministers, which has the prime minister as its head. The president's role is largely ceremonial, much closer to that of the British monarch than to that of the US president. The post-holder can ask the Council to reconsider a particular matter but if they adhere to their advice then the president must act in accordance with it. The president and vice president are elected indirectly by an electoral college for a period of five years and with staggered terms. The vice president does not succeed to the office of president automatically. The electoral college consists of elected members of parliament and state assemblies through a system of proportional representation. The only way the president can be removed is through impeachment by the Houses of Parliament for violating the constitution.

While the Council and prime minister are, theoretically, collectively responsible to the House of the People (*Lok Sabha*), real power has been shifted from these institutions through the operation of political parties. This is rather similar to the way in which the UK prime minister and his/her cabinet have become more accountable to their political party than to parliament. The power of the Council of Ministers with the prime minister as its head is also facilitated by Article 74(1), which requires that it aid and advise the president and that he/she must exercise his/her functions in accordance with that advice (India Gov 2010). The People's Assembly has 543 seats with two being appointed by the president. Members are elected directly by the people through universal adult suffrage and they serve five-year terms. Members of this lower house are known as Members of Parliament as in the UK system. There are reserved constituencies for Scheduled Castes and Scheduled Tribes and a significant number (about 110) of the state representatives are from these. The possibility of reserved seats for women has also been under discussion for some time. Like the UK House of Commons elections, the direct voting system for membership of the *Lok Sabha* is on the basis of a single vote, single constituency and first-past-the-post. This bicameral system provides for not more than 250 members in the Council of States (*Rajya Sabha*) up to 12 of whom are appointed by the president and the others being chosen by the elected members of the state and territorial assemblies serving six-year terms. This territorial, state-based constitution for the Upper House resembles that of the US Senate more closely than that of the British House of Lords. The Council of States is a permanent institution with one-third of members retiring every second year to ensure continuity and the vice president of India is its *ex-officio* chairman.

The powers of the parliament and the 28 states to legislate are given in Article 245 and the 7th Schedule of the constitution. The two Houses are given similar powers by the constitution but each also has special powers that the other does not. There are rules, for example, to enable the *Rajya Sabha*, to make a law in relation to any matter on the State List or to create an All India Service. Similarly, the *Lok Sabha* is given the special power to control the purse strings. All departmental expenditure has to be agreed by this lower House and Money Bills can be introduced only here.

The constitution puts the Indian Supreme Court at the top of the judiciary that it establishes. It has jurisdiction over any dispute between the government and the states or between states. The constitution also gives the Court power to decide matters of Fundamental Rights. It has appellate jurisdiction overall courts and tribunals in India. The Supreme Court has 26 judges, one of whom is the Chief Justice. The High Court is at the head of the judicial system at state level. There are also village council (*Panchayat*) courts (see 'Federal and local government' below) in some states, which determine petty civil and criminal matters. State law governs these. There are District and Session judges for judicial districts.

## The civil service

The bureaucratic roots of the Indian Civil Service were put down long before those of the British system and so there are considerable differences. Subramaniam (1998: 88), for example, argued: 'Of the three fully developed ancient bureaucracies of India, China, and Iran, the Indian legacy has made the strongest and most widespread contribution to modern public administration in the Third World mainly through the agency of the British Empire.' He argues that this was, in part, the result of the British having no

> precedents, experience or ideas available from their own domestic non-bureaucratic arrangements for applying to their new Indian possessions in the late 18th century and hence they picked up, polished, and adapted the relevant practices of Indian administration to their immediate needs.

One aspect of this was a continuance of the idea of 'district overlord', a term that is further explained under 'Federal and local government', below.

Against the background of a greater acceptance of utilitarian values in Britain, the Indian Civil Service was established in 1911 by the British government with the aim of strengthening the control available to the colonial power. Initially, only British people were recruited, by examination in English and in London. Under pressure from the Indian National Congress and political calls for independence, however, Indian nationals were increasingly also recruited with the aim of achieving a 50/50 balance and, towards this end, the examination could, then, be taken in India as well as in London.

After independence, three phases can be identified in the development of India's Civil Service (Mishra 2010). Initially, the role for civil servants was no longer that of running a 'police state', but that of unifying the new state and running a 'welfare state' that aimed to secure minimum living standards for the population, including settling the many refugees. To these ends, and uniquely among constitutions, the Indian Constitution (Article 312) specifically allowed parliament (with a two-thirds majority in the Council of States, the *Rajya Sabha*) to create All India Services to operate at both union and state level. The constitution itself prescribed that the Indian Administrative Service and the Indian Police Service were to be deemed as All India Services created by parliament under the article. Legislation in 1962 established three more All India Services, i.e. the Indian Engineering Service, the Indian Forest Service and the Indian Medical and Health Service.

Central Services were also created to serve the union territories and these are organised into four categories of importance. This division included an A group and a B group. The A Group comprised the Indian Foreign Service, the Indian Railway Service, the Indian Postal Service, Accounts and Auditing Services and the Indian Revenue Service. Group B included Central Secretariat Services (Section Officer Grade), Railway Board Secretariat Services (Section Officer Grade) and State Civil Services. This arrangement continues today. The provinces had their own civil services.

According to Mishra (2010), a second phase arrived when economic planning began in 1951 with the launch of the first Five-Year Plan and the Indian Civil Service took on the huge additional role of socio-economic development planning. This included managing public enterprises, regulating aspects of the private sector, reducing poverty and developing rural areas. This continued until the 1990s when a third phase emerged. In India, as in the UK, for example, politics moved to rolling back the welfare state and it set out to become a facilitator in many services rather than a direct provider.

The independent Union Public Services Commission (UPSC) was established (from the Federal Public Services Commission) by the constitution (Article 135) to help remove nepotism and other corruption in the civil service. Its brief includes recruitment through competitive examinations and interviews, advising the government on promotions and recruitment and dealing with disciplinary matters, pensions etc. The UPSC has to be consulted in relation to recruitment to all higher posts and the Staff Selection Commission recruits to lower-level posts. A third range of bodies, the Public Enterprise Selection Boards, recruit senior staff for the public service enterprises. In the case of Indian Railways, for example, the UPSC recruits to the higher grades by conducting examinations, whereas 19 Railway Recruitment Boards, which report to the Railway Recruitment Control Board, recruit to the lower grades. Training for all staff is done by six centralised training bodies (e.g. Indian Railway Establishment Code 2010).

Lloyd George (British Prime Minister between 1916–22) described the colonial Indian Civil Service as the 'steel frame' of British rule. Upon independence, the Indian Administrative Service (IAS) was designed to perform the same unifying function. This is the highest cadre of the civil service succeeding the Indian (Imperial) Civil Service of British India. A mere 5,600 elite officers serve in the IAS, which, virtually, 'runs' India. Supervised by the Ministry of Home Affairs, IAS officers occupy important government posts at the centre and in the states. This includes 600 or so of these most senior *babus* (civil servants) working on policy, in Whitehall fashion, at the centre with ministers in Delhi (*The Economist* 2008). It also includes the collectors who each lead the (union run) civil services in one of India's 604 districts, and most of its public sector senior managers in the ministries, public corporations, police and railways.

According to *The Economist* (2008) the IAS is both respected (especially as a unifying force) and held in contempt. Evidence of the latter is given in the form of the comment of Sanjoy Bagchi, the author of a recent IAS history and former mandarin, who claimed that:

> Overwhelmed by the constant feed of adulatory ambrosia, the maturing entrant tends to lose his head and balance. The diffident youngster of early idealistic years, in course of time, is transformed into an arrogant senior fond of throwing his weight around; he becomes a conceited prig.

It is also argued that the quality of IAS recruits is deteriorating perhaps, according to *The Economist* (2008), because of increased competition for the best young people from the private sector, more political interference and, most significantly, caste-based restrictions. Half of IAS posts are now reserved for people who are outcaste, low-caste or from tribal communities. With only about 150 recruits into the IAS each year out of 200,000 applicants, however, it is clearly a desirable role. So much so that it is claimed (*The Economist* 2008) that its male officers are among India's most marriageable: more so even than those in the elite of the country's booming computer-services industry.

On the face of it and formally, the Indian political and administrative systems are of the rational-legal ideal type but, in reality and informally, they are, to varying degrees, patrimonial (in terms of Weber's, 1947, 'ideal types'). This has been against all efforts to render them closer to the 'rational-legal' type. The latter is distinguished by a hierarchy based on grades, written policies/procedures and full-time politically neutral, salaried staff. In the 'rational-legal' type, the following of official rules is much valued and any charges for services go to government and not into the pockets of the civil servants. In patrimonial systems, civil servants answer only to the politicians and government jobs are income-producing personal possessions. Subramaniam (2008) offers a partial explanation for this strong tendency in India towards the patrimonial type by observing that the modern 'ideal type' of legal-rational bureaucracy derives from a gesellschaft society (Tönnies 1887) that is organised into impersonal functional associations, whereas the more feudal societies of both India and Britain were, for much of the period of empire, characterised by all-purpose, natural groups of gemeinschaft society (Tönnies 1887). This provided fertile ground for the persistence and growth of the tradition of 'clientelism' and 'patrimonialism' in India after independence.

The idea of 'clientelism' is closely related to that of 'patrimonialism' and Brinkerhoff and Goldsmith (2002: 40) describe it as: 'A political system based on conditional loyalties and involving mutual benefits, in which individuals of unequal power are linked together through the exchange of favors.' Breeding (2008), for example, in her extensive study of 'clientelism' in Bangalore provides as an example, a well-dressed politician promising a group of poor women sewing machines for their votes. Whether offering such simple benefits is a caring act for one's constituents or an attempt to buy political support is debatable. A further example is that given by Jeffrey (2002) and cited by Brinkerhoff and Goldsmith (2002: 29) in relation to the Uttar Pradesh Cane Societies in northern India. The societies are intermediaries between the farmers and the sugar mills. They have locally elected officials and also permanent, government-appointed, staff. The latter send out supply slips on a quota basis to farmers to ask them to deliver cane. They may delay sending the slips or making payment unless the (often Muslim) farmer pays a bribe. It seems that things may be improving since a low-caste political party took control of the Uttar Pradesh government because the face-to-face system has been replaced by direct crediting of bank accounts.

Brinkerhoff and Goldsmith (2002: 1) argue that:

> In many cases, informal systems of clientelism and patrimonialism are key contributors to stifling popular participation, subverting the rule of law, fostering corruption, distorting the delivery of public services, discouraging investment and undermining economic progress. Because they are deeply entrenched, seldom authorized or openly acknowledged, and take different forms depending on their context, clientelistic networks can be both difficult to detect and to remove.

They go on to argue that the Indian system has also been distinguished by 'rent seeking' activity. They define this as (p.41): 'Efforts to get government to create or maintain economic rents, which can then be seized for private gain, without regard for the general good.' They point out (p.15) that in the period of heavy economic regulation, until the early 1990s, this flourished in India, so much so that Indians have a special name for that period, i.e. 'permit raj' and that the Indian economy has grown hugely since its end. They add that the Indian bureaucrats liked the system of licences and quotas because it gave them a job and power as well as offering opportunities for corruption, discussed later.

A more general criticism of the Indian public sector is that it has become grossly bloated and overly bureaucratic. *The Economist* (2008), for example, reported that 'Babu India' (also often known as 'License Raj' for the bureaucracy) employs around 10 million civil servants with three million at central government (including railway workers) and seven million employed by the states. Only 80,000 of these were given as 'decision-makers'. It also argued that, while India has some of the hardest-working bureaucrats in the world, its administration is the most bureaucratic and has an abysmal public service record with 'vast armies of paper-shuffling peons'. An apparent symptom of this bloated and ill-managed service is the serious absenteeism among state employees. This is a huge problem and among the worst in the world, wasting huge amounts of money. Muralidharan (2007: 1) and fellow researchers, for example, reported that 'using representative data from the 19 largest states accounting for 98 percent of India's population – that on any given day 25 per cent of teachers in government schools and 40 per cent of medical workers in government health clinics cannot be found at the facility'. There were wide variations between states, for example, 15 percent of teachers were absent in Maharashtra and 71 per cent in Bihar. The study also made the point that the mere presence of staff is but the first requirement, what they are doing when there is also very important and they reported that 25–30 per cent of the teachers who were in school were not teaching 'and so less than half of the teachers were engaged in teaching activity'. This is despite the fact that teachers in the public sector are paid salaries which are over five times higher than those paid to private sector teachers. While it is often argued that low pay is at the root of non-attendance, Muralidharan and colleagues (2007: 2) found that 'the more highly paid teachers in public schools are in fact more likely to be absent, with absence being higher among more educated teachers, older teachers, and teachers holding higher ranks (all of which are associated with higher pay)'.

## Central government agencies

As explained above, some All India Services are, unusually, created by the constitution. Overall, though, the number and nature of ministries vary in accordance with political and administrative choices. There are usually around 50 ministries with 50 departments under the principal ministries. As Soni (2008) points out, for example, the Ministry of Personnel manages the central government's public services and is directly controlled by the prime minister. It designs polices and procedures in relation to recruitment, training, promotion, employee relations and working conditions.

The constitution also provides for some independent bodies such as the Election Commission (to conduct elections at all levels), the Finance Commission (appointed every five years to determine how revenue is distributed between the central and state governments), the Scheduled Castes and Tribes (SC/ST) Commissioners (to take care of the welfare of these groups) and the Office of the Comptroller and Auditor General (to audit the accounts of both the central and state governments). The latter has been especially bold in drawing attention to apparent corruption in recent years as explained below. The expenses of these bodies are a first charge on the Consolidated Fund of India to help ensure that they remain independent of parliament.

The economic planning regime in India has also produced a hierarchy of advisory bodies. The top body is the National Planning Commission, which works at the centre producing plans, monitoring progress of the plans and, generally, providing the government with expert advice on economic matters. There are also a variety of independent bodies such as Atomic Energy, Space and the Prime Minister's Office. The government of India is also the largest shareholder of the nation's largest bank, the State Bank of India.

## Federal and local governance

The Indian state is quasi-federal. While the constitution provides for some power to reside with the states, it is designed to ensure that the Union dominates. This continues the principle of centralisation from the British era (Jain 2001). As Reddy and Joseph (2004: 2) point out:

> Federalism in India is at once similar and distinct from other federations like that of America; distinct in that it is not a group of independent States coming together to form a federation by conceding a portion of their rights of government, but a distributed entity that derives its power from a single source – the Union.

The form of state government resembles that at Union level. The constitution (Article 153) provides that the executive role in each of the 28 states (but not the seven union territories) rests with the State Governor as the representative of the president. The appointment of governor is made by the president on the advice of the national government. The executive power of the state is carried by an elected chief minister who advises the governor and who heads a Council of Ministers. The chief minister is elected by the members of the legislative assembly. This arrangement mirrors that at the national level with the president, the prime minister and the Council of Ministers. Each state has a State Assembly that formally legislates with the governor, albeit the elected chief minister and the Council of Ministers, effectively deciding on the agenda. Most states have a unicameral legislature, i.e. just a Legislative Assembly, but six states, such as Andhra Pradesh and Tamil Nadu have bicameral legislatures having both a Legislative Assembly (*Vidhan Sabha*) and a Legislative Council (*Vidhan Parishad*) as an upper house. The constitution provides that the Assembly shall have between 60 and 500 members elected by adult suffrage, from the territorial constituencies decided by the Electoral Commission, and it serves for five years. It elects a speaker and deputy speaker. The Legislative Council is permanent, cannot be dissolved and is indirectly elected by the people with one-third of its membership retiring every two years.

The matters on which a state legislature may legislate have been explained above under 'The constitutional arrangement'. A vital function of a state legislative assembly is to approve the annual state budget and all Money Bills without which no expenditure is possible. The State High Court and the Supreme Court of India can challenge and amend decisions of a state legislative assembly if it is seen as unconstitutional. The Union government has more authority on state matters than each state. The governor can call an early election if s/he thinks that the governmental machinery is failing. Also, if the national government decides that matters in a state are in need of intervention, then the president can declare 'President's rule' in that state. At least, in theory, then, the Indian state can transform itself into a unitary one.

As Jain (2001) points out, as well as having the constitutional right to change the distribution of powers between the centre and the states, the Union also has huge powers over the raising and spending of revenues, which leave the state heavily dependent on the centre. He adds, however, that despite this centralising tendency, each state has its own personality and cannot be simply administered from the centre. Jain evidences this claim by citing the fact that the number, size, and composition of states has changed frequently as a result of the demands of the people in the regions. For example, three new states were created early this century, i.e. Uttaraanchal, Jharkhand and Chhatisgarh (lifting the total to 28). Some of the seven Union territories, including Delhi and Pondicherry, have also made claims to be lifted to state status. The Union government has even greater control over the union territories than it does over the states, albeit some have achieved more independence to run their own affairs.

Each state is divided into districts as the basic unit of state administration by the Union. There are about 500 districts with an average population of about two million. Subramaniam (1998) argues that the belief by the British that a powerful local figure was needed to run each district (as opposed to a more bureaucratic approach) caused the institution of district overlord to survive, to one degree or another, from the eighteenth-century Mughal Empire. These days, this is the centrally appointed, district collector (see 'The civil service' section above), who is the most powerful Union officer in the district responsible for services such as law and order, revenue collection, land registration (planning consents), elections, the decennial census and for dealing with natural or man-made emergencies. This idea of 'overlord' was exported to other Afro-Asian British possessions. Subramaniam also argues that it was a consequence of a combination of Indian paternalism and the growth of utilitarianism in Britain, which could not be fully expressed there because of its traditionalist opponents who disliked 'bureaucracy' as a continental disease and who preferred the landed aristocrats who governed, as gentleman-amateurs. The Indian district collector was, thus, revived by the British, albeit to be recruited by competitive examination and still survives as the district collector/co-ordinator, not just relied on for development in India but also in much of Malaysia and Africa.

The role of the district collector has changed over the years, for example, as a result of the Five-Year Plans (especially the welfare projects), an overload of work and the establishment of many more *panchayats* (local councils, see below). The collector's role is now mostly confined to leading the district revenue department and co-ordinating the work of the other departments such as public works, agriculture, public health and forestry, and for promoting social welfare and economic development. Jain (2001) argues that the importance of the 'district' and its chief executive has been reduced as a result of the fragmented expansions of government activity and the rise of the local political 'mafia'. He explains that the district officer now wastes most of his time in the rough and tumble of arguing with anti-social elements while the official work builds up. These shifts, he argues, and the fact that the collectors are usually quite young, have eroded the autonomy and respect once enjoyed in this role; most officers now want to complete their compulsory tenure of the role quickly and get posted back to the state capital. He concludes that the result of all of these changes is that local administration has greatly suffered.

*The Economist* (2008) illustrated some of this by presenting a case study of a district collector in Jalaun. The collector said that he has 65 government departments spending $22.5 million per year to run – without a single computer. While about one-fifth of them are run by competent deputies, he claimed that if he does not put pressure on his juniors 'everything gets largely corrupted'. The law and order aspect of his role is mostly performed by the local police chief but he is often called on in the case of the most serious matters. Directing the form and implementation of huge welfare and development projects is a task that the IAS was not designed for, and it performs abysmally in this respect. This district collector, for example, directs expenditure of another $25m on around 30 welfare schemes and, during the previous year, he had paid $14 million for a charitable ditch-digging project, the National Rural Employment Guarantee Scheme. In the face of a severe drought he had asked for another $13 million for the project. As Jain (2001) points out, a general rigidity, the inflexible adherence to rules and a lack of delegation of authority, hinder the collector's organisation from adapting to changing demands upon it.

The structure of local government below state level is complex and varies between states (See Figure 10.1).

Nevertheless there is an essential division between the governance of the urban/city areas and of the huge rural areas. The latter is known as the *Panchayat Raj* (Rule by Village Committee) and has had a chequered history. Local self-government in India existed in the form of *panchayats* (village councils) until the time of the Bruisers but, in the 1880s, the British tried unsuccessfully to re-establish them. Mahatma Gandhi stressed that local self-government through the establishment of *panchayats* was needed as was the giving of more power to them and Article 40 of the constitution directs states to take measures to organise village *panchayats* and to give them the necessary power to function

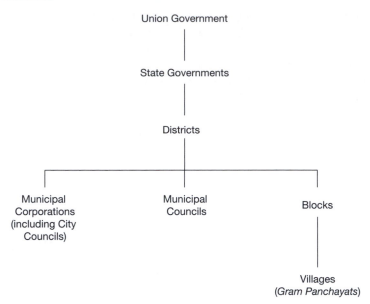

*Figure 10.1* Outline structure of the Indian government system

as units of self-government. In the 1950s the government began experimenting with schemes to develop community involvement and participation, and Jain (2001) describes how, at that time, each district was divided into blocks and *panchayats* of villages. West Bengal led the new push towards *panchayats* by providing significant funds and power to them as well as holding elections at all three levels also, for the first time, allowing the political parties to put up candidates. The State of Karnataka was also a frontrunner. Overall, however, progress with decentralisation was slow and in late 1989 Rajiv Gandhi's government attempted to get the 64th Amendment Bill passed to deliver power and resources to the *panchayat* system but the *Rajya Sabha* rejected it largely because of its hurried introduction in an election year made it look like a gimmick. In 1993, however, the 73rd Constitutional Amendment was made requiring the state legislatures to provide the Panchayati Raj Institutions (PRIs) with sufficient powers and authority to enable them to work as units of local self-governance and to plan and implement economic and development projects. These achieved constitutional status, having been previously considered as simply a state matter. The amendment provided that *panchayat* members are elected for five-year terms in elections under the control of the State Election Commissions. This amendment was not a response to grass-roots pressure but to growing recognition that other attempts to create local self-government in India had failed and that it was needed to help address rural poverty. It was a political initiative by the reforming BJP-led government of P.V. Narasimha Rao. It was, arguably, the largest decentralisation of governance experiment in history.

The *Panchayat Raj* is a three-tier system with elected units at district (*zilla panchayat*), block (*panchayat samati*) and village, or group of villages (*gram panchayat*) levels. Members from the village, *gram panchayats*, are elected to serve on the *Panchayaps samati*. The *tehsildar* serves a similar role at block level as that of the district collector at district level. This officer is the chief of the revenue department. The economic development and social welfare departments typically have offices at this level. There are over 500 district *panchayats* and 6,000 blocks with between 250–600 villages in each. There are about 250,000 *gram panchayats*. All of the states have adopted the changes and the *panchayats* cover almost all of India's villages and rural population with three million elected representatives. The income of the *gram panchayat* is achieved mostly through a property tax on buildings and the open spaces. There are also taxes on professions, pilgrimage and animal trade. Grants are given by the state government and by the Union government for specific purposes or projects. At *samiti* level there are staff and departments; typically seven or eight, including finance, health, education, social welfare and agriculture. There is usually a government-appointed block development officer. The *panchayat* systems main role is to improve the villages through tackling issues such as illiteracy, health, malnutrition, corruption and powerlessness. The responsibilities of *gram panchayats* can include safe and clean drinking water, primary and secondary education, adult education, rural electrification, family welfare, poverty alleviation, rural housing, village roads, records of births, deaths and marriages, tax and revenue collection and libraries.

The members of the *gram panchayats* are elected by locals, and the chairman, the *Sarpanch*, is either elected by the locals or by the *panchayat* members. The amendment required that seats be reserved in *panchayats* for women and SC/ST. A *gram sabha* is usually associated with each *gram panchayat* and it refers to all men and women in the village over 18 years of age. It meets quarterly, usually on public holidays such as Independence Day (15 August) to help achieve maximum participation. The *gram sabha* has to approve the annual budget and development schemes for the village and the *Sarpanch* and his assistants answer the questions put by the people. Other village problems are discussed. Special *gram sabhas* are convened to make decisions on community development schemes.

This level of local government and participation appears to be very encouraging. Unfortunately, progress is slow. *The Economist* (2008), for example, reports, that *panchayats* have significant control of their own budgets in only two states, i.e. communist-ruled Kerala (one of India's least corrupt states) and West Bengal, thus reducing the collectors' role to that of regulator of the land records and of giving advice to the *panchayats*. More positively, Venugopal and Yilmaz (2009) analysed Kerala's new local governments and concluded that they have a very high degree of discretionary power and also a high degree of accountability to citizens. They also found, however, that their administrative accountability and financial management was in need of strengthening. While this appears to be mostly positive for localism,

*The Economist* claimed that, unfortunately, the *panchayat* leaders have been drawn mostly from feudal and political elites and, thus, typically, are acting in as self-serving a way as any *babu*. Moreover, *The Economist* also claims that the official who designed the reform in Kerala accepts that the new approach is weaker as a result of losing the collector's managerial skills saying: 'It's more equitable, more accountable, more democratic, but there's a cost also in efficiency.' Nevertheless, it seems likely that Panchayati Raj Institutions will play an important role in accelerating socio-economic development in the rural areas.

The 73rd Amendment, 1993, also rationalised the municipal bodies by classifying them as *nagar panchayat* serving rural–urban transition areas, municipal councils serving small urban areas and municipal corporations serving larger urban areas and cities. They serve the 26 per cent of the population who live in urban areas and the amendment sought to rectify the problems of limited power and resources, which had been at the root of frequent suspensions of their activities by state governments. Municipal corporations and municipal councils carry out similar functions to each other. While municipal councils are very dependent for their power and funding on their state governments, however, the corporations have, since 2000, become more financially independent and self-sufficient. Nevertheless, there have often been disputes between corporations and their state governments especially about funding. The executive branch of each corporation is headed by a municipal commissioner appointed by the state governor. There are elected councillors and a non-executive mayor. Mandatory responsibilities include supply of clean water, removal of refuse, sanitary and healthcare facilities, registration of births, deaths and marriages, road maintenance and health clinics. Compulsory primary education is the responsibility of the municipalities in many states. Discretionary responsibilities include libraries, leper homes, rescue homes for women and street children, and parks and open spaces. Non-government organisations (NGOs) and agencies also work with both the state government and the municipal corporation for the provision of services. The members of municipal councils include a president, a committee and a chief or executive officer. The president is elected from the councillors and has both political and executive powers. The municipal councils have similar discretionary and obligatory functions to those of municipal corporations.

## Financing the system

Every year, India struggles to reconcile the irreconcilable: stimulate economic growth and investment, alleviate endemic poverty, and feed a ravenous military appetite. The Government must be seen to care about *aam aadmi*, the common man (who votes), while satisfying the needs of businessmen (who keep the economy humming).

Kamdar (2008)

As Kamdar goes on to point out, the result for the 2008–09 budget was for 63 per cent to go to the military, police, administration and debt service and for defence spending to reach a new high US$26.5 billion as part of the military's drive towards modernisation. Agriculture, upon which 70 per cent of the population depends directly, is, according to Kamdar, in crisis. Even though substantial increases were allowed for in the budget, agriculture, education and primary health care need more money and for it to actually reach them rather than being siphoned off through corruption. It has been claimed for example that up to 39 per cent of subsidised kerosene is stolen (*International Herald Tribune* 2005).

Each year, at the end of February, the Finance Minister's annual union budget to the *Lok Sabha* follows an economic survey that explains performance for the last financial year and the proposed direction for the new one. The survey involves various sections of Indian society including NGOs, business, old people and women's associations etc. The budget for 2009–10 was set at US$225.6 billion against expected revenue of US$137 billion. The deficit was US$88.6 billion.

The total tax receipts at all levels of government are approximately 20 per cent of India's national GDP. This is very low in comparison to the 37–45 per cent in the OECD. Moreover, the government subsidises everything from petrol to food. State-owned enterprises losing money are supported by government and many farmers get free electricity. *The International Herald Tribune* (2005) stated, that, overall, subsidies amounted to 14 per cent of GDP. At the same time, however, India spends little on education, health, or infrastructure. According to UNESCO (Hussain 2007), India has the lowest public expenditure on higher education per student in the developing or developed countries. Infrastructure investment, which is greatly needed, is lower than in China. The government says that most spending fails to get to its intended recipients (*International Herald Tribune* 2005). The nation's non-development revenue expenditure in 2003–04 had increased by almost fivefold since 1990–91 and by more than tenfold since 1985–86. Interest payments have become the largest item of expenditure accounting for over 40 per cent of this expenditure in 2003–04. Defence expenditure rose fourfold during the same period (US$26.5 billion in 2007).

The Indian constitution empowers the Union government to levy income tax, tax on capital transactions (e.g. wealth tax and inheritance tax), sales tax, service tax, and customs and excise duties. The state governments are able to levy sales taxes on intrastate sales, entertainment tax, tax on professions, excise duties on alcohol manufacture, stamp duty on property transfers and a levy on land owned. Local governments levy a property tax and charge users for public utilities such as water or sewage. About half of the revenues of the union and the states come from taxes and Bernardi and Fraschini (2005) point out that those on goods and services were the dominant item at 60 per cent of total taxes with direct taxes contributing less than 20 per cent of the total. About one-quarter of the Union's tax income is granted to the state governments. Non-tax income of the central government is from fiscal services, interest, government dividends, and the non-tax revenues of the states derive from central government grants, interest receipts, dividends and income from services.

Bernardi and Fraschini (2005) also argue that the, then, tax system structure was not far beyond the Musgravian 'early stage' drawing, attention to the complex structure of goods and services taxes which dominated the system with direct taxes being very underdeveloped and difficulties being experienced in moving towards a VAT-kind of structure. This was in spite of the reforms and simplifications to the tax system in 1991 to improve compliance and make the system more progressive and the efforts of the Kelkar committees set up in 2002 to lead tax reforms. Income and corporate tax rates were reduced but exemptions and concessions were also reduced. A permanent account number was brought in. In 2005, 21 of the 28 states introduced VAT in place of the previous complex sales tax system. The latter was after many post-ponements, mostly as a result of disagreements between the union government and some states.

## Co-ordinating the system

Co-ordination of the Indian system relies mostly on its centralised nature. India's constitution provides for a federal republic but one, which is strongly unitary with residuary powers of legislation being vested in the federal parliament. This contrasts with the situation in Germany and the USA, for example, where residuary powers are vested in the land and the states. At the Constitutional Assembly, Sarder Patel has argued that the wide diversity of India's population provided centrifugal forces, which could cause the disintegration of the Union unless some centripetal forces were included to counter this. He argued, vehemently, in particular, that an independent and strong civil service was needed and that its members should have security of tenure so that they could be impartial and without fear when offering advice. The All India Services created by Article 312 where a single cadre of officers controlled by the Union (even though its officers occupy all the senior posts in both the Union and the States) can be seen as an effective means of central control and of strengthening the unitary nature of the federation (TI 2003). As Benbabaali (2008, para 42) argues, however, while the Indian Administrative Service is one of the very few administrative systems established as an instrument of federalism, in practice, it seems to be very weak in this respect:

> The contribution of the All-India Services to cementing or safeguarding the Union cannot be reckoned as crucial, compared with the historical, political and cultural factors which make Indians feel that they belong to the same nation, whatever their differences. How could an elite administration itself affected by casteism, communalism and regionalism

offer the perspective of a collective quest for common goals? Vertical solidarity between bureaucrats and politicians seems to prevail over the horizontal solidarity of a composite body of IAS officers, who align themselves with political parties on a caste basis, or simply for opportunist motives of career advancement.

While, under the constitution, the states have some areas of sovereignty in respect of exclusive areas within which they can legislate, the constitution also provides for the governor of each state being appointed by, and accountable only to, the president. This delivers considerable power to the Union especially because, under Article 356, it is the governor who advises whether the constitutional machinery in the state has failed.

The judiciary is a further force of unification. The system is strictly hierarchical in nature from the lowest court to the Supreme Court with no separate state of federal judiciary and any judge can use both state and federal laws. This contrasts with the situation in the USA where state judiciaries are wholly separate from the federal judiciary and each uses only their own laws unless overruled by the Supreme Court. Other institutions such as the Armed Forces and the Comptroller and Auditor General can also be viewed as having co-ordinating and unifying characteristics.

## Managing the system

India's tenth Five-Year Plan noted (p.65) that India has: 'the most endemic and entrenched manifestation of poor government'. Much of the rest of this chapter, likewise, argues that the system is failing especially in the face of corruption. This failure is evident from parliament, at the top, which has, in many respects, lost control of the Union. According to the constitution, parliament should be managing the system because it legislates, supervises the administration, agrees the budget and discusses matters such as international relations and development plans. Kashyap (2003) (former Secretary General, *Lok Sabha*, and author of the six-volume *History of Parliament of India*), however, argued that the legislative role of parliament has much declined and is no longer 'even the most important of its functions either qualitatively or quantitatively. From about 48 per cent, it has come down to occupy less than 13 per cent of its time'.

Still more seriously and generally, he concluded (p.38):

> That representative democracy and parliamentary institutions have endured in India for five decades is a great tribute to their strength and resilience. There has, however, been in recent years quite some thinking and debate about decline of Parliament, devaluation of parliamentary authority, deterioration in the quality of members, poor levels of participation and the like. Today one notices a certain cynicism towards parliamentary institutions and an erosion in the respect for normal parliamentary institutions and the parliamentarians.

Right or wrong, the people feel that the new breed of politicians in all parties are generally selfish, power-hungry, greedy, dishonest hypocrites and power merchants for whom the nation comes last and the welfare of the people is the lowest priority. Their only concern is to amass wealth and somehow get to and stay in power. They are so busy in the struggle for power that they have no time or energy left for serving the people. The people are aghast and, and what is worse, they feel helpless. We must deliberate on the highest priority basis why things have come to such a pass and what can be done to restore the legislatures and legislators to their old glory and bring about a renaissance of democratic faith and parliamentary culture.

## Accountability, secrecy and openness

The Transparency International (TI) 2012 Corruption Perception Index (CPI) for India is given as 3.6 out of 10, ranking it as ninety-fourth 'least corrupt' of the 180 nations listed (slipping from eighty-fourth in 2010). This is against China's CPI of 3.9 (eightieth position), the UK's CPI of 7.4 (seventeenth position) and the USA's CPI of 7.3 (nineteenth position). It has become 'normal' for real decision-making to be 'under-the-table' or 'behind closed doors' and, thus, secret, closed and without the attachment of any accountability.

According to TI (2003: 17) corruption in India has become a social phenomenon being widespread, institutionalised and rapidly growing. It argues that ' bribes, commissions, under-the-table payments and gifts by the politicians or the bureaucrats are no longer frowned upon and even subtle ways have been discovered to create a legitimate veneer and consider these as normal life activities'. 'In short,' the report argues, 'such an ethos has been created in the society that corruption has ceased to be regarded as a crime any longer.' Even more strongly, TI (2003: 18) argues that:

> The entire infrastructure in Indian society is built on the edifice of corruption. It has percolated down from top to bottom. Very often political corruption in India takes place in collusion with the bureaucracy in the shape of huge kickbacks in big national and international deals which go undetected and unpunished for obvious reasons. In India the connection between corruption and the steady deterioration of the basic administrative system has not been adequately understood and focused upon.

A large number of examples are presented as evidence of these claims by TI. As Vohra (2005), a former Union Home and Defence Secretary and Principal Secretary to the prime minister, points out, while post-1947 India was faced with huge financial and social challenges the, then, leadership made good progress and set the country on a path for sustained progress. He argues that:

governance had far fewer failures in the early decades, essentially because our first generation political leaders, who had made large personal sacrifices during the freedom struggle, were persons of proven integrity, committed to higher values and national perspectives. Enjoying the trust of the people and respect of the public services they were able to effectively direct the affairs of the state.

He added, however, that:

In subsequent years, even before the enforcement of Emergency (1975–77), internal feuds and power politics had overtaken commitment to the vital tasks of governance. This period also saw the emergence of a new breed of 'committed' civil servants and coteries of extra-constitutional elements joining the political bandwagon, causing severe damage to Rule by Law and the Constitution.

The failure of national-level political parties and the mushrooming of regional and sub-regional groupings led to splintered electoral outcomes. The consequent emergence of coalition governments, in the states and later at the centre, generated political instability, which had an adverse impact on governance. The new commitment to seize and hold political power at any cost saw the emergence of a frightening nexus between corrupt politicians and public servants and unlawful elements in society.

From around the 1990s there were a series of exposures of scandals relating to large-scale defalcations, embezzlements and cases of corruption, among which were the fodder scam, the hawala case and the Bofors and submarine deals. These scams involved serious allegations against chief ministers and their ministers, ministers at the centre and even prime ministers, besides serving and retired senior functionaries. The latest apparent corruption scandal to blight the Singh government was reported by the Comptroller and Auditor General on 21 August 2012 in respect of the issuing of huge contracts amounting to $34 billion for coal mining through favouritism (*The Economist* 2012).

## Democracy and the administrative system

On the face of it, democratic control of the Union and the states is the intention in India. The constitution, for example, establishes the Election Commission of India, which has a chief electoral commissioner plus two more commissioners all appointed by the president. Their role is to oversee the assembly of electoral rolls and the conduct of elections for Central, State and Union Territories as well as elections for the president and vice president. The Commissioners are accountable to the law of the constitution and can be removed only through the same procedure as that required to remove a Supreme Court Judge. The security of tenure given to senior civil servants by the constitution also appears to help guarantee democratic control against political skulduggery. Unfortunately, as argued throughout this chapter, the administrative system in India is controlled by politicians and civil servants who are frequently corrupt thus acting well outside of any democratic brief. Such corruption is served by the informal system of 'clientelism' and 'patrimonialism', explained, under the section above on the civil service, which seriously compromises democracy, serving as it does only the personal needs of politicians (and sometimes also the civil servants). An aspect of this not yet covered but which makes this case very strongly is the way in which politicians have subverted the laws on 'crime riot'. Buch (2003), for example, argues that, while the constitution requires the executive magistracy and the police to follow the law in dealing with crime riots they have come to abdicate their responsibilities and await orders from the politicians above. He gives two examples. First he cites how in '1984 after the assassination of Mrs Indira Gandhi, the police, especially the Delhi Police, stood by as a mere spectator while rampaging mobs slaughtered thousands of Sikhs'. Second, he points out how, in 2002, in the face of very serious communal riots in Gujarat and with 'honourable exceptions', 'The Police Commissioner of Ahmedabad permitted two ministers to take over his control room and ensure police inaction for three days'.

More generally, Buch argued that 'the civil services are being decreasingly [sic] rendered ineffective and politicians have begun to whimsically apply policy and to implement it in a highly partisan manner', and that 'since nothing pleases the politicians more than a hefty bribe, the next phase is the introduction of a regime of corruption in addition to a regime of favoritism'.

Buch concluded that:

> A regime of favoritism coupled with a regime of corruption, in which the bureaucrats are abused morning, noon and night as servants of red-tape, obstructers of development, bumbling, officious nincompoops, has totally demoralized the civil services. They have become partisan, ineffective and corrupt. The partisanship has even reduced their efficacy as a binding force of our nation. This has degraded the administration to such an extent that one wonders if there is any administration left at all.

A related area of concern is that of the suspension of democracy through the declaration of a state of emergency. The only time this has been done at Union level was in 1975 by Prime Minister Indira Gandhi on the basis of 'internal disturbance' when she was indicted for corruption and ordered to stand down. The declaration enabled her to rule by decree until 1977. Political opposition was oppressed and civil liberties of Indian citizens were suspended. While the prime minister was confident of being re-elected she was easily defeated by a 'Grand coalition' in 1977.

A state emergency can also be declared under Article 356, if the president decides that the constitutional machinery has broken down in a state. Also known as 'President's rule' s/he takes over all of the work of the executive with the governor administering on behalf of the president. Not only does this emphasise the centralised nature of the Indian state but in addition, the nature with which it has been applied strongly suggests that democracy is seen as secondary to the interests of politicians. Tummala (1996) provides evidence of this by considering two cases of states successfully challenging, in the Supreme Court, declarations of emergency made against them (Karnataka in 1989 and Madhya Pradesh in 1992) concluding that:

> while the founding fathers of the Indian constitution argued for a strong federal government, they would probably be surprized and baffled by the arbitrary and capricious way some of the powers have been used by the federal government over the states, particularly those belonging to the opposition.

Reddy and Joseph (2004: 20) expressed the hope that:

> Eventually, the public opinion in India . . . will awaken to the fact that Article 356 may veritably have become a noose that is slowly tightening around the neck of democracy in India, suffocating the right of the people under the Constitution.

In January 2009, the State of Jharkhand had a state of emergency imposed upon it.

## Further developments and issues with the system

Bajpaee (2006) compares the 'rise' of China with the relative failure of India and blames this not only on its corruption, infrastructure 'bottlenecks', bureaucracy and unpredictable democracy with precarious coalitions but also on the large number of conflicts and instabilities on its periphery. Bajpaee sees these conflicts as deterring regional economic integration and perhaps also investor confidence and argues that, in contrast, China has shelved most such conflicts. Bajpaee lists these problems on India's periphery as including Bangladesh, which limits India's access to China and South East Asia, e.g. for a natural gas pipeline from Myanmar. Problems with a politically unstable Nepal, Sri Lanka, Pakistan and Afghanistan also prevent economic co-operation, claims Bajpaee. These issues are significant but it is the self-inflicted shortcomings of its outdated and undeveloped political and administrative system which have resulted in poor governance and a consequent failure to take care of its diverse and, mostly, exceedingly poor, population.

Jain (2001) argues that there are five distinguishing features of public administration in India that were inherited from British rule and have remained largely unchanged since Independence. It seems that, to one degree or another, none of these fits today's needs. These are, first, the district as the basic unit of administration with the District Collector controlling, directing, and co-ordinating all administrative activities in his district. This role has become both overloaded (by the demands of planning) and also compromised by the growth of local self-rule. Second, the centralisation of administration away from the states has become the increasingly dominant ideology of a nation concerned with sustaining the Union, e.g. through declaring 'President's rule', but this has seriously threatened democracy in India. Third, the 'steel frame' of administration through a single powerful civil service aimed at underpinning the Union, has become much weaker especially as a result of corruption by politicians and officers. Fourth, the system of complex rules and regulations invented by the British to help maintain control over the decision-making powers of their Indian subordinates has been perpetuated and deepened in the form of the ever more bureaucratic and inefficient, *'Bubu raj'*. Finally, the divisive system prevailing at both the central and provincial levels remains where civil servants responsible for decisions on policy are clearly distinct from those responsible for administration. This suited the British concerned with control but is still manifested in decisions, very laboriously and inefficiently, being referred up the very high hierarchical tree. Institutional problems, then, blight the Indian system throughout. These include the very high rates of absenteeism of public sector employees, clientelism, patronialism, rent-seeking and widespread corruption, which conspire to hamper progress with tackling poverty and, often caste-based, gross inequality.

Maheshwari (1993) reports that, shortly before she was assassinated, Indira Gandhi said that her greatest failure was an inability to reform the public administration of India. Maheshwari points out that the intention to reform has, nevertheless, been a major aim of successive governments. As Jain (2001) records, this has resulted in many attempts at reform including those recommended by the Gorwala Committee Report of 1951, the Paul Appleby Reports (by a foreign expert) in 1953 and 1956 and, in 1966, the Administrative Reforms Commission (ARC). Only a few cosmetic changes resulted, however. ARC had proposed the re-arrangement of all the services into eight functional categories, ending the generalist service of the IAS. This would have removed the 'steel frame' and it resulted in strong opposition from the top of the civil service and may well have helped to prevent any further such reviews. Since then, different central departments and most states have set up their own review bodies and produced detailed reports causing Maheshwari to argue that the reasons for a lack of reform do not include any shortage of analysis and expert opinion but rather a fear of a loss of control by those benefiting from the present system at all levels.

Maheshwari also argued that advances in information technology should result in the flattening of organisational structures and reductions in bureaucracy. As Bhatnagar (2003) points out, however, many IT experiments have failed especially because of corruption. Tanmoy Chakrabarty, the Vice President of Government Industry Solutions at Tata Consultancy Service, similarly, claimed (Prasad 2008): 'Corruption is the biggest enemy of e-government'; that 'There are vested interests everywhere' and that 'Politicians fear that they will lose control with e-government, and this is coming in the way of successful implementation of e-government projects in India.' According to Prasad, Chakrabarty also noted: 'Out of the 27 projects under the NEGP, only one (the MCA21 program) has been completed. There is a tremendous gap between conceptualization and implementation.' More optimistically, Bhatanger argued that e-government can be used to reduce corruption and that it should be introduced gradually to that effect in developing countries.

Some theorists, such as Maheshwari (2005), argue for gradual change by working within the system towards outcomes such as those recommended by ARC (above), but others, such as Kishwar (2005) argue that the state is seriously to blame for India's failure to deal with the huge problem of poverty, and that radical reforms and the abolition of the status quo is necessary.

Maheshwari emphasises that nepotism, bribery, the abuse of political influence and simple apathy toward public issues are deeply embedded in the culture of India. While he accepts that it will be hard to remove these tendencies, he argues for more rigorous efforts to this end, perhaps beginning by acting on the recommendations of the Fifth Central Pay Commission Report 1997; especially a reduction in government employment through disinvestment in the public sector, contracting out and privatisation, the implementation of job performance evaluations, the upgrading of skills and competencies of civil servants, the abolition of transfers based on political whims and a role for government as evolvers of policy rather than as direct providers. Maheshwari sees shifts towards these changes as necessary to begin to provide India with public service improvements consistent with those being made in most of the rest of the world. Jain (2001) also agreed with most of the Commission's proposals.

Kishwar (2005) argued, more stridently, that while political scientists and economists have seen public administration through the prism of class struggle with the sole protector of the weak being the state, the problems are the fault of the state. This is so, she argues, because the Indian state has opposed globalisation and destroyed people's livelihoods and self-confidence. Kishwar argued that after 60 years of independence, poverty cannot be seen as just natural for the nation in the face of the abundant natural resources and capabilities of its people. Urban elites she argues, have a harsh indifference towards the urban and rural poor and proposes urgent reform of governance, to spread the fruits of globalisation and economic modernisation to the 90 per cent of the population that is self-employed and relies greatly on the unorganised sectors, especially agriculture. Underpinning Kishwar's concern is a belief that the nation has failed to live up to the hopes of its founders in the freedom movement that there would be a sense of 'shared destiny' among people of different religions, castes, regions and economic standing. She blames the national political parties and the centralised administrative set-up for a nation divided by mistrust, polarisation and violence. More specifically, she blames politicians for using the leaders and symbols of religions for largely, secular purposes, e.g. for fighting elections and manipulating votes. The future of Indian democracy is, she argues, tied closely to its ability to resolve minority/majority relations.

Jain (2008: 12–15) argues that 'to meet the challenges of good governance for promoting human security, a seven pronged action plan needs to be adopted'. These can be summarised as:

1    Institutional: The regeneration of the political and administrative institutions from the virtual collapse that they have suffered in the last three decades by restoring 'the legitimacy and effectiveness of the legislature, bureaucracy, the judiciary and the non-state actors of the civil society'.

2    Administrative system: Cut down the size of government, bureaucracy and expenditure as early as possible.

3    Transparency: Jain seeks 'to ensure transparency in the functioning of the government and to fight corruption and mal-administration' through the enactment of a Public Interest Disclosure Act to protect 'whistle blowers'.

4    Bureaucracy: Jain argues for a change of attitude and behaviour because, at present, it sees itself as being: 'the defender of the status quo' and argues for 'a realisation that with the advent of globalisation, liberalisation and privatisation, it has to play a major role of a catalyst for change'. The bureaucracy has to absorb 'the values of participatory democracy, decentralization of authority and power' and 'observe a modicum of transparency and concede an appropriate right of information to the people in its decision-making process' as well as securing 'a balance between a rule-bound administration and an administration that can effectively and quickly deliver results, particularly in developmental and social welfare activities'.

5    Economics: Jain argues for a policy of revamping the public distribution system and disinvesting in public enterprises in key sectors such as power, energy, oil, transport, telecommunication and in ailing industrial units.

6    Social security: Jain sees this as a massive challenge in terms of the need for 'adequate employment generation, good health, universal education system, shelter, and the basic facilities of sanitation and drinking water'. He sees the need for the administration 'to deliver these goods at the lowest costs and in an equitable manner'.

7    Technology: Jain urges its increased use including 'on-line governance': 'wherever feasible, for quick delivery of services, providing information and redressal of grievances', as well as a means 'to achieve transparency – a condition for accountability'.

Above all, however, Jain (2008: 14) argues that none of these things will happen unless 'the governments at all levels of the polity are capable enough to take hard and unpleasant decisions and have the will and capacity to implement and continuously monitor and evaluate their impact'.

Finally, he asserts that:

> the political leadership has to demonstrate its strong determination to undertake reforms by first cleaning its own stable from corrupt and criminal influences, and setting ethical standards of quality governance both at the political and administrative levels. For changes to come, it is necessary to change the mindset and attitudes of both the public administrators and the politicians in power.

# References

Bajpaee, C. (2006) 'India Held Back by Wall of Instability', *Asia Times*, 1 June. Online, available at: www.atimes.com/atimes/South_Asia/HF01Df01.html (accessed 13 October 2010).

Benbabaali, D. (2008) 'Questioning the Role of the Indian Administrative Service in National Integration', *South Asia Multidisciplinary Academic Journal*. Online, available at: http://samaj.revues.org/633 (accessed 22 January 2014).

Bernardi, L. and Fraschini, A. (2005) 'Tax System and Tax Reforms in India', Working paper no. 51, Department of Public Policy and Public Choice, Pavia, Italy, University of Pavia and University of Eastern Piedmont.

Bhatnagar, S. (2003) 'Transparency and Corruption: Does E-Government Help?', Indian Institute of Management, at: www.iimahd.ernet.in/~subhash/pdfs/CHRIDraftPaper2003.pdf (accessed 9 October 2010).

Bidwai, P. (2002) 'Reality of Dalit oppression: The urgency of social reform', *Transnational Institute: A worldwide fellowship of scholar activists*, 22 October, posted 1 May 2006, at: www.tni.org/article/reality-dalit-oppression-urgency-social-reform (accessed 13 October 2010).

Breeding, M. E. (2008) 'The Influence of Clientelism on Policy Representation: Evidence from Bangalore, India', at: www.allacademic.com/meta/p266993_index.html (accessed 27 September 2010).

Brinkerhoff, D. W. and Goldsmith, A. A. (2002) 'Clientelism, Patrimonialism and Democratic Governance: An Overview and Framework for Assessment and Programming', Abt Associates Inc., Bethesda, Maryland at: http://pdf.usaid.gov/pdf_docs/Pnacr426.pdf (accessed 6 December 2010).

Buch, M. N. (2003) 'Why India Needs A Strong and Impartial Civil Service', Bolo, 2 February, at: www.boloji.com/opinion/0034.htm (accessed 6 December 2012).

Business Standard (2010) 'P.M. sets 10% growth for 12th Plan', at: www.business-standard.com/india/news/pm-sets-10-growth-target-for-12th-plan/389568/ (accessed 12 October 2010).

CIA (Central Intelligence Agency) (2012) 'Factbook', Washington, CIA, at: www.cia.gov/library/publications/the-world-factbook/geos/in.htm (accessed 13 December 2012).

Deutsche Bank Research (2005) 'Outsourcing to India: Crouching Tiger Set to Pounce', Frankfurt, Deutsche Bank Research, at: www.dbresearch.de/PROD/DBR_INTERNET_DE-PROD/PROD0000000000192125.pdf (accessed 28 August 2010).

*The Economist* (2008) 'Briefing: Battling the babu raj', Anonymous, 8 March, vol. 386, issue 8570, pp. 27–30, at: www.economist.com/node/10804248 (accessed 6 December 2012).

*The Economist* (2008a) 'What is Holding India back', Anonymous, 8 March, vol. 386, issue 8570, p. 11 (cover story), at: www.economist.com/node/10804248 (accessed 6 December 2012).

*The Economist* (2012), blog, at: www.economist.com/blogs/banyan/2012/08/corruption-india (accessed 8 November 2012).

Election Commission of India (2009) 'Archive of General Elections 2009', at: http://eci.nic.in.eci.eci.ht (accessed 21 January 2014).

Eleventh 5-year Plan (2007–2012) *Vol.1 – Inclusive Growth, Vol 2 – Social Sector, Vol 3 – Agriculture, Rural Development, Industry, Services and Physical Infrastructure*, New Dehli. Oxford University Press, at: http://planningcommission.nic.in/plans/planrel/fiveyr/11th/11_vi/11th_vol1.pdf (accessed 13 August 2010).

Heitzman, J. and Worden, L. R. (eds) (1995) *India: A Country Study*, Washington: Library of Congress, at: http://countrystudies.us/india/ (accessed 20 July 2010).

Hussain, S. (2007) 'Higher Education Spending: India at the Bottom of BRIC', *Rediff India Abroad Home*, at: www.rediff.com/money/2007/feb/05edu.htm (accessed 15 October 2010).

India Gov (2010) at: http://india.gov.in/govt/constitutions_india.php (accessed 15 January 2010).

IMF (International Monetary Fund) (2010) World Economic Outlook Database, at: www.imf.org/external/country/IND/index.htm (accessed 12 December 2010).

*International Herald Tribune* (2005) The Global Edition of the *New York Times*, 8 October, at: www.nytimes.com/ (accessed 12 July 2010).

Jain, R. B. (2001) 'Towards Good Governance: A Half Century of India's Administrative Development', *International Journal of Public Administration*, 24: 1299–334.

Jain, R. B. (2008) 'Towards Good Governance: A South Asian Perspective', Paper presented to *the International Conference on 'Challenges of Governance in South Asia' in Kathmandu*, Nepal, December 15–16.

Jeffrey, C. (2002) 'Caste, Class, and Clientelism: A Political Economy of Everyday Corruption in Rural North India', *Economic Geography*, 78: 21–42.

Kamdar, M. (2008) 'India's Budget May Backfire', *The Australian*, 3 April, at: www.theaustralian.com.au/news/executive-lifestyle/indias-budget-may-backfire/story-e6frga06-1111115957453 (accessed 17 October 2010).

Kashyap, S. C. (2003) 'Parliament, Reform Thyself', *Indian Tribune*, 24 September, at: www.tribuneindia.com/2005/specials/tribune_125/main5.htm (accessed 8 August 2010).

Kishwar, M. P. (2005) *Deepening Democracy: Challenges of Governance and Globalization in India*, Delhi: Oxford University Press.

National Portal of India (2010) at: www.india.gov.in/ (accessed 17 August 2010).

Maheshwari, S. R. (1993) *Administrative Reform in India*, New Delhi: Jawahar Publishers & Distributors.

Maheshwari, S. R. (2005) *Public Administration in India: The Higher Civil Service*, New Delhi: Oxford University Press.

Mishra, R. K. (2010) 'National Civil Service System in India: A Critical View', at: http://citeseerx.ist.psu.edu/viewdoc/download?doi=10.1.1.130.2920&rep=rep1&type=pdf (accessed 20 August 2010).

Moore, B. Jnr. (1966) *Social Origins of Dictatorship and Democracy*, Harmondsworth: Allen Lane.

Muralidharan, K. (2007) *Teachers and Medical Worker Incentives in India*, Cambridge, Mass.: Harvard University Press.

NDTV (New Delhi Television) (2012) at: www.ndtv.com/article/india/pratibha-patil-demits-office-says-corruption-the-enemy-of-good-governance-247249 (accessed 13 December 2012).

Planning Commission of India (2002) 'Report of the Committee on 20/20 Vision', October, Planning Commission, Yojana Bhawan, New Delhi.

Prasad, S. (2008) 'Corruption Slowing India's E-govt Growth', ZDNetAsia, 12 August, at: www.zdnetasia.com/corruption-slowing-india-s-e-govt-growth-62044787.htm (accessed 15 September 2010).

Reddy, J. K. and Joseph, J. V. (2004) 'Executive Discretion and Article 356 of the Constitution of India: A Comparative Critique', *Electronic Journal of Comparative Law*, 8 (1), at: www.ejcl.org (accessed 5 September 2010).

Shashi Tharoor (2003) 'India: From Midnight to the Millennium' in Dahlstrom, E. and O'Neill, B. E. *Homespun and Microchips: India's Economic Dichotomy*, Washington DC, National War College, at: www.dtic.mil/cgi-bin/GetTRDoc?Location=U2&doc=GetTRDoc.pdf&AD=ADA441587 (accessed 9 September 2010).

Soni, V. (2008) 'A Portrait of Public Administration in India: Challenges of Governance in the World's Largest Democracy', *Public Administration Review*, 68: 1158–161.

Subramaniam, V. (1998) 'The Administrative Legacy of Ancient India', *International Journal of Public Administration*, 21: 87–108.

*The Times of India* (2010) The Economic Times, 'India Can Become 3rd Largest Economy by 2012: PwC', 24 January, at: http://economictimes.indiatimes.com/news/economy/indicators/India-can-become-3rd-largest-economy-by-2012-PwC/articleshow/5491011.cms (accessed 8 June 2010).

Tönnies, F. (1887) *Community and Society: Gemeinschaft und Gesellschaft*, Charles P. Loomis (ed.) (1957), The Michigan State University Press, pp. 223–31, at: http://media.pfeiffer.edu/lridener/courses/GEMEIN.HTML (accessed 2 July 2010).

TI (Transparency International) (2003) 'The National Integrity Systems TI Country Studies Report India', Transparency International Secretariat, Berlin, at: http://www.transparency.org/policy_research/nis/nis_reports_by_country (accessed 8 August 2010).

Transparency International (2010) 'Surveys and Indices', at: www.transparency.org/policy_research/surveys_indices/cpi/2009/cpi_2009_table (accessed 12 December 2012).

Twelfth 5-year Plan (2012–17) vol. 1 'Faster, More Sustainable Growth', vol. 2 'Economic Sectors', vol. 3 'Social Sector', New Delhi: Sage Publications. Also online, at: http://planningcommission.nic.in/plans/planrel/fiveyr/12th/pdf/12fyp_vol1.pdf (accessed 21 January 2014).

Tummala, K. K. (1996) 'New Trends in Federalism. Les nouvelles formes du fédéralisme', *International Political Science Review / Revue internationale de science politique*, 17 (4): 373–84, at: www.jstor.org/stable/1601275 (accessed 7 July 2010).

UNEP (Union Public Service Commission), at: www.upsc.gov.in/ (accessed 12 July 2010).

United Nations (2006) 'Republic of India, Public Administration Country Profile', at: http://unpan1.un.org/intradoc/groups/public/documents/un/unpan023311.pdf (accessed 15 January 2010).

United Nations Food and Agriculture Organisation: United Nations World Food
    Programme (WFP) and MS Swaminathan Research Foundation (MSSRF) (2008)
    'The Report on the State of Food Insecurity in Rural India', at: http://home.
    wfp.org/stellent/groups/public/documents/newsroom/wfp197348.pdf (accessed
    3 October 2010).
Venugopal, V. and Yilmaz, S. (2009) 'Decentralization in Kerala: Panchayat
    Government Discretion and Accountability', *Public Administration and Development*,
    29 (4): 316–29.
Vohra, N. N. (2005) 'Governance: Make the system responsive', *Indian Tribune*, 24
    September, at: www.tribuneindia.com/2005/specials/tribune_125/main5.htm
    (accessed 8 October 2010).
Weber, Max (1947) *The Theory of Social and Economic Organization*, trans. A. M. Henderson
    and Talcott Parsons. New York: Free Press.

# 11 Conclusion

*J. A. Chandler*

To what extent is public administration similar in most developed or rapidly developing countries? The tendency, certainly within Anglo-American political structuring, is to assume that globalisation is producing an increasingly homogeneous method for undertaking business. Many western theorists of business management tend to produce substantive textbooks on issues such as strategic management or international business that suggest there are similar forms of successful administration irrespective of the role of the organisation and its environment. In most circumstances this assumes they should be operating in a competitive environment and should adopt similar structures and follow similar processes. New Public Management rhetoric transfers this trend to the public sector suggesting that all administration is management and all management is generic.

It will be suggested in this summary that while globalisation is a reality it may take forms other than the creation of a world blueprint for successful organisation and performance. Specific cultures and individual interests may remain a central part of social and organisational life and that, as a result, systems of public administration will continue to differ among nations and the sub-divisions of nations. Indeed, since different people have different values, we cannot expect that one size of administrative outlook fits all.

## The nature of globalisation

The idea that social forces will, over time, create a uniform society in which social, political and economic behaviour and institutions are common for everyone is not particularly new. Marx and Engels argued that ideological differences would be irrelevant between nations after the revolution to overthrow capitalism. Max Weber suggested that developed nations would be governed by similar modes of legal-rational thought through hierarchic rule-based bureaucracies. Post Second World War, Daniel Bell (1960) expressed the tendency of capitalist ideas to predominate as 'the end of ideology'. Fukuyama (1992) argues that liberal-democratic political and social values based around competitive capitalism built on high levels of trust between individuals in society has become the dominant culture throughout the world.

Giddens (1999) observes that there has been an explosion in discussing the development of social sciences in terms of globalisation over the last 10 years which 'has been influenced above all by developments in systems of communication, dating back only to the late 1960s'. It is now possible through the Internet to communicate with little difficulty with individuals throughout the world and to secure information on an international scale. Globalisation should, however, not be interpreted as simply a communications revolution but, as the consequence of these changes. These have resulted in an enhanced capacity for the media and hence markets to access the majority of people throughout the world. Thus, individuals are increasingly exposed to consumer goods and their associated cultural values that are pushed through the media predominantly by large multinational business corporations. The offerings of McDonald's and Toyota, Lady Gaga, the football World Cup or Olympic Games appear to form elements of a bland and homogenised world culture of consumption. Theorists of globalisation argue over the extent to which this development will extend to creating similar social and political values, although few suggest it will lead to wholesale and absolute uniformity. The ability to transfer mass information across the globe enables the spread of a vast number of different values and lifestyles to individuals who in previous ages may never have been exposed to any differing cultures than those that characterised their local society. Thus, it is possible for societies to become far more pluralist as particular groups of individuals in the same communities adopt differing ideas and cultural values. Globalisation is a process that, for example, makes it increasingly difficult for the Chinese government to prevent its citizens from being aware of Christianity and has ensured that Buddhist or Muslim ideas are widely practised in formally predominantly Christian Europe. The process of globalisation facilitates changing values and cultural paradigms in once more isolated states. A major tension in the development of public society in the twenty-first century is, therefore, between demands for cultural individuality and localised traditions and a more homogeneous pluralist world of cultural values.

Politically, these developments pose the question of the role of the state. Will the mass communication age dominated by large businesses that need to reconcile differences between many political cultures lead to the demise of the nation state and the development of common pluralistic systems of policy-making and administration? It is widely argued that the nation state is now far less autonomous than 100 years ago. Multinational companies, with budgets far greater than many of the nation states in the less developed world, can have a powerful effect on the direction of national and regional economies. There has also been a huge growth in the number and strength of international agencies and organisations that diminish the power of the nation state. Held (1991) observed four major factors decreasing state sovereignty. First, the influence of multinational companies operating in a global economy, second the resultant growth of transnational regulatory authorities such as the United Nations, the International Monetary Fund and even more extensive regional bodies such as the European Union, and third, the growth of international law often promulgated or defended by these transnational agencies. Held also saw the global effects of the cold war, now a greatly diminished source of tension, as a further factor undermining national sovereignty through organisations such as NATO. Nevertheless, the importance of these external global factors on national states can be exaggerated given the legacy of values and beliefs that underwrite the formation and structure of individual states. The 'Arab Spring' that since 2011 has created major changes in governance in the Middle East has yet to resolve into new forms of governance that will have some permanence and it is far from clear that these will necessarily be more western in approach when the dust settles. As Helen Thompson (2010, 147) remarks, 'we have to conceive of states as confronting a fundamental political problem of legitimising rule that arises out of the clash of interests and beliefs among their citizens'.

## The ideological centre of globalisation

Although globalisation does not in itself create a more homogeneous social and economic environment, certain values have, since the nineteenth century, become increasingly dominant while others founded on a more protected regional base, have declined. The rise of laissez faire capitalism was an important development in global thought but by the twentieth century this view was challenged by collectivist ideology ranging from Marxist Leninism to fascism. The later twentieth century has seen a decline in the collectivist values of both the far right and left, to be replaced, at least for the present, by widespread support for more individualist market-led competitive capitalism that is based largely on the thinking of New Right theorists and economists. The emergence of New Right values allied to neo-conservative thought that accompanies many agencies promoting globalisation has markedly restructured the scope of public administration and how the process is internally managed across the globe. The source of these values lies within European thought in the early twentieth century and particularly the Viennese school of thinkers who opposed both the socialist and fascist ideas that they saw as an assault by an over-powerful state on individual rights and liberty. This train of thought after the Second World War fitted the mood of right-wing thought in the United States with its ideological critique of communism and social democracy and many of the proponents of the school found eventual refuge in American universities where their ideas could be implanted on fertile ground. Suspicion of an over-powerful state lies deep within the development of the United States constitution through its balance of powers and was seen to create a powerful means of developing the nation's wealth on the basis of free enterprise through market competition. Predominantly such values promote minimal control over society by the state, which itself should be broken up into decentralised units that were accountable to a local electorate. The provision of services to the governing units should be left largely to private sector enterprises contracting through bargaining within the marketplace to federal, state and local governments. At its extreme it presages the minimal state as most extensively outlined by Robert Nozick (1980).

By the 1980s Republican values in the United States that strongly endorsed a view that the state should have less dominance in the American economy were taken up by President Reagan. This ideological position has been upheld by most subsequent leading republicans and respected by not a few Democrats. The values were however divided between libertarian concerns of the New Right and a neo-conservative outlook that argued that the capitalist state needed to retain powerful means of control in order to confront the enemies of free-market capitalism both within and outside the state. While neo-conservatives can take on board many of the market capitalist economic ideas of the New Right, their ideas on the role of the state are not fully compatible. Neo-conservatism in many circumstances looks to the state to protect the existing status of wealthy and powerful interests in society. These lines of thought in Europe were in the 1970s focused into the values of the right wing of the British Conservative Party and emerged as a powerful governing force in 1979 with the election of the government of Margaret Thatcher that preached the idea, as characterised by Andrew Gamble (1988), as the 'Free Economy and the Strong State'. During the subsequent 18 years of conservative government the role of the state in the provision of services and development of the economy was severely reduced with the sale of nationalised industries and an increasing demand for public sector services to be delivered by contracted private companies. At the same time, however, care was taken to increase the role of the public sector in ensuring law and order and ensuring the decline of collective non-governmental public power through the trade unions and professional associations.

The values of the Anglo Saxon countries in the 1980s were initially an anathema to most West European States but what could not be denied was that a formula of privatisation of public industries created sufficient wealth for central government to be a successful electoral tool as a means of keeping taxation on an even keel. In France, Mitterand quickly abandoned his strongly socialist values that propelled him to his first term as president and began adopting policies of privatisation and efficiency drives aimed at decreasing the cost of public services. Other European Union states began also to follow this trend and, following the collapse of the Berlin Wall and the Warsaw Pact, the newly independent states of Eastern Europe followed the New Right pattern with ideological enthusiasm as the antidote to authoritarian state ownership. As is evident from the chapters on China and India in this book, both of these populous and economically powerful states realised that the New Right formula of market competition was essential for developing their economies and, especially in China, the ruling class realised also that a neo-conservative focus on retaining law and order through an authoritarian government was compatible with a framework that inevitably exacerbated the inequalities between wealth and poverty.

Neo-conservatism is, however, a central factor that may ensure that globalising tendencies of New Right liberalism will not bring international homogeneity of small-scale regulatory government to all developed states. It is an ideology concerned with the protection of the interests and classes that benefit from an established traditional network of power and wealth to ensure that they and their fellow travellers retain their privileged position. As part and parcel of this concern it is a position that retains a strong nationalist sentiment wedded to an assumption that nations are in competition with one another within the world economy, if not also in terms of cultural values. While many classical liberals, such as the father figure Adam Smith and also Hayek, were comfortable with what they thought to be a system that could ensure that the most able should rise to positions of power and economic privilege, a neo-conservative view of the liberal capitalist state as established in the United States, maintains that this is a superior system that should be imposed on the rest of the world. Such pretensions have in the early years of the twenty-first century done much to alienate American power from much of the world and in particular the Middle East (Drysek and Dunleavy 2009: 282–6). As such neo-conservatism is not a new phenomenon and has been a characteristic of nationalism at least since its development during the European enlightenment. As a new movement it is perhaps only intelligible through the attachment of nationalist and conservative values to work alongside the potentially more radical aspects of New Right or perhaps better put, neo-liberal, values. From a Marxist position both neo-liberal and neo-conservative positions can be seen as rationalisation that informs the capacity of the ruling class to shape the state to secure their hegemony over power while ensuring the need for social stability and a class structuring of society.

The development and globalisation of New Right and conservative ideology has produced mainstream trends in public administration and management that have in the countries studied in this volume increasingly been pushing the more collective social democratic values to one side. It may be possible that future problems in the stability or power of major businesses or popular demands for greater control over public services might lead to a cyclical return to policies of nationalisation or even the development of completely novel relationships between business and government. Should such changes develop it is even more problematic to predict whether any new realignment of public and private interests will involve all liberal-democratic regimes or affect some and not others.

What is more certain is that the preceding three decades have witnessed the retreat of collective social democrat values in the face of neo-liberal and neo-conservative onslaughts. The patterns of thought as regards public administration within these more dominant right wing can be summarised in the box below.

The development of New Right and neo-conservative values have pushed the structuring of administration within states in two not wholly compatible directions. Neo-conservative interests that uphold the status quo, of usually

---

### New Right and Conservative values

Reduced size of the state through:

- privatisation;
- delivery of public services by private contractors;
- adoption of private sector management techniques;
- decentralisation and de-concentration of power.

### Neo-Conservatism

Ensuring central control of the structures of power through:

- strengthened means of government control;
- concentration of power;
- support for established institutions.

---

imagined or over-exaggerated civic virtues, embeds more firmly the specific characteristics of the formal constitutional machinery of many states. At the root of this attitude is, as suggested above, the desire of those classes and business interests exerting power and enjoying unequal shares in the riches of the state, to defend their political position. However, the economics of New Right competition is also of value in retaining the wealth needed to defend both internally and internationally the status of those who control the political, economic and administrative powers of the state. Thus, the states reviewed in this study show within their administrative structure a dual aspect. In terms of the formal constitutional aspects of government they largely demonstrate stability. On the other hand, within a stable constitutional framework the less formal processes of public administration are undergoing rapid changes as the formal structures are exposed to private sector practices. The public provision of services and resource allocation within a firmly structured system of public regulation is increasingly undertaken by the private sector using private sector marketing techniques. The role of the state is to set not just the rules of the economic game but who should compete at the highest level of the system within a stable system of power relations within a set constitutional arrangement.

## The constitutional framework

Although there has been an extensive growth of international regulation and constraint and the movement of capital by private multinational companies, many commentators do not perceive an immediate end to the nation (Thompson 2010; Holton 1998). Since the 1960s there has been a major expansion in the number of nation states following the end of colonial empires and this has continued with, for example, the break up of the USSR and the fractionating of the Balkans. The constraints established by supra-national bodies may often be the result of an institutionalisation of diplomacy that formerly was undertaken in a more anarchic and violent form. The European Union, although a highly complex entity that modifies many of the procedures and policies of member states still conducts its crucial negotiations through bargaining between nation states and, as Robert Jones (2000) emphasised in his contribution to the first edition of this book, relies on member states to implement the policies developed in Brussels and sanctioned by the Council of Ministers. What has changed is any propensity for members to pursue rivalry through trade wars or bloody wars rather than debate and mutual bargaining. A further factor that demonstrates the retention, for the foreseeable future, of the nation state is the propensity of most transnational organisations or multinational companies to operate through the medium of the nation state as the means for implementing agreed policies. Policies, that may have been determined through national bargaining within transnational bodies or as a consequence of pressure from multinational companies are, nevertheless, implemented through the medium of administrative organisations that are specific to each particular nation state and established to protect long evolved and evolving systems of power and self-interest among ruling or would-be ruling elites.

There is, therefore, little evidence of rapid convergence in the constitutional structures of the developed nations. The developing nations of China and India appear in the twenty-first century to steadfastly cling on to the arrangements of their constitutional framework that emerged in the 1950s. Formal change through amendments set within existing constitutions seems a rare procedure in most developed states reviewed in this study. The last amendment to the United States constitution was the 27th in July 1992 on the relatively minor issue of preventing Congressmen raising their pay and other forms of compensation until after an election of a new House of Representatives. More recent constitutions such as the unworkable document produced by de Gaulle for France (Hayward 1983, 1–20) have had a number of significant changes but still retains its built-in propensity to develop tensions between the president and Assembly. Russia has emerged as a democracy but with the rise of Putin still retains elements of central domination. Since the 1980s the unwritten constitution of the United Kingdom has adopted the European Convention on Rights and devolved power to the provinces of Scotland and Wales but has yet to resolve the purpose and constitution of the House of Lords and despite much agitation not changed the first-past-the-post electoral system.

## The civil service and central government agencies

The stability of most national constitutions is echoed within the administrative organisation of the state such as the civil service and central government agencies. The basic models of civil service structures that were recognised by Weber still remain on the surface structurally the same. The United States' framework of appointments for the policy-making hierarchy in the civil service that are made by the president and his cabinet Secretaries of State, subject to the Senate's approval, has been strongly established for over 100 years. Similarly the French and German systems are structured much as they were reformed 60 years previously with guarantees of permanency until retirement for most civil servants. Britain and Ireland in contrast have, despite some efforts to enhance the role of political advisers, kept the appearance of political neutrality among leading bureaucrats. The Indian Civil Service also retains its structural similarities to the British system although within this framework has, since independence, a strong clientelist tendency and has become far more politicised. Italy is one of the few systems in which there has been significant structural change within the civil service machinery that coalesced after independence with the development of a contractual system of appointment rather than the expectation that a position of civil servant was a position for life.

Modern public administration systems in established stable states tend, however, to manipulate the central bureaucratic structure more readily through a fluid use of ad hoc public agencies. It may be argued that ad hoc state agencies, which were created outside a constitutional framework or through legislation establishing common recruitment, promotion and remuneration frameworks within civil services, pre-dated the Weberian-style bureaucracies that were in many states in this study established in the nineteenth century. The capacity to create and remove a stand-alone agency outside the necessity for constitutional change, or legislation, has wide ramifications for established bureaucratic interests, ensuring that the ad hoc agency is a highly flexible instrument of administration. The use of ad hoc agencies has been particularly prevalent in the Anglo Saxon states such as Britain, which have insidiously created such agencies only to rein in their number in a bonfire of the quangos at times of budgetary retrenchment. In federal systems such as the United States there is even less control of ad hoc agencies at the level of state and local government. It is often necessary to develop ad hoc agencies to co-ordinate and implement policy on a regional level or use private companies, as Elcock shows in the United States, to ensure that small city and county authorities can share tasks either with each other or state governments. Such a tendency is also the case within the Indian federal system. The trend to semi-independent agencies remains less marked in the Mediterranean states that are more influenced by the French prefectoral and centrist models, while states such as China and Russia retain a strong authoritarian central framework that ensures that national agencies outside the civil service remain closely tied to central controls and may appear in practice as if they were specialist elements of the central civil service.

## Public management

The preceding paragraphs suggest that in the nations studied in this volume an attitude of conservatism surrounds the formal structures of public administration. This may be thought to reflect the embedded neo-conservative faith in the values of a specific national culture which, in its most aggressive forms is currently exhibited by the United States and some global sectors of governance such as the IMF, as an unquestioned faith in the value to all of their culture of a strong state and free economy. In reality this attitude may more effectively be cast in the Marxist terms of the state being the representative institution of the economic dominant class. Thus, neo-conservatism is in many cases the values of those who, rightly or, for many, wholly mistakenly, believe they have power and authority that requires their resolute defence. Given that constitutions, the relationship between senior civil servants and elected politicians, and the uncertain balance of power between central governments, regions and localities, are based on power relations that benefit the most wealthy and resourced individuals and groups, in an era of capitalist values, it is not surprising that the formal structures of governance and administration in most states are slow to change.

Despite generally slow change in administrative structures, the previous three decades has led to substantive change in how the power elites manage their empires of governance. It has been argued by Rhodes (1997) that states are being hollowed out as increasingly governments turn to the private sector to deliver services. However, this view must be accepted with some caution given that in most pluralist states and autocracies power in the public sector rests with those who also have economic power. In many regimes public services are privatised but those in government who enable such a trend are largely representatives of the private interests that control the economic networks within the state. In the United States election to Congress and the White House requires huge financial support from business and in Britain Thatcher's conservatives, New Labour or the millionaire majority within Cameron's cabinet are similarly beholden to and apologists for the New Right competitive capitalist society.

Within developed states much has changed in terms of how public systems are managed that is based on largely New Right values that are interpreted in the sphere of government as New Public Management. The trend towards privatisation has been accompanied by a restructuring of the role of the state towards production. Governments are increasingly becoming regulators of business, ensuring that there is open competition among major corporations to avoid the dangers inherent in the creation of private sector monopolies. Much greater emphasis is placed on public–private partnerships to provide large-scale services and infrastructure projects. Governments will, therefore, sponsor and help secure and guarantee the capital necessary for allowing private sector businesses to meet identified public needs. Alongside the move towards outright privatisation are the elements of NPM in which public sector organisations are seen to turn away from the rigid rule-bound hierarchy of Weberian management towards more flexible and entrepreneurial management styles of the modern private sector. Hood (1991), paraphrased by Rhodes (1991, 548) characterised these features as:

- a focus on management, not policy, and on performance appraisal and efficiency;
- the disaggregation of public bureaucracies into agencies which deal with each other on a user pay basis;
- the use of quasi markets and contracting out to foster competition;
- cost-cutting;
- a style of management which emphasises inter alia out-put targets, limited term contracts, monetary incentives and freedom to manage.

NPM derives largely from management practices developed predominantly by United States theorists such as Mintzberg, Kantor and Peters and Waterman who argued that organisational control through strictly regulated hierarchies of ordered tasks and duties suggested by classical management theory was inappropriate for securing effective service delivery in a highly diverse and changing environment. Thus, flexibility and empowerment of managers within the confines of a widely accepted vision and strategy for an organisation became the watchword for the new management style. Such an arrangement was rapidly adapted for the public sector and sanctified in the United States context in Osborne and Gaebler's (1992) *Re-inventing Government*. In a rather ill-defined style they set the idea of decentralised, flexible and entrepreneurial management for the public sector within constraints of accountability, requiring managers to secure the goals set for them by politicians acting on behalf of the citizens who elect them.

But there must be a measure of doubt as to whether the adoption of these practices represent a universal trend to some homogeneous private and public style of management that is being forced on all states by the economic and social consequences of globalisation. Although states may readily learn from one another about the differing management innovations that each is adopting, they may take very different messages from the process. As Guyomarch (1999) shows in the context of new management reforms in the French Civil Service, these have been accepted only in sectors that are consonant with existing cultural values within the French bureaucracy, such as greater decentralisation of decision-making, but not in sectors such as recruitment to elite *corps* that is embedded in the values of the bureaucracy. In some cases adoption of a technique or current aphorism may be useful for providing the impression of active pursuit of efficiency, economy and effectiveness. Indeed these watchwords of managerialism cannot in themselves be opposed. Cost-cutting and financial parsimony has been a feature of conservative governments throughout the century. Like sin, we are against inefficiency, but may differ greatly as to the goals that should be made efficient. Bureaucrats must, therefore, appear to adopt new managerial techniques to give the impression of a concern for greater efficiency in order to retain their prestige and legitimacy with the public and their political masters. They are, however, unlikely to adopt these techniques in a form that would undermine their status and influence within the state.

## Privatisation

Privatisation must similarly be seen as a far from identical process in developing countries since it may be shaped by the need to restructure differing inherited structures. The process of nationalisation is in itself a relatively new phenomena developed by ideologically opposed regimes for very different purposes. On the one hand fascist regimes in the 1930s nationalised monopolies and financial organisations to secure central control by the state and was, on the other hand, adopted by the social democratic governments to keep in operation productive services that were highly inefficient under private ownership or to secure welfare facilities that were not sufficiently profitable to interest the private sector. The tendency to privatise in many European liberal democracies is only possible as a process reversing a similar global movement to nationalise industries and expand the role of the state that began in the 1930s.

The points of incompatibility between libertarian New Right values have been played out in different forms within the countries studied in this volume. On the New Right scale privatisation has not followed identical procedures. Britain pioneered under the Thatcher governments the sale of many of the profitable public enterprises through marketing of shares to the public. In Italy, however, businesses have tended to be sold to large private sector companies. In Britain governments established regulation to control monopolies and did not usually retain any interest by way of ownership in the privatised businesses whereas in Italy and France the government has much more frequently retained veto powers over the decisions of companies by holding a controlling 'golden share'. The motives behind privatisation also differ widely among European states. In Britain the sales of public assets as shares were, in part, designed to foster a society of many shareholders that, it was thought by the New Right Thatcher governments, would tend to produce substantially more right-wing electors. In Italy and Greece, for example, the much more recent trend towards privatisation among state-owned companies occurred not so much as a consequence of adulation of Thatcherism but as a means of raising capital to alleviate a huge burden of public debt and through a recognition that an inefficient bureaucracy had, unlike in Britain, created unprofitable and sometimes corrupt state businesses. Significantly the generally efficiently run municipal businesses operated by many northern Italian cities that range from milk supply to electricity and gas generation, have not been widely subject to privatisation.

Privatisation has already been an even more dramatic feature of governments in the former command economies of China and Russia. While still retaining strong central governments in these populous emerging economies, they have opened up their societies to capitalist modes of competition and growth. Russia under the guidance of Putin and the post-Mao Chinese State engineered after 1978 by Deng Xiaoping have fully adopted the 'Free Economy and the Strong State' as characterised by Andrew Gamble. In both countries, while many state industries have been privatised, there remains considerable capacity for the dominant party and bureaucratic structures to ensure that those managing the major private industries are supporters on the dominant political system. In Russia this has been developed as support for Putin and may not, however, be as long-lasting as the more embedded institutional control of the Chinese Communist Party within the state. India, as a more fragmented democracy at its creation, followed a rather different path but, as David Pell observes, at the price of a huge differential in wealth, created a more privatised economy with a rate of economic expansion not far behind that of China.

## Decentralisation

The juxtaposition of new-liberal and neo-conservative values is most clearly at odds over the trend towards decentralisation. While allowing localities greater power may lead to the democratic value of allowing citizens greater liberty to develop their own values and interests, this aim may for some interests mark a dangerous erosion of the existing power relations in society that could ensure that local and regional interests have the power to challenge the state and even undermine its capitalist values. A number of states and particularly the United Kingdom and Russia exhibit a highly ambiguous and fractured policy towards localism and citizenship as a result of these contending pressures.

Federalism is firmly established in four of the states surveyed in this book, the United States, Germany, Russia and India. These systems appear constitutionally to be subject to few changes since their creation despite considerable changes in the demography of these areas and the, at times, rather bizarre political circumstances in which they were created. A number of states in this survey, such as Italy, have a partially federated structure with small enclaves given a special regional status and, most recently, the United Kingdom devolved a measure of self-government to Scotland and to a lesser extent Northern Ireland and Wales that suggests a federated system in all but name. Behind the discretion of federal governments are also the political relationships that can secure a state considerable autonomy from the centre or require it to bend to federal government values. The more established federal structures are based in many cases, as in India or in West Europe, Spain or Belgium, on the need for the state to recognise strongly held cultural and linguistic differences that if suppressed lead to endemic and potentially violent revolt that could seriously destabilise the country as a whole. Nevertheless, in other countries such as Germany or the United States the framework of federalism has, over time, become an accepted and often assumed pattern of political power that remains substantially in place since, despite serious cultural divisions, it is a successful structure for devolving and de-concentrating power in order to avoid an overwhelming dominance of the national government.

Behind the federal relationships lies the issue of managing resources. In many cases the move towards globalisation in financial markets covering huge populations requires central governments to exert strong controls over levels of spending and borrowing from substantive divisions in the state. The economic recession in Europe has also led to states such as Spain and Italy having to bail out regional government that cannot now balance their budgets. The diverse populations and needs of some of the most populous states, in practice, necessitates devolution of power in respect to how the funding is spent and the extent to which a central government can accept accountability for spending. Thus the unitary Chinese system effectively allows, within spending limits, considerable autonomy to its provinces, while, converging from the opposite direction, the federal system of India is more of a quasi-federal state given the funding controls placed on them by their central governments.

Superficially the local government systems in the countries covered by this study appear to show traditional diverse patterns of structuring, which in legal and constitutional terms retain structures that were in place at the beginning of the twentieth century and, in as much as changes occur, with the exception of Britain, appear to devolve greater powers to localities. There has been only a slight reduction since 1945 in the huge number, around 36,000, of French communes, the minuscule township and city governments in the United States with very few exceptions have since 1945 refused to merge into larger local authorities. Britain has been the most assiduous of the countries surveyed in this study that has required smaller authorities to merge. If the New Labour governments of Blair and Brown had stayed much longer in office, they would have divided the country into less than a hundred unitary authorities that, in terms of population, would be difficult to be seriously seen as 'local'.

The British pattern of local government reform appears unique among liberal democracies. The pattern of local government in the countries highlighted in this book, nevertheless, tend to demonstrate a decline in small, community-based local governments. Communes in France and Italy, *Gemeinden* in Germany and in the United States 'city' and township governments, are increasingly merging in larger district or provincial blocks to share major services usually by jointly contracting with corporate private sector contracts for local service provision. Through this framework there is a trend towards the more formal arrangement of the British and Irish local government system into larger unitary authorities, in practice, if not a through legislative compulsion. The driver of such change is predominantly a symptom of the growth in multinational business that can use economies of scale to provide services such as refuse collection or the provision of utilities. Ideologically such trends are also supported through greater enthusiasm for

New Right market capitalism and its public administrative adjunct New Public Management.

It may be argued that such developments are offset by the New Right and communitarian enthusiasm for personal freedom and the hollowing out of central government. There is a tendency especially in Britain and the United States to support such ideas by ad hoc community developments that are only partially connected to local government given that such co-ordinated and electorally representative institutions are as public institutions seen as potential affronts to individual liberty. Thus in the United States there is a continuous invention of new ad hoc local government organisations for specific purposes ranging from irrigation to collective outsourcing of cable television and phone connections (Burns 1994). In Britain this trend has been enforced through legislation that has sought to deal with issues such as urban deprivation by central government financing, in partnership with private sector organisations, Local Strategic Partnerships. There is in China and India an increasing tendency to subvert local government to the needs of the party in power through legislative and financial controls that make it impossible for lower tier bodies to develop policies not acceptable to central government values. In more centralised western states such as the United Kingdom, the Irish Republic and Poland this is increasingly achieved through by-passing local government by privatising local services and creating ad hoc centrally financed development agencies.

## The economic crash

Since the last edition of this book the reach and effectiveness of public administration in western states has been seriously challenged by the post-2008 recession, while economic growth in the major Asian economies has been largely stabilised by lower demand from the western economies that as a consequence decreases the chance of reform of the public sector in these states. It may be argued that spendthrift civic cultures in, for example, Greece and Italy, were to blame as a consequence of long-term public policies that featherbedded public sector agencies and their workforce and allowed endemic avoidance of taxation. However, these Mediterranean states only became fiscally vulnerable when faced by a downturn in the world economy. Despite their failings they were able to survive recession until events in other wealthier countries such as America and Britain tipped their rather fragile economies over the edge. Another line of attack on the public sector is that poor systems for state regulation of finance did not alert national banks and ministries of finance to rein in the borrowing practices of their major banks. However, the global basis of larger banks and their link with each other made it problematic for most public regulatory agencies to police at a national level what were global networks of interdependency that concealed ill-considered attempts to insure their financial gambles. Moreover, if the private sector cannot be trusted to regulate itself this hardly absolves the sector from much of the blame for the financial crash. While governments could have been more aware of an impending crisis, the prime cause of the recession lies within the private sector rather than public sector agencies. The collapse of major privately owned banks largely in the United States but also in Britain and Ireland was a result of reckless speculation that greatly inflated property prices and private borrowing. Despite its largely private sector origins in western liberal democracies the consequences of private recklessness has, however, been borne as much, if not more, by the public sector that took on the responsibility of bailing out the private financial sector. The failure of the private sector required governments to over borrow in order to prevent the meltdown of the private financial system and later to pay for greater demands on welfare payment and a decrease in taxable economic activity that were a consequence of the resultant decline in the world economy. The consequence has been a requirement for governments to retrench public sector spending through creating a smaller public sector or, through higher taxation and a more robust system of collection, ensure some rebalancing of an increasing trend towards private affluence and public squalor. The strategies used by states to rebalance the role of the private and public sectors of the economies have not surprisingly differed among the Anglo Saxon, Mediterranean and former command economy countries just as much as other aspects of their administrative public practices have been shown to differ in character.

It is difficult to characterise the extent to which the recession may re-shape the public sector within post-communist states. Russia and China, through the dismemberment of the command economies, have undergone substantive cut backs in the role of the state in the provision of social welfare that dwarf the extent of any more incremental cut backs being made by the liberal democracies facing economic recession. How far these regimes will follow the path of Britain or a Republican-dominated United States remains to be seen should the economic recession place these economies in reverse gear. In India the growth in the economy may have been stabilised as in China and Russia by the downturn in western economic output but the country is not facing a recession that would be in itself sufficient to change its largely mixed economy outlook.

Demands from the IMF, the European Central Bank, and, in effect Germany, that the Mediterranean states of Greece, Italy, Spain and Portugal should privatise have been countered by substantive opposition. Greek governments may have been obliged to avoid further economic meltdown through a programme of austerity and the sale of state-owned businesses, but there has been substantial mass opposition to these demands. In Italy the government of Mario Monti similarly raised taxes and increased the pension age but did not drive very far down the route to privatisation. In France the accession of the more left-wing Hollande to the presidency has initiated an attempt to balance the books not so much by cutting the public sector, which is to contribute one-third of the proposed savings, but by raising individual taxation especially for the middle and moneyed classes and on large businesses.

Rebalancing the increasing gulf between the richest and poorest in most western economies might from a Rawlsian view of fairness be the better approach.

In those predominantly Anglo Saxon countries where the profitable nationalised industries and utilities such as electricity production or water supplies have already been sold off, the burden of cuts is beginning to fall on those elements of the economy that are cherished by neo-conservatives. Thus, expenditure on the armed forces, police and, in many states, the central civil services is beginning to create serious challenges to some governments. Within sectors of public provision the trend to cut costs has also promoted privatisation of the delivery of services that strategically are still under public ownership and control. The recent restructuring of the British National Health Service is substantially geared around an interest, cautiously introduced by the Blair and Brown governments, in throwing open health care to private sector operations. Similar trends are being adopted for education and even within the police services.

In contrast to the Mediterranean states facing potential economic meltdown, the reaction to the problem in the Anglo Saxon states is strikingly in contrast to the Keynesian values that in the last western economic recession of the 1930s prompted countries such as the United States and Britain to push forward in the following three decades major growth in the public sector through nationalisation of failing or over-priced utility companies and increasing the provision of health care and public housing. The consequence was an unprecedented period of economic growth, notwithstanding the devastation of the Second World War, that has been punctuated by the present crisis that began with the loosening of the reins in public regulation of finance and the growth in privatisation stemming from the New Right values implemented by the Reagan and Thatcher administrations that were then widely copied both in Western Europe and Asia. Should privatisation of public sector resources continue unabated it would be the unwitting triumph of those New Right and neo-conservative forces that created the global crisis in the first place. This may well be a pyrrhic victory.

# References

Bell, D. (1960) *The End of Ideology*, Glencoe, Illinois: Free Press.
Burns, N. (1994) *The Formation of American Local Governments*, New York: Oxford University Press.
Drysek, J. and Dunleavy, P. (2009) *Theories of the Democratic State*, Basingstoke: Palgrave.
Fukuyama, F. (1992) *The End of History and the Last Man*, London: Hamish Hamilton.
Gamble, A. (1988) *The Free Economy and the Strong State*, Basingstoke: Macmillan.
Giddens, A. (1999) Reith Lectures, No. 1. Online, available at: http://news.bbc.co.uk/radio4/reith1999/lecture1/.shtml (last accessed 17 February 2014).
Guyomarch, A. (1999) '"Public Service", "Public Management" and the "Modernisation" of French Public Administration', *Public Administration*, 77: 171–93.

Hayward, J. (1983) *Governing France: The One and Indivisible French Republic*, 2nd edn, London: Weidenfeld and Nicolson.

Held, D. (1991) 'Democracy, The National State and the Global System', in Held, D. (ed.) *Political Theory Today*, Oxford: Polity Press, pp. 197–235.

Holton, R. J. (1998) *Globalization and the Nation State*, Basingstoke: Macmillan.

Hood, C. (1991) 'A Public Management for All Seasons', *Public Administration*, 69: 3–19.

Jones, R. A. (2000) 'The European Union' in Chandler, J. A. (ed.) *Comparative Public Administration*, 1st edn, London: Routledge, pp. 171–99.

Nozick. R. (1980) *Anarchy, State and Utopia*, Oxford: Basil Blackwell.

Osborne, D. and Gaebler, T. (1992) *Reinventing Government*, Reading, M.A.: Addison Wesley.

Rhodes, R. A. W. (1991) 'Theory and Methods in British Public Administration: The View from Political Science', *Political Studies*, 39: 533–54.

Rhodes, R. A. W. (1997) *Understanding Governance: Policy Networks, Governance, Reflexivity and Accountability*, Buckingham: Open University Press.

Thompson, H. (2010) 'The Character of the State', in Hay C. (ed.) *New Directions in Political Science*, Basingstoke: Palgrave, pp. 130–47.

# Index